PUBLIC SECTOR STRATEGY DESIGN

Within the public sector, strategies are not designed to influence markets, but instead to guide operations within a complex environment of multilateral power, influence, bargaining, and voting. In this book, authors David McNabb and Chung-Shingh Lee examine five frameworks public sector organization managers have followed when designing public sector strategies. Its purpose is to serve as a guide for managers and administrators of large and small public organizations and agencies. This book is the product of a combined more than 60 years of researching, teaching, and leading organizational seminars on the theory and practice of management applications in industrial, commercial, nonprofit, and public sector organizations.

The book consists of four parts: Strategic Management and Strategy Fundamentals; Frameworks for Designing Strategies; Public Sector Strategies; and Implementing Strategic Management. Throughout, the focus is on the widespread value of strategic management and adopting the strategy appropriate for the organization. Including chapters on game theory, competitive forces, resources-based view, dynamic capabilities, and network governance, the authors demonstrate ways that real managers of public sector and civil society organizations have put strategic management to work in their organizations. This book will be of interest to both practicing and aspiring public servants.

David E. McNabb is Professor Emeritus in the School of Business, Pacific Lutheran University, USA. He has taught undergraduate and graduate business management and public administration courses for Edmonds Community College, Olympic College, Oregon State University, the University of Maryland-University College (Europe), the American University in Bulgaria, the Stockholm School of Economics in Riga, Latvia, a regional business education program in Northern France, and the MPA program at Evergreen State College. He has worked for the cities of Fullerton, California and the Washington State House of Representatives. He is author of *Research Methods for Public Administration and Non-Profit Organizations*, 4th edition (Routledge, 2017).

Chung-Shing Lee is Professor and Dean of the School of Business at Saint Martin's University, USA. Prior to his current position, he was a Professor of Technology and Innovation Management and Dean of the School of Business at Pacific Lutheran University, USA. Dr. Lee has been a visiting Professor in the College of Management and a Research Associate in the Institute of Knowledge Service and Innovation at Yuan Ze University in Taiwan, and a faculty research associate at the Center for Advanced Lifecycle Engineering (CALCE) at the University of Maryland. Dr. Lee is a member of the editorial boards of *Technological Forecasting and Social Change*, *International Journal of Innovation and Technology Management*, *Journal of Competitive Studies*, and the *Competitiveness Review*. Dr. Lee is the recipient of numerous teaching and research awards. He has been helping organizations design and implement innovation strategies for more than two decades.

"In this book, David McNabb and Chung-Shing Lee provide a significant and valuable contribution to the body of knowledge in public sector strategy and management, as well as offering public administrators and practitioners a useful framework for them to design and implement strategy for sustainability and success."

Dr. Jonathan C. Ho, *Yuan Ze University, Taiwan*

"Although the process of strategic management has been enthusiastically adopted by many public sector managers, the guidance on how best to develop the strategies necessary to put those processes into the task of running a government agency has been essentially missing. This book by David McNabb and Chung Shing-Lee appropriately fills that void. They have produced the only book I am aware of that blends strategic management theories with the practical skills needed for designing strategies."

Mohamad (Mo) Sepehri, *University of the District of Columbia, Washington DC, USA*

"Modern public administration in today's complex and challenging environment is well-served by this important book on the core elements of strategic management. Its combination of theory and practical applications makes it a meaningful contribution to strategic planning for executives and administrators in all public organizations. Elected officials and leaders in the non-profit sector also need to understand the challenges their staffs and organizations are facing. After reading this book, their leadership will be more insightful and valuable."

Clare Petrich, *President of the Port of Tacoma Commission, Washington, USA*

PUBLIC SECTOR STRATEGY DESIGN

Theory and Practice for Government and Nonprofit Organizations

David E. McNabb
and Chung-Shing Lee

Routledge
Taylor & Francis Group

NEW YORK AND LONDON

First published 2021
by Routledge
52 Vanderbilt Avenue, New York, NY 10017

and by Routledge
2 Park Square, Milton Park, Abingdon, Oxon, OX14 4RN

Routledge is an imprint of the Taylor & Francis Group, an informa business

© 2021 Taylor & Francis

Library of Congress Cataloging-in-Publication Data
A catalog record for this title has been requested

ISBN: 978-0-367-55680-8 (hbk)
ISBN: 978-0-367-55677-8 (pbk)
ISBN: 978-1-000-19386-2 (ebk)

Typeset in Bembo
by Wearset Ltd, Boldon, Tyne and Wear

CONTENTS

ILLUSTRATIONS

Boxes

Figures

Tables

PREFACE

Public sector, nonprofit and civil society organizations globally face a daunting convergence of the challenges of increasing operating costs, limited and declining budgets, the need to replace failing infrastructure, find and replace qualified employees, improve the quality of their services, meet the needs of an increasing population. At the same time, they must invest huge sums in ever-changing technology as they plan for meeting the need for new and innovative services to their citizens. All this and more must be done while delivering reliable public services through a variety of new channels and media. As leaders in government continue planning for ways to overcome these challenges, public and civil society organizations are increasingly constrained by their limited budgets in what they can provide their citizens. They are constantly looking for new and better ways to put their resources and organizational capabilities to work.

Public sector managers and leaders of nonprofit organizations are seldom confronted with the need to develop strategies for dealing with competition. As Bozeman and Straussman warned:

> By its very nature, public strategic management cannot and should not be as warlike as business strategy. Rarely is the quashing of a competitor an acceptable option.... The external control of public organizations by political authorities ensures that warlike strategy will, in the long run, be self-defeating.
>
> *(1990, 51)*

This absence of an entrepreneurial culture, insufficient knowledge of market and technological changes, and an outdated managerial mindset are further constraints. Private sector frameworks for organizational strategy are limited in their applicability to government and nonprofit organizations. In this book, we analyze five of the chief strategic management frameworks in our search for what concepts are best suited to overcoming these challenges facing public sector organizations. Our conclusions are our own and, to the best of our ability, we have given credit to the research and conclusions of international strategic management researchers. We respectfully apologize for any accidental omission.

The reason for writing this book was to provide public organization management practitioners working at the level of strategy formation or about to be promoted to that level, a guide to the major frameworks available to them in the development of strategies. This includes managers who have some experience in management of nonprofit organizations—what is increasingly referred to as the civil society or third sector.

David McNabb and Chung-Shing Lee

ACKNOWLEDGMENTS

We want to take this opportunity to thank the fine editorial staff at Routledge Taylor & Francis for their continued support during the preparation of this and previous books. We are particularly indebted to our long-time senior publisher Laura Stearns Varley in New York and editorial assistant Katie Horsfall in Great Britain for their encouragement and assistance throughout the development of the concept and preparation of the final manuscript.

In addition, we wish also to thank the anonymous reviewers who examined the concept and descriptive data prior to the go-ahead for writing the book. Pre-production reviews are a difficult and time-consuming task. We owe them a deep debt of gratitude for their reviews and valuable suggestions.

We also thank the senior administrators of our universities for their willingness to support the concept from the beginning. The School of Business at Pacific Lutheran University has long provided emeritus professor McNabb with a fully supplied office and access to school materials, research access, and technical assistance throughout the preparation of the work.

Finally, for their support and understanding throughout the research and writing of such a book as this, we owe an enormous debt of gratitude to our families. We can never thank them enough for all that they do.

David McNabb, PhD
Professor and Dean Chung-Shing Lee, PhD

PART I
Strategic Management and Strategy Fundamentals

1

INTRODUCTION

The first chapter introduces the core concepts inherent in strategic management and strategic planning (Figure 1.1). Its purpose is to serve as a guide for managers and administrators of large and small industrial, commercial, civil society and public organizations and agencies. This book is the product of a combined more than 60 years of researching, teaching and leading organizational seminars on the theory and practice of management applications in industrial, commercial, non-profit and public sector organizations. It is rooted in this history and our interpretations of recent thinking on strategic management theory and application.

The public sector includes all government organizations that provide services to a variety of publics without reference to a profit motive. This does not mean that public services are given away. Rather, most services provided by public organizations come with a cost. A more detailed definition compiled by contributions of many researchers might be: The public sector includes organizations owned and operated by some level of government that exists for providing a service for its citizens and is usually funded raised through taxes, fees for service, or by financial transfers from other levels of government.

In a paper in the *Academy of Management Journal*, Ellen Chaffee (1985) explained that researchers and managers in general have been using the term *strategy* for more than 20 years. Chaffee added that while there was general agreement on the definition of what the term referred to (its "anchoring concept"), at the time, no general agreement on a more definitive definition of the term existed. Citing Donald Hambrick (1983), Chaffee named two reasons for the lack of agreement on a definition: (1) strategy is multidimensional, and (2) strategy must be situational and, therefore, will vary from industry to industry and from organization to organization.

It was recognized as early as the 1960s that public sector, nonprofit and civil society organizations, like their for-profit cousins, must regularly plan and devise and revise strategies for carrying out the missions for which they were formed (Chandler 1962; Miles, Snow, Meyer and Coleman 1978; Nutt and Backoff 1991; Hough 2011). Chandler chronicled the evolution of organizations' attention to strategy in his many books and papers on business history. Alfred Chandler had defined strategy as "the determination of the basic long-term goals of an enterprise, and the adoption of courses of action and the allocation of resources necessary for carrying out these goals" (Chandler 1962, 13). Box 1.1 includes a definition of strategy from Chandler's 1962 *Strategy and Structure*. The section includes what organizations must do to remain sustainable and was modified to apply to public sector organizations.

Despite the early lack of agreement on a definition of strategy, an extensive search of the literature suggests that general agreement has been reached on what the term strategy implies. An example of that agreement was offered by Aldea, Iacob, Hillegersberg, Quartel and Franken in 2018. They explained that strategies are simply the action plans that managers use to guide their activities, and that strategies can help shape the way the organization employs its assets and capabilities. Managers base strategies from the conclusions they gain from their analysis of the

---

BOX 1.1 DEFINITION OF STRATEGY AND THE EFFECTS OF CHANGE IN THE OPERATIONAL ENVIRONMENT

This definition of strategy included in the introduction to Chandler's *Strategy and Structure* (1962), repeated here, has been briefly modified to reflect our focus on public sector organizations.

Strategy can be defined as the determination of the basic long-term goals and objectives of an [organization], and the adoption of courses of action and the allocation of resources necessary for carrying out these goals. Decisions to expand the volume of activities, to set up distant [branch operations] and offices, to move into new [social or political] functions or become diversified along many lines of [public value] functions involve the defining of new basic goals. New courses of action must be devised and resources allocated and reallocated in order to achieve these goals and to maintain and expand the [organization's] activities in the new areas in response to shifting [public or political] demands, changing sources of supply, fluctuating [fiscal] conditions, new technological developments, and the [changes occurring in society]. As the adoption of a new strategy may add new types of personnel and facilities and alter the [operational] horizons of [personnel] responsible for the [organization], it can have a profound effect on the form of its organization.

Source: Alfred Chandler (1962)

environment in which they operate. The strategy selected "must identify, protect, acquire, and sustain critical capabilities, in order to provide mitigation against future uncertainties" (Aldea et al. 2018, 86).

Designing strategies for government and nonprofit organizations is made difficult by the multidimensional aspect of strategies and use across many activities of many different organizations. A strategy for a government or nonprofit organization relies on understanding the limited choices available and the resulting restricted economic, legal and politically influenced action options. With the strategic management approach, strategies are not designed to influence markets, but instead for guiding operations within a complex environment of "multilateral power, influence, bargaining, voting and exchange relationships and the norm" (Wechsler and Backoff 1986, 321). Box 1.1 describes the forces that help guide public sector strategies.

UCLA Professor Richard Rumelt (2011) addressed the question of a meaning of strategy by describing what it is not. He emphasized that it was not about what management wanted to happen, charismatic leadership, vision or planning. Rather, it is about an organization's coherent action that is supported by thorough understanding and intelligent decision-making:

> A strategy is a way through a difficulty, an approach to overcoming an obstacle, a response to a challenge. If the challenge is not defined, it is difficult or impossible to assess the quality of the strategy … if you fail to identify and analyze the obstacles, you do not have a strategy. Instead, you have a stretch goal or a budget or a list of things you wish would happen.
>
> *(Rumelt 2011, 42–3)*

A further contribution was his defining the distinction between a bad strategy and what is a good strategy. Four characteristics characterize a bad strategy:

1. **Failure to define specific challenges.** These challenges must be explicitly defined if a plan for overcoming them and obstacles are to be removed can be put into effect. Neither a "stretched goal," a budget, nor a wish list is a strategy.
2. Mistaking goals for a strategy. Goals are not strategies. For example, an aggressive goal of improving relationships with stakeholders by 10% is not a strategy; it is a goal. The manager's task is to create the environment that will make achieving the goal possible.
3. Bad strategic objectives. Objectives that are wishes or that cannot be measured or are simple restatements of the problem provide no guidance. Adding the phrase "long term" does not make them an objective. Nor should the objectives be just a laundry list of a committee's wishful "blue sky" idea that no one knows how to accomplish:

> Good strategy, in contrast, works by focusing energy and resources on one, or a very few, pivotal objectives whose accomplishment will lead

to a cascade of favorable outcomes. It also builds a bridge between the critical challenge at the heart of the strategy and action—between desire and immediate objectives that lie within grasp. Thus, the objectives that a good strategy sets stand a good chance of being accomplished, given existing resources and competencies.

(Rumelt 2011, 53)

4. Fluff. Fluff describes objectives that have no real meaning; they are just restatements of the obvious. They are simple statements and provide no strategic guidance.

To counter the list of what makes a bad strategy, Rumelt listed just three things (Wauters 2017):

1. **A diagnosis:** an explanation of the nature of the challenge; simplifying the often-overwhelming complexity of the problem; identifying the critical aspects of the situation.
2. **A guiding policy:** an approach that meaningfully copes with and overcomes the barriers identified in the analysis.
3. **Coherent actions:** clear and logical actions that are coordinated with relevant others to ensure accomplishment of the guiding strategy.

Structure of the Book

The rest of this chapter begins with brief introductions to public sector strategic management concepts and the guiding principles of strategy formation. These introductory chapters are followed by descriptions of the chief frameworks for implementing public sector strategies. These are game theory, the competitive forces, resource-based view, and dynamic capabilities frameworks. The next section includes five chapters with examples of strategies based on the frameworks. The last two chapters are refreshers on strategic management and strategic planning concepts.

Many previous authors have helped to build what is our interpretation of the latest stage in these theories. As in all research, current research builds on what others have earlier contributed toward or disagreed with in the theory or theories under examination. We recognize their contributions and give full credit for their work. The final text is also an extension of some of our earlier research, elements of which are cited throughout the text. However, the final product represents our interpretations and extensions of the latest on innovation in general and particularly on the theory of strategic innovation. We take full responsibility for our assertions and conclusions.

The book consists of four parts: Strategic Management and Strategy Fundamentals; Frameworks for Designing Strategies; Public Sector Strategies; and Implementing

BOX 1.2 THE PUBLIC SECTOR STRATEGIC MANAGEMENT AND STRATEGY SHAPING TASK

"The strategic management task for the general-purpose government agency ... involves not only the development of strategies for implementing policy and for the internal and external management of the agency, but also for the establishment of organizational purpose and character [its mission, vision and values]. The available strategies and forms of action are restricted ... by various factors including constitutional arrangements, legislative and judicial mandates, jurisdictional boundaries, resource constraints, political climate ... and client and constitutional interests. In this context, strategic choice and action taking by individual agencies is highly dependent on external influences and environmental forces. Since the primary goal of strategic management in public organizations is to provide direction [with specific strategies] for the organization ... strategic management involves the joining together of external demands, constraints, and mandates with agency-specific goals, objectives, and operational procedures."

Source: Wechsler and Backoff (1986, 321–2)

Strategic Management. Throughout, the focus is on the need to recognize the widespread value of strategic management and adopting the strategy appropriate for the internal and external operating environments of the organization. The goal should be to design strategies with the highest probability of success and sustainability.

After a review of the core concepts of strategic management, we include a chapter on how strategic management has come to be adopted by all levels of government and civil society organizations. The second section includes a chapter each on the five basic frameworks extant in strategic management: game theory, competitive forces, resource-based view, dynamic capabilities, and network governance. We include chapters that describe some of the ways that the managers of public sector and civil society organization are benefiting from strategic management.

Chapter 1: Introduction

The first chapter introduces the core concepts inherent in strategic management and strategic planning (Figure 1.1). Its purpose is to serve as a guide for managers and administrators of large and small industrial, commercial, civil society and public organizations and agencies. This book is the product of a combined more

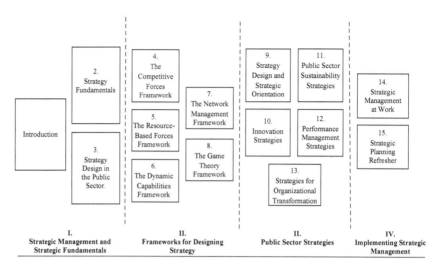

FIGURE 1.1 Strategic management in public sector organizations.

than 60 years of researching, teaching and leading organizational seminars on the theory and practice of management applications in industrial, commercial, non-profit and public sector organizations. It is rooted in this history and our interpretations of recent thinking on strategic management theory and application.

The final section includes guides for public sector managers planning to adopt strategic management, three of which focus on managing strategic innovation in all types of organizations. Figure 1.1 shows the full structure of the strategic innovation management process as we present it in the book.

Chapter 2: Strategy Fundamentals

In this introductory chapter, we review the fundamental concepts of strategic management and the dominant design paradigms for analyzing and forming operations strategies. Basic concepts include organizational strategy formulation, strategic orientation, strategic management, strategic management frameworks, strategic innovation, transformational change for implementing strategic management, and sustainability planning. Strategy design frameworks include game theory, competitive forces, resource-based designs, dynamic capabilities and network governance.

Chapter 3: Strategy Design in the Public Sector

Strategies are selected guidelines for managing both private and public sector organizations. In the private sector, competition drives strategy formation, whereas in the public sector, the motivator is public service. The public sector provides a wide variety of goods and services to a diverse clientele. The strategies adopted are shaped by policies set by elected stakeholders beyond their control. In this chapter, we review five of the major theories that underlie creation of organizational strategies for private sector organizations. Throughout the chapter, we introduce descriptions of how these theories have been transposed for application to strategy design and management in public sector organizations.

Chapter 4: The Competitive Forces Framework

Chapter 4 reviews the influence of competitive forces frameworks on strategy formulation, combining product-market-based strategies introduced by H. Igor Ansoff in 1957 and Michael Porter in 1979. As in Chapter 3, we illustrate how these, with industry-based approaches, have been shown to also have relevance for public sector organizations.

Chapter 5: The Resource-Based Framework

In this chapter we describe how private sector employment of an organization's physical, human, information, organizational and capital resources are also employed in the design of public sector operational strategies. Building on earlier concepts, Jay Barney expanded this framework in 1991 by adding that the resources must be valuable, rare, inimitable and nonsubstitutable.

Chapter 6: The Dynamic Capabilities Framework

The dynamic capabilities framework described in Chapter 6 is an organization's "ability to integrate, build, and reconfigure internal and external competencies to address rapidly changing environments. Dynamic capabilities thus reflect an organization's ability to achieve new and innovative operational forms quickly and apply them to advantage" (Teece et al. 1997). This approach focuses on development of capabilities for developing and managing functional, organizational and technology skills that enable superior performance. In this light, the dynamic capabilities paradigm is particularly suited for application in public sector strategic management.

Chapter 7: The Network Management Framework

The network management framework in Chapter 7 focuses on designing strategy to take full advantage of the organization's dynamic capabilities. This focus of this chapter is designing strategies that employ as much of any or all of the strategy design frameworks in collaborative and cooperative strategic strategy. The combination of strategic frameworks expands the organization's capabilities far beyond any one framework can possibly produce. Openness to new and different strategic frameworks enables design of operational strategies that include the contributions of all members of a partnership, alliance, network or cooperative agreement of like-minded organizations for accomplishing its operational tasks and achieving its goals.

The collaborative framework model is considered particularly well suited to public sector strategic management. The framework assumes that government is no longer the influence of a single public policy organization but is more governing through accommodating the influences of internal and external stakeholders. It does not necessarily mean a large number of stakeholders but, rather, refers to a variety of different actors that often includes a combination of public, private and civil society contributors.

Chapter 8: The Game Theory Framework

As designed by John von Neumann and Oskar Morgenstern in 1944, game theory is a procedure for achieving optimal decision outcomes between two or more competing individuals or organizations in zero-sum games. As designed, it can also be used with correlations of players. This approach to strategy design for optimal strategies is based on an evaluation or estimate of the effects of strategy decisions adopted by opponents. The actions and choices of all players affect the outcome to each. John Nash contributed to the theory in 1950 with the concept of a decision–outcome equilibrium point that will eventually arise between all choices. From this point, no player can increase a payoff by unilaterally making decisions.

Chapter 9: Strategy Design and Strategic Orientation

In this chapter we examine some of the ways an organization's strategic orientation impacts the strategies it adopts. This orientation is the guiding principle that underlies all strategic decisions. It shapes the direction that a public sector organization takes in planning to perform its mission and the way it plans to continue to function over the foreseeable time period. It therefore influences both current operational plans and schedules and the proposed human and administrative capital investments that must be available. There are two major components to this idea. The first is the sense that an organization does indeed have a plan that delineates its strategic goals and for the tasks and performance objectives that relate to the long-term goals. The second is the regular monitoring and measuring performance progress gained toward achieving its short-term objectives and longer-term goals.

Chapter 10: Innovation Strategies

This chapter focuses on how public organizations develop and implement strategies for adopting services and process innovation. Both private and public organizations make many changes during their operational life. Most of those changes are easy to manage, informal and ad hoc adjustments to existing operations. Others, however, are transformational. They are deliberate, sometimes radical, often difficult to manage, and are the result of adopting an innovation in some way. Adopting an innovation-friendly policy is often an example of a transformational change. When innovations result in the need for a transformational change, research suggests that successful innovations occur most often when five organizational conditions and management practices are in place. These conditions and practices are described in this chapter.

Chapter 11: Public Sector Sustainability Strategies

Public organizations are increasingly encouraged to also develop a sustainability strategy along with their operational and strategic plans. This chapter looks at the need for sustainability planning and some of the development processes. The sustainability plan includes three components or tools: a self-assessment, development of a strategy for accomplishing goals and rectifying problems, and an action plan of how to accomplish its sustainability goals. A recent definition of a sustainability strategy describes the concept thus:

> Sustainability is often likened to democracy, in that it is not a problem to be solved, but a challenge that requires constant innovation, commitment, vigilance, and learning. Thus, it is not another thing to do, or another box to be checked. It asks us to discern our contribution to this challenge of our time, delivered in the context of our passion and purposes. When sustainability is understood and "owned" at the unit level, and when it is strongly linked to the unit's mission and unique expertise, innovation takes place.
>
> *(Foley 2014)*

Chapter 12: Performance Management Strategies

This chapter focuses on the strategic management processes associated with programs for improving government organizations' performance. The current concentrated performance improvement mandate took root in the federal government with passage of the Government Performance and Results Act (GPRA) in 1993. Application of performance improvement programs at the state and municipal levels followed shortly after. This chapter discusses the movement and how successful implementation and strategic management are associated. Three strategic planning projects required by the GPRA were an agency strategic plan, specification of agency performance goals, and an agency performance plan for achieving those goals. All three were required to be updated every four years, beginning the first year of every four-year presidential term of office.

Chapter 13: Strategies for Organizational Transformation

Organizations can go through different types of change depending on changes in their internal or external environments. The organization can make the small incremental adjustments associated with maintaining stability in its operational environment, or it can suffer through the larger discontinuous changes necessary to adjust to instability or uncertainty in its environment. It can be a planned adaptation to meet an anticipated shift in the external environment, or it can be an unplanned transformation requiring a fundamental re-creation brought on by a threat to the organization's existence. This chapter discusses the reasons and processes associated with strategic transformation change.

Chapter 14: Strategic Management at Work

This chapter looks at examples of how some public sector organizations have put strategic management to work. Government administrators regularly employ environmental analysis, strategic planning, strategy formulation and implementation, performance measurement, and strategic allocation of resources—admittedly sometimes in piecemeal fashion, but increasingly together in a comprehensive application of the strategic management concept. Strategic management has been adopted as an integrative approach to managing an organization. It centers on designing enterprise-wide strategies and focusing agency activities toward accomplishment of management-established goals and objectives; it is managing with a purpose. It is particularly important in the public sector in light of the far-reaching shifts taking place in the internal and external environments of government.

Chapter 15: Strategic Planning Refresher

Strategic planning (SP) is the physical demonstration of how to implement strategic goals. It is a required activity in most budget units in the federal, state agency and major municipal departments. SP consists of a combination of elements from three planning models: The combination adopts elements of capital planning, asset management planning, and financial planning. There is no one best way to combine these planning tools, although a traditional set of activities has evolved. This chapter is included as a refresher on the core elements of strategic planning for agency managers by helping guide mission strategies and tactics.

Summary

The use of strategic management concepts is in common use in government agencies and support organizations in nations big and small around the world. This system is now one of the most widely used managerial practices in government. The management system integrates operating environment analysis, planning, implementation, measurement, and provision of public sector goods and services. A results-oriented approach, it has been adopted by government managers in all levels of government and human services organizations. Designing strategies is an essential product of the strategic management process. In the following chapters, we look at five of the extant frameworks public sector organization managers have followed when designing public sector strategies.

2
STRATEGY FUNDAMENTALS

Strategic management is the set of management actions and decisions that guide the ongoing performance of an organization. It includes analyses of an organization's internal and external environments and the setting of long-term objectives deciding on the strategy or strategies for their achievement, and the progress evaluation and control by performance monitoring and measurement (Hunger and Wheelen 1997, 2015). Although the tools associated with strategic management have been available at least since the 1940s, if not earlier (Drucker 1974), it was not until the 1980s and 1990s that its practices and processes became widely used in government (Bracker 1980). The widespread application of the federal government's adoption of strategic management took root in the 1990s with passage of the Government Performance and Results Act of 1993 (GPRA). The GPRA required federal agency managers to submit a strategic plan for reaching their performance goals and agency program activities to Congress and to the Office of Management and Budget (OMB). The strategic plans were to cover at least a five-year period and to be updated at least every three years. Only agencies with budgets of $20 million or less were exempt from the reporting requirements. To ensure compliance, the Office of Personnel Management was ordered to include a strategic planning and performance measurement training component in its management training.

State, county and city governments then began to include strategic planning components with their budget proposals, bringing the planning tools for facilitating strategic transformation management practices in public and civil society organizations (Taffinder 1998; Joyce 2000; Kang, 2005). Managers and administrators in all sectors now regularly employ internal and external environmental analyses, strategic planning, strategy formulation and implementation, performance measurement, and strategic allocation of resources. That adoption admittedly sometimes occurs in piecemeal fashion, but increasingly comes together in a comprehensive application of the strategic management concept.

Planning for Rapid Change

Strategic management has been shown to be particularly important in the public sector as a consequence of the extensive shifts taking place in the internal and external environments of government. In this era of rapid change and international competition, strategic management is required for successful achievement of government sustainability goals. There is an ongoing need for organizations to quickly recognize failing strategies and structures and create new ones that will enable them to adapt to a digital world. In our view, this means creating an improved organizational capacity for crafting strategies that embrace innovation. These include improving the capacity for learning and the techniques of knowledge management, an emphasis on e-government, as well as skills at working with stakeholders.

Strategy vs. Strategic Management

The term *strategy* is used in many ways in private and public sector management, thus reflecting a variety of meanings. Examples include strategy as decisions on where, when and how to offer particular services and public goods; strategies for approaches to accomplishing important public objectives; strategies as patterns of actions over time; and strategy as both vision and direction (Mintzberg 1994; Nutt and Backoff 1995; Halachmi 1996; Joyce 2000; Wauters 2017). In his book on strategic management, Frank Rothaermel (2015, 4) described strategy as "the set of goal-directed actions a firm takes to gain and sustain superior performance *relative* to competitors" (emphasis in the original).

At its most basic sense, strategy is the set of key decisions made to meet an organization's goals and objectives. A comprehensive master plan includes three levels of strategy: a corporate strategy, a business-level strategy, and organizational function strategies. The corporate strategy describes the organization's overall long-term direction. For a business firm, this could mean planned actions in pursuit of market growth. For a government or civil society organization, this could mean a strategy for attaining sustainability. At the business level, this includes strategies for each of the businesses in which a firm competes. In a government agency, it could mean the several major service fields that organization serves. At the functional level for all organizations are the strategies for all units that support the strategies. Together, these strategies outline how the organization will achieve its mission and objectives.

Strategic management has both a process and a content dimension. Public sector strategies have offered both broad definitions that define what government does, as the ends to be achieved through public action, as the mission and vision goals determined through political processes, as well as the processes taken to implement these goals. Paraphrasing Fred Nichols (2019), there are three kinds of strategy in both business and public sector organizations: In business, these are strategy in general, corporate strategy and competitive strategy. In the public sector, there is primary organization strategy, agency strategy and specific program strategy. At the federal or state level, this is department-level strategy (such as for the Department of Agriculture), agency level within a department (such as the USDA Food Nutrition Service), and a program level within an agency (such as the Child Nutrition Program). At the municipal level, this could be New York City government, the NYC Department of City Planning, and the specific program example of strategy for the Bronx Metro-North Station Area Study (BMNS).

For adopters of strategic management, strategy refers to two fundamental management activities: strategic management (SM) and strategic planning (SP). Although closely related, strategic management and strategic planning are not the same. Strategic planning occurs when organizations, working with important stakeholders, review their actions, gather data on relevant changes in their environment and on their internal capacities, and craft missions, visions and goals and specify the practices and policies for accomplishing those goals. Strategic planning is an active, ongoing process, the set of decisions and activities that business leaders, politicians, administrators and civil society organization managers use to guide the long-term direction and performance of the public sector and government agencies, with the added ability to be able to anticipate and react to changing environmental conditions.

The following technology-oriented definition of strategic management was provided by a global network of information technology websites: "Strategic management is the continuous planning, monitoring, analysis and assessment of all that is necessary for an organization to meet its goals and objectives" (TechTarget 2018). The importance of product and process innovation, new technologies and citizen expectations and entitlements force public sector organizations to make decisions strategically to remain relevant. The strategic management process helps agency leaders evaluate their present situation, establish goals and objectives, design and implement strategies, and monitor the effectiveness of the implemented strategies. Strategic management typically includes the following elements:

- Strategies exist for guiding the policies and functional actions of an organization.
- A strategy should have a long-term focus, usually within a range of three to ten years.
- The strategy should direct actions in all organizational departments.
- A strategy should be based on a thorough analysis of the external environment and the strengths and weaknesses of the organization.
- The strategy or strategies should reflect the best fit between the organization's mission and the uncontrollable environment.

- In evolving and adverse environments, a strategy may focus on gaining and maintaining sustainability.
- A strategy should include a focus on identification and implementation of innovation.
- A strategy is transformational; it should focus on doing something that the organization is not currently doing.

Levels of Strategies

Strategies are designed for three levels of private sector organizations: principal department (the corporate level); program level (specific activity); and strategies for each of the organization's management functions. Strategies at the department level answer the question: "What is our core area of responsibility?" Strategies at the program-line level answer the question: "How do we design and implement operational strategies that contribute to successful delivery of primary services?" Strategies at the functional level answer the questions: "How are we organized and how do we operate to provide the best possible support for each of our program strategies?"

An operational strategy is the path organizations take to accomplish an objective or goal. It is the underlying sense and direction of an organization's mission and the way in which its strategic plans are implemented. Strategic management includes the decisions made for the ways that resources are applied to operational activities. Private, public and civil society sector organizations use strategic management tools to coordinate and align their mission, vision and strategies with their resources and capabilities. Strategic management activities transform random activities into a planned operational system that provides for performance feedback and enables the organization to evolve and grow as environments and circumstances change.

The execution of an organization's strategies is synonymous with strategy management and amounts to the systematic implementation of a strategic plan. The conceptual framework for implementation of a strategy depends upon what an organization's leaders feel is most important for the success of the organization's mission (Johanson 2009). Strategic management has evolved alongside the changes that have occurred in organizations and the economic and political environments in which management activities are implemented. The chosen strategy and the way that the organization's activities are applied are products of its strategic orientation. An organization's strategic orientation is the direction and focus the organization follows as it directs and employs its assets for designing and implementing present and future operations. In addition to the more commonly used term of strategic orientation, it is described in a variety of ways: strategic fit, strategic disposition, strategic thrust, and strategic choice (Morgan and Strong 2003; Lee, Chan, McNabb and Khalifa 2019).

Strategic Management Fundamentals

Rothaermel (2015, 4) defines strategic management as "the integrative management field that combines *analysis, formulation*, and *implementation* in the quest for competitive advantage" (emphasis in the original). Mastery of strategic management enables you to view a firm (or a public sector organization) in its entirety. It also enables you to think like a general manager to help position your firm (or government organization) for superior performance. Figure 2.1 displays a verso

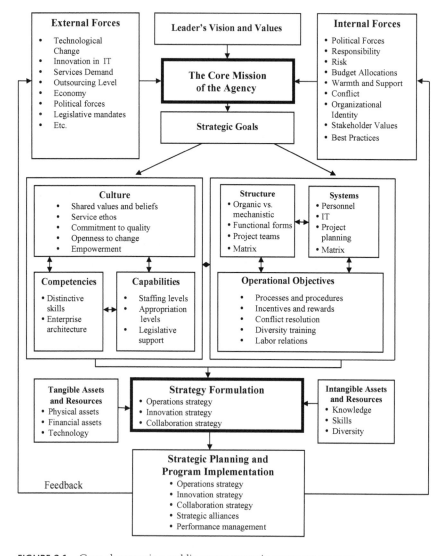

FIGURE 2.1   Core elements in a public sector strategic management system.

of the core operations factors in a public sector strategic management system. It illustrates the components in the strategic management system as applied to a public sector organization.

Strategic orientation is the focus of an organization's multi-functional, goal-oriented strategies. It is established during a process by which an organization brings plans for the strategic application of its assets, capabilities and functions. An organization's strategic orientation is a reflection of management's vision of how the organization will focus its energies and make the changes needed to get to its objectives, and how and where the organization will achieve its future goals. Thus, it is both a plan and a policy that includes a vision for the future and a course of action to follow.

Role of Strategy in Strategic Management

The term *strategy* is one of the most contested words in the public administration lexicon. The term is used in many ways, reflecting a variety of meanings: strategy as decisions (to offer particular services and public goods), *approaches* (to accomplishing important public objectives), *patterns* (of actions over time), and both vision and direction (Mintzberg, 1994). Thus, strategy has both process and content dimensions (Nutt and Backoff, 1995). Halachmi (1996) notes that authors on this subject have offered both broad definitions that determine what government does and the ends to be achieved through public action, and narrower approaches that take missions and policies as fixed (since they are set through political processes) and focus on how to implement them.

The purpose of strategic management is the need for building an ability to function in rapidly changing environments and for reinventing or redesigning the core mission. Change requires organizations to improve performance, design ways for growth, increase the value of its services or products, or create competitive advantage. The change may involve new or improved products, services, or operational processes. Whatever the focus of the adopted strategy, adoption of strategic management to implement and monitor the strategy will require changes to the way managers operate.

Strategic Management Process

Strategic management is an active, ongoing process, the set of decisions and activities that politicians, administrators and managers use to guide the long-term direction and performance of the public sector and government agencies, with the added ability to be able to anticipate and react to changing environmental conditions (Wheelen and Hunger, 2010; Hempel and LaPlaca, 1975). Hunger and Wheelen defined strategic management as a set of management actions and decisions that—when correctly implemented—guide the long-term performance of an organization. The management actions include analyses of the organization's internal and external environments, setting long-term objectives, and forming strategies to accomplish those objectives. It includes the activities of environmental scanning, establishing objectives, strategy formulation, strategy implementation, progress evaluation, and performance measurement and control.

Similarly, Poister and Streib (1999) defined strategic management as a process whereby organization managers engage in strategically managing a government organization to ensure that strategic plans are up to date and are sustainably effective. This model emphasizes ongoing planning and monitoring by a strategic management group, not necessarily the organization's leaders and top managers.

The process requires more than simply determining strategies through strategic planning, but also internal and external monitoring of important trends plus performance measurement, performance management, and results-oriented budgeting, all done in the context of the organization's values, mission and vision. Although the SM process was developed as a tool to help private sector organizations be more competitive in the global marketplace, a growing number of public administrators have concluded that it can be as beneficial to government agencies and civil society organizations as it is to managers in private enterprise.

The strategic management process consists of two activity characteristics. First, the strategy must be designed and adopted. Second, it must be implemented. Creating the strategy begins with agreement on the organization's mission, establishment of a vision that will guide all long-term goals, and elaborating the values that guide everything it does. Putting the strategy into action means selecting the activities and management systems that will enable the organization to achieve the objectives that lead to attainment of its long-term goals. Together, the strategy-making, strategy-implementing process consists of nine inter-related managerial tasks (Table 2.1).

Foundations for Strategies: Mission, Vision and Values

Strategies that are formed can have meaning and be achievable if they are designed on a foundation of the organization's core mission and what it wants to achieve. In planning terms, these are an organization's mission and its vision. Along the way, the way it operates will be shaped by the values by which it operates. A mission statement for a government organization is a statement of the reason for which it was formed, for whom it will perform those duties, and by what performance accomplishments it will be measured. These themes are based on the statutory requirements established by the appropriate elected body under which it functions. The strategies that follow explain how the agency will perform its functions. Spelled out, they help to ensure the mandated goals are achieved.

There are no rules for what should be said in either an organization's mission statement, or what its long-term vision or values should be. The wide variety of versions employed in different levels of government agencies illustrate these differences. While the mission statement of the U.S. Department of Energy's Project Leadership Institute tends to follow the general trend at all levels, the

TABLE 2.1 The strategy-making, strategy-implementing process

Step	Action	Discussion
1	Clarify the mission	Set the organization's mission, vision and values for period of 10 to 20 years in the future
2	Sense of purpose	Provide a sense of purpose by converting mission to measurable goals and objectives
3	Evaluate environment	Evaluate the external environment; forecast future client needs and wants and shifting legal and political environments
4	Analyze capabilities	Analyze the organization's resources, capabilities and capacities for meeting current and future demand for services
5	Set long-term goals	Set long-term goals balanced with expected environmental changes, resources and capabilities
6	Set task objectives	Set short-term operational objectives that match resources with mission goal requirements and long-term goals
7	Fashion strategies	Identify strategies possible for achieving desired results within scheduled time periods
8	Implement strategies	Implement chosen strategies with planned efficiencies and performance goals tempered with regular progress analyses; implement necessary changes to strategy
9	Evaluate performance	Implement performance measurement metrics with room for adjustments in directional objectives, the basic strategy; monitor and react to new ideas with new opportunities

Source: The authors

vision section of this organization illustrates the wide variety of interpretations of the concept. Examples of these positions at the federal, state and local levels of government are shown in Boxes 2.1 and 2.2.

Federal Agency Mission and Vision Statements

The mission of the U.S. Department of Energy is "to ensure America's security and prosperity by addressing its energy, environmental and nuclear challenges through transformative science and technology solutions" (DOE n/d). A brief search could not reveal a traditional vision statement for the DOE. However, the mission of just one of its many agencies and offices, the Project Leadership Institute (PLI), included both statements. The purpose of the PLI is to provide management training and knowledge-sharing for new workers and newly appointed project managers.

The PLI's purpose is to address and reverse the problems associated with the traditional relying on "ad hoc interactions and project peer reviews to make connections outside of their home institution" (PLI n/d). The program was established to provide a way for new project managers to gain access to the DOE's collective experiences and perspectives through the network of PLI alumni, board members, and instructors/speakers. Alumni will continue to contribute to and derive value from the network well beyond their cohort participation. The PLI network will amplify support of project delivery excellence through individual service exemplified by peer review and mentorship.

[Program] participants and administrators will, over time, accelerate the pace of learning. Together they will build a library of knowledge in the form of publications, recordings, case studies, reflections, and other materials that will articulate insights and lessons learned from DOE projects. This knowledge will have broad benefit, not only to the PLI network, but also to the wider DOE complex. The PLI will promote the development of tools and informational resources that aid DOE project executives, project teams, and other key participants in major projects.

The mission and vision statements of the PLI management-training program are shown in Box 2.1.

BOX 2.1 MISSION AND VISION STATEMENTS OF A US DOE TRAINING PROGRAM

Mission

The mission of the U.S. Department of Energy (DOE) Project Leadership Institute (PLI) program is to cultivate a diverse network of successful DOE project delivery practitioners—those capable of delivering major high-risk projects. The PLI program participants contribute to building a culture of project management excellence across DOE.

Vision

The vision for the PLI program is to provide cohort participants with a prestigious, transformational professional development experience that is simultaneously both a leadership development and project delivery course of study and practice, tailored to the DOE context. The program is rigorous and intensive. It will include experiential learning components and interaction with leaders from a variety of fields. Participants will undertake self-assessment activities to reveal strengths and potential weaknesses in the project leadership context. The PLI program will emphasize critical leadership development principles including stakeholder communications, perspective taking, ethics, service, and self-reflection.

Source: U.S. Department of Energy PLI

State Agency Mission and Vision Statements

The South Carolina Public Service Commission (PSC) is typical of the state-level public utilities oversight agencies (PSCSC 2019). The Commission holds hearings on issues pertaining to rates and other issues affecting the electric, gas, telecommunications, transportation, water, and wastewater industries in South Carolina. There continues to be a steady number of hearings within the electric industry on issues that must be addressed from a regulatory standpoint. Some of these issues include solar programs and energy efficiency programs, and a nuclear power generating facility. Sections of the Commission's report are shown in Box 2.2.

Environmental Analyses

SWOT analysis is the acronym for the analysis of both the internal and external environments of an organization. These analyses are applicable to organizations in all sectors. Two targets of the internal analysis are the assets, resources

---

BOX 2.2 ACTIVITIES OF THE PUBLIC SERVICE COMMISSION OF SOUTH CAROLINA

"The PSC regulates the rates and services of investor-owned public utilities in the State of South Carolina and establishes just and reasonable standards for their rates and services…. The State Regulation of Public Utilities Review Committee serves as the joint legislative committee that oversees the operations of the Commission. In order for the Public Service Commission of South Carolina to carry out its mission, the Commission must be alert to and anticipate emerging issues in the industries it regulates, including federal regulatory developments. Maintaining effective communications with its customers and participation in national organizations integrated into the utility sectors will aid in achieving this goal…. With growing pressure for the generation of energy using alternative energy sources, the Commission must effectively regulate these industries, safeguarding the ratepayers without unduly burdening the industries or stifling competition…. The Commission's primary duty is to adjudicate cases involving the state's investor-owned utilities. This past fiscal year, the Commission opened 427 new dockets, including non-docketed items, held 60 hearings, issued 327 orders, and 475 directive orders. In 2016–2017, the PSC issued 385 orders and 476 directive orders. A total of 5,690 matters were posted on the Commission's Docket Management System (DMS). The Commission also held 35 Commission Business Meetings during the year."

Source: PSCSC (2019)

and capabilities—its strengths (S)—that contribute to the organization's ability to succeed in its mission or its inability to carry out the tasks needed for achieving its goals and carrying out its mission—its weaknesses (W). The strengths and weaknesses of an organization are found in or the lack or ineffectiveness of the resources and capabilities that reside in the organization itself.

Similarly, two classes of factors need to be identified in the organization's external environment: the opportunities (O) that can be divined from the extant characteristics of the factors beyond the control of the managers and administrators, together with the threats (T) to the organization's mission and its goals and objectives lurking within the current and changing environments.

External Environment

These are the forces in an organization's external or non-controllable environment that may positively or negatively affect its ability to provide the goods and services in ways in which the best possible value for the organization is achieved. The six general forces originally identified for profit-oriented organizations are the political, economic, sociocultural, technological, ecological (or natural), and the legal environment.

Analysis of the political environment is a major influencing force within the external environment of public sector and civil society organizations. As with many of the private sector external environment factors, political factors influence many of the strategy decisions made by government organizations. Political forces that influence an organization's operations can take two different forms. One type is shaped by stakeholder power changes that result in the need for administrative adjustments. These political forces include the political pressure on organizations resulting from political decisions, and the regulations and laws under which organizations can operate. The second type of politically oriented strategies is brought on by shifts in partisan politics. These pressures can result in transformational changes, including changes in agency leadership, staffing, and policy emphases (Wechler and Bachoff 1986).

Technology factors include the advances and impact on markets and operations; an example is the initiation of E-Government and the effects on retail firms by the growth in Internet shopping. The impact of environmental factors such as global warming and air, water and soil pollution affects public and private sector organizations in all societies, creating economic opportunities for some and devastation for others. Sociocultural factors, such as the rapid changes in cultural norms and values of diverse populations, mass migration movements from poor and endangered societies to developed regions, are having far-reaching impacts on governments and the economic environment of all sectors.

The Internal Environment

The internal environment consists of the resources that an organization can manipulate and the capabilities and core competencies that it can employ to achieve its strategic goals. The organization applies these skills and assets to overcome areas of operational weaknesses and to take maximum advantage of its strengths. For businesses, the goal is to achieve competitive advantage. For public sector organizations, the goal is to provide maximum attainable value for citizens and related stakeholders.

In his popular book on strategic management, Frank T. Rothaermel (2015) referred to two of the five planning frameworks we describe in the following chapters to explain how managers can compensate for their operational weaknesses while implementing strategic moves that take advantage of their organizational strengths: the core competency and the resource-based frameworks. Although both of these frameworks were designed as ways of gaining and competing in the private sector, they are equally applicable for use with strategic management in public sector organizations. Core competencies are defined as the organizational and leadership knowledge and skills in guiding activities that help to differentiate the firm's products and services from the offerings of the firm's competitors. Resources are the tangible and intangible assets held by the firm that can be used when implementing its operational strategies.

Strategic Goals and Operational Objectives

A primary activity of an organization's senior management is setting long-term goals and designing achievable operational strategies. Once these goals are established, the objectives for the operational tasks that will make the goals achievable will be structured to coincide with the organization's capabilities and resources. Every goal-oriented action will be influenced by the strategic fit between the task-oriented objectives and plans for achieving those long-term goals.

Establishing Long-Term Goals

Federal government agencies, political parties, states, counties, cities and hamlets, and other sector organizations need to prepare plans and programs each year with the annual budgets they believe they will need—and be able to raise—for the planned programs. The following example of Plymouth, Minnesota, 2019 population of 70,576, illustrates a city government's goals and identifies selected key task-oriented objectives for achieving the goals (City of Plymouth 2019):

- **Protect Plymouth's Strong Financial Position.**
  Maintain Plymouth's fiscal health by implementing long-term revenue and expenditure plans to ensure sustainable operations with a reasonable tax level. Utilize non-property tax funding sources where appropriate.
- **Monitor Economic Challenges.**
  Continue to evaluate and prioritize services. Seek innovative solutions to maintain high quality core services, promote financial transparency and protect Plymouth's strong financial position and quality of life.

- **Provide Efficient and Effective Services.**
  Continue to explore partnerships with neighboring communities, school districts, businesses, watersheds and other agencies to decrease costs through shared services and eliminate duplicate efforts. Streamline processes through the use of technology. Evaluate community trends and consider associated facility and service needs.
- **Promote Transportation Solutions.**
  Focus on improvements to Highway 169, Highway 55 and continue to explore other transportation options. Seek funding partners for rail crossing improvements and I-494 crossing improvements.
- **Develop Northwest Greenway.**
  Continue development of northwest Plymouth as it progresses, continue planning and construction of the Northwest Greenway and park system amenities.
- **Implement Environmental Initiatives.**
  Collaborate with City EQC, watershed commissions, and district to ensure effective progress on water quality mandates. Continue energy conservation efforts in city buildings and promote recycling.
- **Implement Proactive Public Safety Initiatives.**
  Continue proactive policing strategies using technology and collaboration to promote and enhance livability. Build on the successes of fire prevention and fire service programs for a safe community.
- **Protect the City's Infrastructure Investment.**
  Ensure that the city can protect and enhance the useful life of city assets (streets, utilities, parks, trails, facilities and fleet). Continue to monitor financial resources and economic conditions and consider timing with regard to infrastructure needs as identified in the Capital Improvement Program.
- **Consider Development and Redevelopment Requests.**
  Continue to carefully consider land use related to development and redevelopment to ensure a well-planned community with a varied tax base. Build on Plymouth Proud business initiatives.
- **Develop a Renewed Vision for City Center.**
  Explore options for continued development and redevelopment of City Center. This would include placemaking efforts, beautification, and safety. Pursue public-private partnerships to bring additional community activities/ uses to City Center.

In planning and managing their operations, public organizations use the same internal and external environment analyses as private sector firms, although the focus of government's strategic activities is not for competing for market share as it is for private firms. Rather, public sector organizations need information for maximizing results from their allocated budgets and for greater efficiency and performance in the delivery of their services. W. Edwards Deming reminded planners in 1988 that in the public sector, there is no market to capture. In place of a larger share of a market share captured, "a government agency should deliver economically the service prescribed by law or regulation. The aim should be based upon distinction in service," not in market share or profit (Deming 2018, 5).

In its handbook for strategic planning by state agencies, the Arizona state government defines the two-environment analyses as

> a basic management tool that is used not only in strategic planning, but also in policy development and problem solving. It provides a baseline assessment of the organization.... The data gathered during the assessment will often lead to the identification of strategic issues.
>
> *(AOSPB 2011, 10)*

The internal assessment weighs the organization's capacity to respond to problems associated with the core mission, additional issues, problems and opportunities. The assessment "throws light on administrative and managerial policies and procedures that help or inhibit" performance while looking for "patterns of beliefs and values" that influence and drive current operations.

The Arizona guide described an external analysis as the process of identifying and evaluating both the opportunities and threats in the then current environment and the changes that might occur in the foreseeable future. This analysis then provides the input necessary for long-term goals and for designing future strategies for achieving those goals.

The Arizona environmental analysis guide also includes a section on the need for identifying the organization's "customers" and stakeholders. Customers are defined as anyone who receives the agency's services, uses the products or services, or benefits from actions of the agency or result of a program. It also includes individuals or organizations whose interests are served or influenced by an organization's operations. Stakeholders are individuals or organizations that have a "vested interest in or with expectations of a certain level of performance or compliance from an agency, program or subprogram."

Adopting Strategic Management

Adoption of strategic management processes in most organizations is an evolutionary process rather than a revolutionary activity. Hunger and Wheelen (2015) identified four distinct stages in the path toward full-blown strategic management. Each is discussed below.

First Stage: Annual Budgeting

Agency administrators follow the traditional government financial planning processes known everywhere as *annual* (or *bi-annual*) *budgeting*. However, eventually managers following the traditional budgeting process alone soon find it difficult to manage programs that extend beyond one- or two-year planning cycles. In this stage, operational plans are reflections of the immediate tasks and activities upon which the budget is based. Public administrators in this budget-setting mode often give little or no consideration to setting long-term objectives because they have no way of knowing whether legislative bodies will agree to fund their programs.

Second Stage: Department-based Planning and Budgeting

In the second stage, budgets are still department or unit focused; they still lack the synergies that can be created when the work of all units is coordinated into a larger, unified and focused whole. Unit administrators still devote much of their time and effort to justifying their position that their needs for resources are greater than that of other units in the agency. This competition for resources that pits unit against unit can severely limit the effectiveness and efficiency of government agencies. This requires preparation of more detailed and coordinated plans than the annual budgeting process can provide. It also requires administrators to start planning with a longer horizon, predicting future states of nature, and planning the agency activities that will extend from three to five years beyond the annual budget cycle.

Third Stage: Organization-level Planning and Budgeting

The agency enters the third stage when the senior administrators come to recognize that the political infighting for resources among agency units is severely curtailing the effectiveness of the organization. Instead, they come to believe that the agency would be better served if all planning and budgeting were brought together under a single *team* of managers with skills in planning activities, but which will continue to work under the direction of the agency's top administrator.

The planning focus in this third stage shifts from simple resource allocation to ensuring that resources are available to carry out the agency's mission and serve its external stakeholders and clients. Hunger and Wheelen call this shift in planning focus *externally oriented planning* and see it as an important step on the road to eventual full implementation of the strategic management concept.

Fourth Stage: Adopting Strategic Management

In the Hunger and Wheelen model, the agency enters the fourth, strategic management phase as an effort to transform the limitations on organizational operations associated with top–down planning. In this stage, planning teams work together to design the transformation tactics that will enable the agency to maintain a culture that embraces change, accomplish its mission strategies, and how those strategies evolve to meet the needs of future generations.

Coordinated, long-term plans now include detailed discussion on how strategies are implemented, transformation is achieved, performance evaluated, and how processes and activities are to be controlled and altered when necessary to meet changed conditions. Moreover, the emphasis is no longer on trying to simply predict future events, but rather on anticipating a variety of future conditions and determining how the agency will need to function under those changed conditions.

Summary

The advantages of employing the tested principles and processes of strategic management have been shown to be as advantageous to public administration organizations as it is for enterprises in the private sector. An operational strategy is the path organizations take to accomplish an objective or goal. It is the underlying sense and direction of an organization's mission and the way in which its strategic plans are implemented. Strategic management includes the decisions made for the ways that resources are applied to operational activities.

Private, public and civil society sector organizations use strategic management tools to coordinate and align their mission, vision and strategies with their resources and capabilities. Strategic management activities transform random activities into a planned operational system that provides for performance feedback and enables the organization to evolve and grow as environments and circumstances change.

As these principles and processes are reviewed in this chapter, we include extant approaches to the several dominant paradigms for analyzing and forming operations strategies. The basic concepts of strategic management include organizational strategy formulation, strategic orientation, strategic management, strategic management frameworks, strategic innovation, transformational change for implementing strategic management, and sustainability planning. The operational paradigms employed for analyzing and implementing these principles are the traditional competitive forces model and a resource-based model, a dynamic capabilities model and a network governance model.

Adopting strategic management typically occurs through a series of four stages in organization management. It begins with short-term budgeting for basic operational activities. In the second stage, planning and budgeting progress to a department or unit asset analysis and unit planning. Planning and budgeting still occurs in unit top–down form. In the third stage, plans and budgets are expanded to cover projected overall organization outlays, which includes evaluation over a period of three to five years. Asset lifespan and replacement costs and schedules are identified in a capital improvement plan. In the fourth stage, planning and budgeting is not conducted at the organization or enterprise level, occurring with the cooperation and collaboration of all unit managers.

3

STRATEGY DESIGN IN THE PUBLIC SECTOR

Strategies are selected guidelines for managing both private and public sector organizations (Watson 2008). In the private sector, competition drives strategy formation, whereas in the public sector, the motivator is public service. The public sector provides a wide variety of goods and services to a diverse clientele, as the following description of the sector illustrates:

> [The public sector] provides firms and households with services, such as health and education, housing, transport, electricity or security, through direct provision and through funding. It manages infrastructure and other public investments that the private sector may be unable to finance or for which the private sector may be unwilling to bear all the risk. It regulates social and economic behavior when necessary, such as food or road transport safety. Equally importantly, it develops and manages competing policy proposals, pro-actively (ideally) identifying emerging social and economic challenges and proposing solutions and it sets sector policy objectives, such as reimbursement methods for allocating recurrent budgets to hospitals, or incentives for water use efficiency.
>
> *(World Bank 2012, 6)*

Designing Strategy

Approaches to the designing of strategies for accomplishing these services and more are developed using the underlying interpretations and preferences of analysis frameworks and management themes that function as focal points in designing the sector organization's strategies. We were not the first to follow a underlying framework approach to analysis of organizational strategy. Keig and Brouthers (2013) employed this approach in their chapter on some of the major theories of business strategy. They grouped the theories according to four paradigms: product-market perspectives, industry-based theories, resource-based theories and competition-based theories. They then looked at representative approaches following a roughly chronological order.

Product-based Frameworks

Three important advances in research on product-based frameworks were the 1957 product-market growth matrix developed by J. Igor Ansoff, a three-dimensional view of product-market strategies introduced by Derek Abell in 1980, and the four different organizational behaviors model proposed by Raymond Miles, Charles Snow and colleagues in 1978. Ansoff identified four strategic approaches based on a 2×2 matrix of either new or modified products or services within new or old markets. Abell followed the product-market approach, but grouped strategies by customer groups, customer functions served, and product technology. Miles and Snow grouped strategies based on four types of organizations: defenders, prospectors, analyzers and reactors.

Industry-based Frameworks

Keig and Brouthers then looked at the competitive-forces concept found in industry-based frameworks. This framework was introduced by Michael Porter in 1979. He saw strategies determined or influenced by five competitive forces: the bargaining power of buyers, the same for suppliers, the threat of new entrants into the market, the threat of substitute products, and the existing competitive rivalry among firms. Porter added another concept a year later—the concept of three generic strategies that firms could follow: cost leadership, differentiation, or focus strategies. George Day added a four generic strategy model in 1990, based on a 2×2 matrix of different prices and quality.

Resource-based Framework

Subsequent researchers shifted from the outside view of organizational strategy formulation frameworks to several different tales on an inside the organization approach to strategy design. The three such frameworks reviewed by Keig and Brouthers were a resource-based view model, a knowledge-based view, and a dynamic capabilities framework. Jay Barney (1991) was the strongest early promoter of the resource-based approach. The strategy-related resources include all the tangible and intangible assets of the organization that can contribute to the successful result of a strategic approach. The assets are particularly important when they are valuable, rare, impossible to imitate, and nontransferable to another organization. We devote a full chapter to this framework.

Knowledge-based Framework

This framework was promoted by Robert Grant in 1996 to overcome the weaknesses of the resource view. An organization's knowledge base affords the organization to design strategies unique to it, its managers, and its employees. Competencies are born and nurtured from individuals' tacit and explicit knowledge. Tacit knowledge is gained by the activities and experiences of the individual. Explicit knowledge is recorded in documents, patents and other means of collecting, transmitting and recording information. The knowledge management movement of the late 20th century grew from managers' awareness of the need for retaining and using the institutional knowledge gained by its employees.

Dynamic Capabilities Frameworks

The dynamic capabilities strategy design framework was promoted by David Teece, Gary Pisano and Amy Shuen in 1997. They saw the capabilities of the organization's managers to adapt their resources in ways that they could be exploited for gaining competitive advantage. In many ways, the capability to see how the existing knowledge held by the organization's personnel could be used to find new and better uses for the organization's resources, this framework appears to be a logical unification of both the resource and knowledge models. Box 3.1 is an example of a dynamic capabilities-based strategy.

BOX 3.1 EPA-VICTORIA LAUNCHES NEW FIVE-YEAR STRATEGY

Environment Protection Authority Victoria (EPA) has launched a new five-year strategy that sets it up as a world-class regulator of pollution and waste. The strategy, titled *Our Environment, Our Health*, sets out the five goals EPA will focus on to create a healthy environment that supports a livable and prosperous Victoria now and always. The five goals are: prevent harm, equip community and business, be an influential authority, respond to harm, and organizational excellence. EPA will focus on several complex pollution and waste issues. These include:

- Implementation of specific leachate management conditions in landfill licenses to reduce off-site and amenity impacts that pose risks to the community and the environment;
- Addressing illegal dumping of hazardous materials, including asbestos, through EPA's Illegal Dumping Strikeforce Program;
- Improving industry practices to reduce and prevent the contamination of land, groundwater and stormwater through strategic compliance and engagement programs;

- Prevention of land and groundwater contamination from underground petroleum storage tanks through targeted compliance and education activities;
- Improving EPA's knowledge and capability to manage emerging contaminants of concern such as PFAS (per-and polyfluorinated alkyl substances);
- Further developing our knowledge and approach to assessing the impact of air pollutants on the environment and public health;
- Developing a management strategy for the environmental and human health impacts of lead contamination at current and former shooting ranges.

Source: EPA (Environmental Protection Authority) Victoria, Canada (2017)

Competition-based Strategy Frameworks

Keig and Brouthers discussed two versions of what they saw as competition dynamics theories: strategic conflict and competitive dynamics theory. Proposed by Carl Shapiro in 1989, the strategic conflict approach uses game theory to provide managers with help to identify preferred positions in the market and to identify potential actions of their competitors. The competitive dynamics model of Ken Smith, Walter Ferrier and Hermann Ndofor (2001) addresses the impact of the organization's action and competitors' reactions to events in the industry and its position in the industry. For example, the position changes that may occur as a result of introducing a new product or entering upon a price war.

Five Public Sector Strategy Frameworks

The five major strategy design frameworks often seen in studies of public sector organization strategies selected for discussion here have evolved since the last decades of the 20th century: (1) game theory, (2) the competitive forces framework, (3) the resource-based framework, (4) the dynamic capabilities framework, and (5) the network governance framework. These five management frameworks originated as private sector strategic design frameworks and are shown in Table 3.1.

Each approach continues to have its own supporters, with portions of all five frameworks often found in all types of organizations in all sectors. Modern strategic management is thus an integrative approach to managing an organization. It centers on designing enterprise-wide strategies and focusing the organization's activities toward accomplishing management-established goals and objectives. In sum, an organization's strategic orientation is shaped by management's focus on one or more strategic frameworks. This orientation is an expression of the way in which the organization's leaders align its actions with its position in the market, its operational focus, and its capabilities and capacities for meeting the demands of its current and future operations.

TABLE 3.1 Public sector strategic management planning and strategy selection

Frameworks for Public Organization Strategy

Framework	Inputs	Maximize Budget Allocation	Maximize Strategic Objectives	Outputs
Game Theory Approach	Results of zero-sum gaming among agencies for budget allocations	Focus on achieving greater resources by gaming with other agency managers	Focus on achieving sustainability by seeking new missions and additional mandates	Strategies for strict budget controls for maximum benefit from limited resources
Competitive Forces Framework	Society's needs, wants; political influence; executive mandates, etc.	Focus on achieving greater value by contracting service delivery with civil society	Focus on improving process efficiency goals by investing in staff training and education	Strategies for identifying operational strengths and weaknesses for success in competitive environments
Resource-Based View Framework	Tangible and intangible resources applied to strategic planning	Focus on increasing resources for adding services with existing staff	Focus on addressing high-visibility, limited goals for powerful stakeholders	Strategies designed for receiving maximum benefits from strategic application of existing resources
Dynamic Capabilities Framework	Organization's basic competencies applied to short-term problem solutions	Focus on developing management capabilities in organizational and technological capabilities	Focus on expanding, coordinating and integrating internal capabilities, technological skills and special knowledge	Strategies for guiding application of the knowledge and management skills and capabilities
Network Governance Framework	Network contributions to knowledge-sharing and cooperative problem-solving	Focus on combining assets, knowledge and skills with other institutions and levels of government through cooperative membership in informal personal and organizational networks	Focus on goal achievement by networking with other agencies and non-government stakeholders in cooperative governance as a leading agent in the governance of networks and strategic partners	Expansion of decision resources, capabilities and knowledge; development of strategies for addressing society's goals and solving common problems

The frameworks briefly presented here provide evidence that a strategic approach and the organizational transformation for implementing it have evolved since the late 20th century to today, and include at least four different but related orientations to the implementation of strategic management in the public sector. Aspects of the concept can result in serious organizational discontinuity and curtailing of organizational outcomes. The challenges to successful implementation of the approach to strategic management we have described here are formidable. There is no longer any justification for organizational inertia. Significant change often occurs only after catastrophic failure that forces political and policy leaders to adapt to changed circumstances and failed policies.

The various factors affecting an organization's capacity to engage in strategic management and adopt a strategic orientation have been thoroughly analyzed in the strategic management literature. There are many barriers to full adoption of strategic management by government agencies. Vinzant and Vinzant (1996) have noted that public agencies have varying levels of fiscal and statutory autonomy, factors that limit their ability to have full control over important elements of strategy development and implementation. However, governments large and small have successfully adjusted the basic concepts to their own operations, thereby benefiting largely from management concepts once thought to only be applicable to the private sector. They have overcome leadership deficiencies, a culture resistant to change, and strategies inappropriate to the capacities and competencies of the organization. In addition, they also realized that an inefficient implementation may result in failure of even the best-designed strategy.

Strategic Management Frameworks

Strategic management requires understanding of an organization's position in its external environment and its ability to successfully apply its internal strengths and operational weaknesses. Analysis of the firm's external environment is necessary for identifying the opportunities and threats that improve or hinder successful performance of its mission. Analysis of its internal environment identifies its operational strengths and weaknesses. Acquiring both bodies of knowledge are necessary precursors for designing strategies for achieving its performance goals. Managers of public sector organizations have many different analysis frameworks available for designing operations strategies. Among the analysis frameworks available for aiding strategy decisions are analysis based on game theory, the competitive forces framework, the organization's resource base, the dynamic capabilities of the organization's management, and a network governance approach.

The Competitive Forces Framework

This approach to strategic management grew primarily out of the work of Harvard professor Michael Porter (1980, 1985 and 1991). Porter wrote that five competitive forces shape an organization's position in a market. These forces are the bargaining power of its suppliers, the threat of new entrants into the market, the bargaining power of customers, the threat of substitute products or services, and the rivalry among existing competitors. Within the industry, identifying a company's strengths and weaknesses includes establishing where the company stands against the underlying causes of each competitive force. A firm's leaders can devise a plan of action that may include:

1. **positioning** the organization so that its capabilities provide the best defense against the competitive force; and/or
2. **influencing** the balance of the forces through strategic moves (e.g., innovation), thereby improving the company's position; and/or
3. **anticipating** shifts in the factors underlying the forces and responding to them, with the hope of exploiting change by choosing a strategy appropriate for the new competitive balance before opponents recognize it.

Applying the information gained in the analyses of their clientele and of their capacity for delivering their mandated services, Porter also introduced the value chain concept. A value chain includes the activities required for producing a product or service from start to finish. Later authors expanded on this concept by adding the service chain concept, which includes all the activities necessary for distributing a finished good or service to the persons or organizations for which it was designed. Both of these concepts are discussed in greater detail in the next chapter.

The Resource-Based View Framework

Eisenhardt and Martin (2000) defined the resource-based model as: "The firm's processes that use resources—specifically the processes to integrate, reconfigure, gain, and release resources—to match and even create market change." The resources-based view (RBV) of inputs for government organizations' strategic planning is based on the belief that tangible and intangible resources and capabilities should be considered critical elements for achieving superior performance.

Selection of these strategic resources for determining operational strategies should be "valuable, rare, inimitable and non-substitutable." By themselves, these resources cannot ensure success; the organization's management must be capable of organizing and employing the resources effectively and efficiently if they are to be considered valuable. Some critics of the model claim that an organization's strategy that is based on application of the identified resources

> should align with the environment where the firm are operating. This can be performed using the Porter's framework. RBV support the view that resources use and capabilities developed are hard to imitate by rivals.

The firm can achieve core competence by developing expertise and resource strengths, being a low-cost provider or focus on niche market.

(Essays, UK 2018)

The Dynamic Capabilities Framework

The dynamic capabilities conceptual model of an organization has generated great interest in the business, management and economic literature. "Dynamic capabilities are the organizational and strategic knowledge, skills and routines by which it configures its strategies as markets emerge, collide, split, evolve and die" (Bridges, Coughlan and Kalish 1991). The model that was considered the first to focus on dynamic capabilities was introduced in an article by Teece, Pisano and Shuen (1997, 516). They defined the approach as "the firm's ability to integrate, build, and reconfigure internal and external competencies to address rapidly changing environments." Between 1991 and 2015, 3852 research papers were published on the topic, with the annual number peaking at 397 in 2012. As expected with this much research, a variety of alternative definitions have emerged (Albort-Morant et al. 2018).

The Network Governance Framework

Governments and government agencies are finding it increasingly necessary to work with other governments and agencies to deal with the increasingly severe problems facing society. To make that collaboration and cooperation possible, they are forming strategic networks with like-minded units. A network has been defined as a group of

> three or more legally autonomous organizations that work together to achieve not only their own goals but also a collective goal. Such networks may be self-initiated, by network members themselves, or may be mandated or contracted, as is often the case in the public sector. When defined in this way, as multilateral collectivities, networks can become extremely complex entities that require explanations that go well beyond the dyadic approaches that have been traditionally discussed in the organization theory and strategic management literatures.
>
> *(Provan and Kenis 2008, 229)*

The Game Theory Framework

Game theory's contribution to strategy decision-making has been described as:

> the branch of mathematics concerned with the analysis of strategies for dealing with competitive situations where the outcome of a participant's

> choice of action depends critically on the actions of other participants. Game theory has been applied to strategic contexts in war, economics, business, government, politics, and biology, among other disciplines.
>
> *(Oxford Dictionary of English 1998)*

In mathematics, it is the study of mathematical models of strategic interaction between rational decision-makers, logic, and computer science.

It has a long history in the decision-making of managers in both civil society organizations and all levels of government. When described by von Neumann and Morgenstern in 1944, it referred to decisions in two-person zero-sum games, in which one person's gains result in losses for the other participant. It has subsequently been shown to apply equally to multi-organization decision-making situations.

Game theory is the study of how players (people, organizations, governments, nations, etc.) compete or cooperate to achieve an outcome which results in achieving desired or preferred payoffs. For the game to occur, the following requirements must be met (Straffin 1993, 4):

1. There must be at least two players. The players may be firms, investors, government agencies, or any social organization.
2. Each player must have a number of possible courses of action—strategies—that may or may not guide the player's actions.
3. The strategies chosen by each player will determine the outcome of the game.
4. Outcomes are signified by a numeric system assigned as the payoff for each player (the numbers are ordinal, not quantities).

Adopting Strategic Management

Adopting a new and different management framework with its resulting strategic orientation often requires large-scale changes in an organization's mission and strategic vision. However, the increasing rapidity of environmental changes and international competition are compressing the time between large-scale changes. This rapid pace of change has made the need for change to no longer be incremental; organizational change must now be transformational. Viewing the increasingly rapid changes occurring in organizations during the decade of the 1970s, Henry Mintzberg (1979) analyzed what he saw as the human and organizational reasons behind the nature of transformational change. He believed that patterns of change

> seem to be consistent with human cognition. We do not react to phenomena continuously, but rather in discreet steps, in response to changes large enough for us to perceive. Likewise, strategic decision processes in

organizations are not continuous, but irregular. They must be specifically evoked; they proceed for a time; and then they terminate.

In a word, they must be transformative.

The transformational challenge for organizations in all sectors is that the societal pace of change throughout the world continues to accelerate, driven by technology, economics and other forces. Data are accumulating that suggest that the increasingly linked nature of the globalized economy increases the risk of sudden systemic crises. In addition, important changes in the environment of public agencies are discontinuous, and as a result require that on occasion public agencies make abrupt changes in their mission, structure and operations. Organizations must be prepared to make these transformational changes quickly and often.

After operational goals are set and prioritized, managers must design the strategies to follow for accomplishing the objectives. Since many different strategies are possible, this requires a careful decision process. Leadership is needed to select the strategies that best fit the environmental conditions, long-term trends, recent developments, existing and future capabilities, and both the costs to complete the strategic actions and the cost that will accrue from a failed implementation.

Teams of managers, administrators and stakeholders come together in common-goal networks to visualize possible scenarios or states of nature, and then estimate what demands will be placed on society and members of the network if and when those scenarios come to pass. Although the senior network administrator may still initiate the primary mission strategy, the planning team or teams now must interact with managers and staff in all units at all levels. Contributions to the continually evolving strategic plans of the network and its constituent term must plan together. Members from all sectors are now working together to develop success strategies. The strategic management process is now an evolutionary, transformative process, with contributions, evaluations and changes occurring at any time. Table 3.2 illustrates some of the underlying strategy design frameworks.

Strategic Management Focus

A core concept underlying strategic management is its focus on helping to shape an organization to achieve sustainability. To accomplish this, it includes strategic planning, continuous performance improvement, budgeting, resource management, and performance monitoring and reporting. These activities need not occur in sequence; rather, they function in concert, integrating analyses and conclusions.

Strategic management in the public and civil society organizations have much the same fundamental justifications and programmatic processes as organizations in the commercial and industrial sectors: For all organizations, SM is a systematic process of analyzing the internal and external environments of an organization and then making and implementing strategic decisions to meet short-term objectives and longer-term goals.

TABLE 3.2 Comparisons of frameworks for strategic analysis, planning and implementation

Framework Characteristics	Game Theory Approach	Competitive Forces Approach	Resource-Based View of the Firm Approach	Dynamic Capabilities Approach	Network Governance Approach
Champions	J.Von Neumann and O. Morgenstern (1944); J. Nash (1951)	M. Porter (1980, 1985)	Penrose (1959); Rumelt (1984); Barney (1986, 1991)	Teece and Pisano (1994); Teece, Pisano and Shuen (1997)	Agranoff and McGuire (2003); Goldsmith and Eggers (2004)
Unit of analysis	Decision outcomes	Industry, firm, product	Resource, capabilities, competences	Innovation processes or capabilities	Strategic networks
Strategic re-orientation capacity	Moderate	High	Very low	Low	Moderate
Role of industry structure	Exogenous	Exogenous	Endogenous	Endogenous	Exogenous
Focal concern	Potential decision payoffs	Structural conditions and competitor positioning	Asset fungibility[1]	Asset accumulation and replicability; organizational learning	Cooperation and collaboration in problem-solving networks
Strategic changes	Incremental	Strategic leaps	Incremental (Path dependence)	Incremental (Path dependence)	Strategic leaps
Economic rent[2]	Nashian[6]	Monopoly[3]	Ricardian[4]	Schumpeterian[5]	Network
Strategic payoffs	Best payoff alternative	Unconstrained search for new businesses	Similar to existing business	Similar to existing business	Substantial
Program diversification	New product decisions for diversification	Acquisitions to raise rivals' costs or to erect entry barriers	Build upon or extend existing capabilities	Innovation streams	Different network memberships for different problems

Notes:

1 The characteristic of interchangeability, i.e., asset must be flexible in its deployment.

2 The difference between what a strategy (e.g., labor, capital) decision generates and the payment that would be necessary for its employment.

3 Rents generated from monopolist deliberately limiting supply or erecting entry barriers.

4 Ricardian rents accruing to the owners of scarce, firm-specific resources.

5 Rents reward to the creators of product or process innovations.

6 Nashian rents reward the "winner" of non-collaborative games determined at the natural equilibrium between all options.

Consistent application of the process leads managers through the steps needed to achieve success and gain sustainability for public sector organizations and competitive advantage and growth for private sector organizations. Bruce Perrott recognized this late in the last century, noting the value of strategic management to public sector organizations:

> Strategic management is ... a useful discipline as it creates the basis for allocating resources, evaluating performance, resolving conflicts, recruiting support, justifying decisions to legislators, explaining the organization to the public and performing a wide variety of other management chores.... Strategic management broadens the traditional notions of strategic planning to include strategic thinking, strategy formulation and implementation. It merges short-term and long-term planning by seeking immediate actions which simultaneously address issues in a dynamic, evolving environment.
>
> *(Perrot 1996, 338)*

Strategic Issues

Strategic issues are the stuff from which strategies are formed and implemented. The strategies themselves are designed with an appropriate mix of elements of each of the relevant management frameworks, environmental constraints, stakeholder power to shape policy and the interests of the organization's customers.

Strategic issues are important future or ongoing operational positive or negative themes, opportunities or problems that require planning specifically for dealing with their resolution. Strategic issues are high-priority issues that call for careful strategies and program decisions that are included in an organization's strategic plan. Because strategic issues can have significant critical impact on the performance of the organization, they require designing specific strategies and preparing budget allocations for programs and resources for dealing with them. They may require a long-term solution using a framework or frameworks commensurate with their impact on the sustainability of the organization. The solution requires identifying the organizational structure, the goods or services distribution involved, customer service, resource management, strategic networks or partnerships, and the strategic management strategies to be implemented, the goals to be accomplished and the objectives for the tasks to be performed.

Evaluating Potential Strategies

Members of the faculty at Harvard's Kennedy School of Government identified three underlying principles necessary for the design and implementation of a strategy by a public sector organization. First, the underlying concept of the strategy must be based on the overall mission or purpose of the organization. Moreover, the mission should be stated in terms of public values. Second, the strategy has to be a sustainable reflection of society's willingness to support the program or activity. Third, the strategy must explain how its goals will be achieved through implementation of the organization's core competencies and resources (Moore 1997). From this foundation, to achieve legitimacy, it has to meet these three tests:

1. The strategy has to be "substantively valuable." That is, the actions taken under the scope of the strategy must result in things or ideas that stakeholders, clients and recipients value and are commensurate with the costs.
2. The strategy must be "legitimate and politically sustainable." That is, the underlying mission and goal of the strategy must have the long-term ideological and financial support of its political overseers and public served.
3. The strategy must be "operationally and administratively feasible." That is, it can be brought to fruition with the existing assets, capabilities and personnel of the organization.

It is often difficult to determine whether the goals, objectives and even the strategies are the right ones considering the possible reactions from important stakeholders or policymakers. A possible pathway toward a solution to this decision problem may be addressed with use of a simple two-question evaluation metric introduced by Prusty, Mohapatra and Mukherjee in 2017 and repeated in Table 3.3.

TABLE 3.3 Selection guidance criteria and example metrics

Factor	Criteria	Example Evaluation Metrics
Goal		
	Desirability	How applicable to the mission is this goal?
		How much is pursuing this goal worth in the long run?
	Feasibility	Is this goal sustainable in the long run?
		Is this goal feasible with our current resources?
Objective		
	Desirability	How much is this objective worth pursuing in the short run?
		How much does this objective contribute to the goal?
	Feasibility	Is achieving the objective possible with current resources?
		Is achieving the objective with our management capabilities feasible in the short run?
Strategy		
	Effectiveness	When implemented, will this strategy produce the desired results?
		Will this strategy result in more harm than benefits?
	Feasibility	Is this strategy politically implementable?
		Will this strategy be supported by policymakers?

Sources: Prusty, Mohapatra and Mukherjee (2017); Arundel, Bloch and Ferguson (2019).

For evaluating possible goals and objectives, weighing the desirability and feasibility on a five-point scale can provide some guidance. In addition to the tests for evaluating a potential strategy described by Moore (1997), rating and comparing scores for all proposed strategies on their expected effectiveness and the feasibility of their successful implementation helps avoid making the wrong strategic choice and alignment with existing policy (Arundel, Bloch and Ferguson 2019).

Summary

Strategies are selected guidelines for managing both private and public sector organizations (Watson 2008). In the private sector, competition drives strategy formation, whereas in the public sector, the motivator is public service. The public sector provides a wide variety of goods and services to a diverse group of citizens, firms and non-governmental organizations. Government departments and agencies must depend on the electorate for approval. The strategies agencies adopt are influenced by policies set by competing elected governing bodies, influential stakeholders, and the electorate. These policies are beyond the control of agency managers. Therefore, strategy formulation and implementation becomes a complicated balancing activity that may be aided by management principles and processes put forth in strategic management.

Strategic management is a toolbox of potential strategies that are best aligned with the organization's resources and management capabilities that make it possible for achieving the long-term goals of the organization's mission. Analysis of the organization's internal capacities is joined by analysis of the current social, economic and political environmental and operational envelopes within which the agency is mandated to operate. This information then allows the organization's managers to design the strategies they determine are most likely to allow the organization to accomplish its goals. Program and task objectives commensurate with the strategic orientation and available resources are then planned and implemented. Procedures must be designed for monitoring the organization's performance toward achieving those objectives. Performance monitoring is incomplete without management's preparedness to respond to stakeholder-required shifts in procedures when objectives are not met, when resources are insufficient, or mission direction is augmented or redirected. For this to happen, learning is a core concept in strategic management.

PART II

Frameworks for Designing Strategy

4

THE COMPETITIVE FORCES FRAMEWORK

The competitive forces framework (also known as the *strategic positioning approach* or as *Porter's five forces approach*) to strategic management developed. Credit for introducing the framework is given to Michael Porter, who in 1979 and 1980 emphasized the importance of managing an organization's value chain and adoption of a competitive positioning in the marketplace. The five forces that Porter said make up an organization's competitive environment are: (1) the firm's competitive rivalry, (2) the power of its suppliers, (3) the power of buyers of the organization's goods or services, (4) the threat of substitute products, and (5) the threat of new suppliers entering the market. The five forces are all external environment factors. Porter then named four types of generic strategies that organizations adopt to deal with these forces: differentiation, cost leadership, cost focus, and differentiation focus. Many alternative strategies have been added since the 1980s, including a combination strategy, innovation strategy, technology strategy, learning strategy, and others.

Writing on game theory as studied in economics, Samuelson and Nordhaus (1985) saw the variety in the paths followed by researchers in the social sciences as different not so much by what the researchers studied, but by how they studied their subject. The same idea can help explain the differences in the organizing frameworks preferred by researchers in public sector management. The framework followed for several decades beginning in the 1970s was patterned after the private sector's competitive advantage concept and how to adjust operating in a competitive environment to public sector operations.

The competitive forces framework was developed as a means of analyzing the competitive environment faced by a firm in a given industry. The approach has also been modified for use for in-depth analysis of a public sector organization's operation environment. In both applications, designing strategy using the Porter five forces framework is generally conducted after a SWOT environmental analysis. The applications process includes the following seven steps.

SWOT Environmental Analysis

The decision to adopt any strategy begins with a complete analysis of the organization's internal and external environments. The tool used in this process is "SWOT analysis." SWOT, the acronym for the framework that appeared in a number of different management guides sometime in the 1960s, is formed from the first letters of four environment characteristics: strengths, weaknesses, opportunities and threats. A SWOT analysis looks at both internal and external factors during the foundational research for beginning a strategic plan (Figure 4.1). Strengths and weaknesses are considered internal factors, whereas opportunities and threats are considered external forces. As discussed in the next two chapters, strengths can be either tangible or intangible resources or capabilities. Weaknesses are factors that limit an organization's ability to improve services or meet threats (Figure 4.1).

Public–Private Sector Value Chain Example

Buttigieg, Schuetz and Bezzina (2016) employed a traditional external and internal environment analysis framework in their preparatory analysis of a combined public and private healthcare system. The participants examined the external environment of both sectors following the traditional strengths and weaknesses, opportunities and threats (SWOT) analysis framework. Overall, the major factors that set the two systems apart included the client-centered resources, management skills, comfort and technology of the private sector, and the regulatory actions and protection of the public interest of the public sector. "The public sector aims for

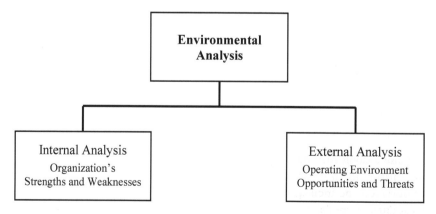

FIGURE 4.1 The SWOT analysis framework.

patient satisfaction through quality, free access, and availability, whereas the private sector aims for quality and client satisfaction to secure return on investment and shareholder value" (Buttigieg, Schuetz and Bezzina 2016).

The objective of the study was to provide recommendations for improving collaboration and cooperation between the two system-governance models. Malta's universal healthcare system was patterned after that of Great Britain, with the added collaboration between public and private hospitals/clinics a priority of the Maltese Government. The study followed a value chain analysis mixed-system model developed at the Wharton School and published by Jossey-Bass in 2002 (Burns et al. 2002).

To identify separate value chains, the researchers collected data aired at a workshop with 28 professionals from the public and private healthcare sectors. They then analyzed strengths, weaknesses, opportunities, and threats in the Porter SWOT model. That analysis revealed several strengths and opportunities with which they can better equip policymakers to maximize provision of healthcare services.

The public healthcare system provides for free medical service for all citizens and for qualified individuals. Not included are elective dental care, optical services, and some medicines. Low-income residents and some citizens with chronic illnesses receive free medicines and some medical devices. A private sector system that operates in parallel to the public system provides the majority of available primary care in the nation.

Analysis Illustration

A SWOT analysis conducted for the strategic planning of a five forces value chain illustrates how the two management tools work in practices. Porter's five forces framework was applied in strategy planning for the emergency medical service, a mixed public and private sector healthcare industry (Pine 2006). Table 4.1 shows example analysis results for a partial list of the steps in the value change of an emergency medical services agency. The five forces cost leadership and differentiation strategies used for industry planning are not easily adaptable to public sector strategic management. However, Hansen and Ferlie (2016) found that some parts of Porter's theories fit successfully to public organization strategic planning. They saw particular relevance for the theory's emphasis on two strategies: a focus on improving value creation for all relevant stakeholders and aligning the value chain activities with those strategies.

Five Forces Framework

Because analysis methods in the five forces framework are designed to provide information in an organization's internal environment, instead focusing on the organization's position against competition in the external environment, a somewhat different model is used (Figure 4.2). In this case, the medical service system analyzed was a commercial rather than a government operation.

TABLE 4.1 Example of public sector health facility SWOT analysis along value chain

SWOT Stage	Value Chain Steps				
	Pre-hospital	Facilities	Treatment	Outcome	Follow-up
Strengths	Health education	Accessible Full service Infrastructure	Affordable diagnosis spectrum	National Cancer Institute	Scheduled check-up
Weaknesses	Ad hoc Not well structured Budget constraints	No free access High cost	Easy access No unnecessary treatment Variation in care	Delayed discharge Lack of community support	Lack of monitoring
Opportunities	Social media	Restructuring along care pathways	Organization along care pathways AlgorithmsSpace	Planned process Information exchange	Follow-up management
Threats	Undisciplined culture	–	Risk aversion	–	–

Source: Concepts in Buttigieg, Schuetz and Bezzina (2016).

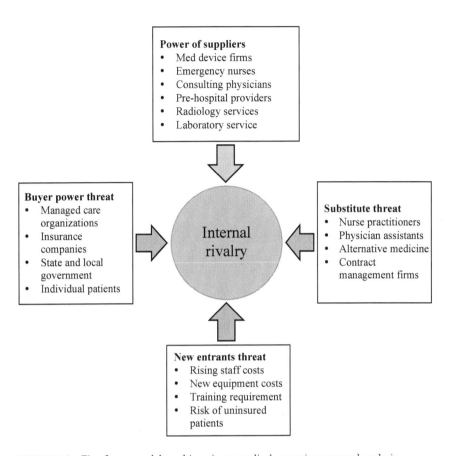

Power of suppliers
- Med device firms
- Emergency nurses
- Consulting physicians
- Pre-hospital providers
- Radiology services
- Laboratory service

Buyer power threat
- Managed care organizations
- Insurance companies
- State and local government
- Individual patients

Internal rivalry

Substitute threat
- Nurse practitioners
- Physician assistants
- Alternative medicine
- Contract management firms

New entrants threat
- Rising staff costs
- New equipment costs
- Training requirement
- Risk of uninsured patients

FIGURE 4.2   Five forces model used in private medical operation external analysis.

Organizations at the federal, state and local levels of government have also found the strategic fit and value chain concepts applicable to their strategy selection and management planning frameworks. Strategic fit defines the extent to which an organization's resources and capabilities are such that its strategies best contribute to the achievement of its mandates and strategic goals. The benefits of good strategic fit include implementation of available best practices, efficient skill application, and the transfer of knowledge and skills. A value chain is the combination of the activities that best add value to recipients of a government service. Each process in a government agency's value chain becomes a source for strategic management decisions that result in improved performance efficiency, cost reduction, and a contribution to better performance ratings.

Overall performance can be improved by closely monitoring and managing activities in each of the five operational processes (the "five forces") that add to superior performance: inbound logistics, value-creating operations in developing services for implementation, the outbound logistics activities required for delivering a government service, the integrated information activities for informing clients and stakeholders of the service, and the support activities that augment service delivery.

The Public Sector Value Strategies

A public sector value chain has the same goal of adding value to primary and support activities as do businesses and industries. The nature of the value and how it is measured is not the same. For private sector organizations, value is measured in sales, market share, or profits. For public sector organizations, value is reflected in the degree that public services meet the needs of citizens, private organizations and society in general. For both, the value chain is the combination of activities performed for producing and delivering a product or service and the enterprise functions that support these primary activities. Porter identified the private sector support activities as consisting of firm infrastructure, human resources management, technology and procurement. Porter's primary activities consist of inbound logistics, operations, outbound logistics, marketing, sales and customer service. Figure 4.3 shows how these activities might be included in a municipal public utility. Value is added at each position on the central line from a source of the water to receiving and processing wastewater.

Value Chain Applicability Questions

A variety of sources have questions on the applicability of the value chain concept to public sector organizations (Stabel and Fjeldstad 1998; Ajuaj 2003; Woiceshyn and Falkenberg 2008). An alternative approach patterned is the three distinctive configurations of the value chain described by Stabel and Fjeldstad: the traditional value chain, value networks and value shops. Porter's value chain was originally developed to illustrate how the various activities in a manufacturing firm create value by development and sale of products.

Most public sector organizations do not distribute products. They are more likely to provide services designed to solve a class of problems affecting a segment of society. Thus, the government agency or agencies assigned with the solution apply a combination of their resources and competencies in what has been termed a "value shop" to come up with the appropriate solution. Often, the organization works with different organizations in and outside of government, other government levels, and civil society organizations for the service to be distributed. In these situations, a value network more closely describes the value creation process.

Yang (2016) addressed public sector values in his study of four best-practice cases in which public values were examined. However, earlier definitions of public value had been proposed in work by Moore (1997) and Bozeman (2007).

Moore saw public values as desirable outcomes from government delivery of services for individual and social groups. These services were described as falling into one or more of these three categories (Bozeman 2007): (1) the rights, benefits and prerogatives that citizens should or should not be entitled, (2) the obligations of citizens to society, the nation, and one another, and (3) the principles on which government's policies are based or are not followed. The Yang study was designed to determine whether a consensus could be found on answers to the following question: What does an effective public value creation process consist of?

The four public sector organizations were selected on the basis of prior reputations as being highly committed to providing public value. They were the City of Albuquerque, New Mexico; the Children's Services Council of Broward County, Florida; Truckee Meadows Tomorrow and Washoe County, Nevada; and South Australia. The public values outcomes for each organization are shown in Table 4.2.

TABLE 4.2 Examples of outcome categories evaluated as public values

Organization	Public Value Outcomes Tested
Albuquerque, NM	1 8 categories: human and family development, public safety, public infrastructure, sustainable community development, environmental protection and enhancement, economic vitality, community and cultural engagement, government excellence and effectiveness 2 46 desired community conditions 3 99 indicators[1]
Children's Services Council of Broward County, FL	1 7 categories: abuse and neglect, domestic violence, juvenile justice, prosperity, safety, school readiness, and youth employment 2 About 90 indicators[2]
Truckee Meadows Tomorrow and Washoe County, NV	1 Category examples: arts and cultural vitality, civic engagement, economic well-being, education and lifelong learning, enrichment, innovation, land use and infrastructure, natural environment, and public well-being 2 33 indicators[3]
South Australia	1 6 categories: growing prosperity, improving well-being, attaining sustainability, fostering creativity and innovation, building communities, and expanding opportunity 2 98 indicators[4]

Source: Yang (2016)

Notes:
1 proposed by Mayor, City Council and Progress Commission
2 proposed by public participation
3 proposed by Truckee Meadows Tomorrow organization of area groups
4 proposed by Community Engagement Board

Identifying Public Values Processes

Yang concluded that the value creation process involves both universal values and public values. It is therefore necessary to establish goals through a process that includes public participation, perceptions of legitimation, and possible reactions to implementation. The process developed in the Yang study is shown in Table 4.2. Yang saw that a combination of universal and personal values were held by the majority of the different social groups studied. These combinations of values appeared to function as the basis for all public sector value chains.

The 10 nearly universal values identified by Shalom Schwartz (1992, 2012) are self-direction, stimulation, hedonism, achievement, power, security, conformity, tradition, benevolence and universalism. Schwartz stressed that these values usually occur in tandem with others and may be further classified into four broad categories:

- **Openness to change**
  - stimulation
  - self-direction
  - hedonism (shared with self-enhancement)
- **Self-transcendence**
  - universalism
  - benevolence
- **Conservation**
  - security
  - conformity and tradition (combined)
- **Self-enhancement**
  - achievement
  - power
  - hedonism (shared with openness to change)

Public values are values created by government agencies and organizations which are valued by the recipients of the services provided. According to Mark A. Moore, for a public service

> to be judged worthwhile, it must pass a test beyond the mere demonstration that the value of its products (i.e., services) exceeds the value of the resources used in producing the results: it must explain why the [agency] should be public rather than private.
>
> *(Moore 1997, 43)*

The next level in the public sector value creation process involves the planning and management contribution of the agencies to be assigned for developing and delivering the service. Successful agreement results in legitimation: providers and

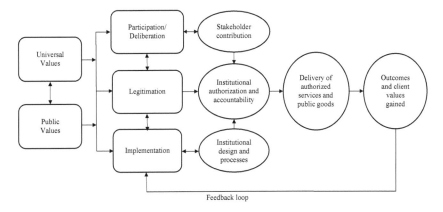

FIGURE 4.3 Model of the public value creation process.

Source: After concepts in Yang (2016).

recipient bodies assure the delivered product is fully in agreement with the service concept and is to be provided in ways and levels that are valued. Stakeholders and agency management participate in the design deliberation. Implementation of the program and delivery of the service cannot succeed without knowing the outcomes and values provided are achieved. Figure 4.3 is a model of the public sector value creation system built on Yang's conceptual views.

Two basic value creation strategies available to public sector organizations are (1) taking actions to maximize value from provision of a public service or (2) concentrating on maximizing the benefits accruing from investments in such public goods as transportation, defense, etc. Public goods are things that the private sector cannot or does not produce in sufficient quantity. An example of a public *service* value is health research and monitoring conducted by the Centers for Disease Control and Prevention (CDC). Public goods are things that are non-rival (everyone has access) and non-excludable (no one can be excluded from its use). An example of a public good is funding the Federal Highway Administration's (FHWA) Department of Transportation that supports state and local governments in the design, construction, and maintenance of the U.S. highway system (Federal Aid Highway Program) through financial and technical assistance to state and local governments.

Porter's strategic positioning framework calls for organizations to focus on finding a niche in the market that is not successfully served by competitors. This implies selective focus on customers who can be better served by a product and marketing effort designed to provide the customers greater value which, in turn, results in greater profits for the firm. However, although they are also affected by changes in their environments, public organizations cannot choose their markets or customers. Beyond their mission's mandated focus (such as social security recipients), public sector organizations usually do not have the luxury of picking and choosing whom they will serve. Nor are they able to offer their services for customers willing to pay more for the service. The payoff for public organizations is not increased profit; it is in achieving sustainability by continuously improving their performance. For this to happen, their "overall focus should be on value creation for all relevant stakeholders" (Hansen and Ferlie 2016, 8).

Public Sector Supply Chains

Supply chain management has as much relevance for public sector organizations as it does for private sector organizations. A supply chain includes the activities that come after the value chain brings an agency's service up to the point of provision (Larson 2009). This includes all the products and services and budget allocations needed to bring the service from it preparation stage to actual receipt by appropriate recipients in society. Its value is immediately apparent when the delivery of the service, adherence to regulations and monitoring effects flows from federal departments through state-level distribution organizations to the city, regional, municipal and civic society organizations into the hands of individual citizens. The goal of supply chain management is the assurance that legislated services reach the audiences for which they were intended and do so in the most cost-effective manner.

Public organizations that follow value chain/supply chain/positioning strategies focus on improving performance at all steps of delivery of the agency's core services. An effective value and supply chain strategy adds value to the service, taking advantage of the organization's strengths of its planning and delivery partners and overcoming the weaknesses of all partners in the strategic network. A major benefit of a positioning strategy is that it allows the agency to increase the efficiency and effectiveness of its limited resources.

While there is general agreement on the value of the strategic management approach, other approaches to successfully designing strategy in public organizations and implementing strategic management have taken precedence. The paradigm that was developed by Michael Porter (1980, 1991 and 1996) was responsible for the surge in interest in strategic management. This model focuses on how to position an organization to take advantage of opportunities in the market. The model suggests that the actions an organization takes to identify and adopt a defensible position against competitive forces should result in a competitive advantage. The concept concludes that the most successful organizations position themselves in external "environments where they can enjoy sustainable competitive advantages" (Priem and Butler 2001).

Management decisions in public sector organizations are often influenced by forces in their external environment more so than managers in commerce and industry. This was pointed out in 1990 in the following way:

Public management is not identical to government management or to public administration. Public management involves management under the influence of political authority ... public management necessarily requires attention to the organization's environment because the influence of external political authority emanates from the environment. For this reason, effective public management requires attention to strategy.

(Bozeman and Straussman 1990, 27–8)

Generic Strategy Limitations

The competitive forces paradigm of Michael Porter is limited in its total applicability in public sector organizations. This is because the concept focuses on adopting a strategy and position in an industrial setting that achieves success in the marketplace through exploitation in market imperfections (Hansen and Ferlie 2016). The elements of the management concept that are applicable in the public sector include strategic positioning, generic strategies that focus on superior performance, the five-step approach, and value chain and service chain analysis.

Strategic positioning in the public sector focuses not on profit, but on creating greater value for the public. Private sector organizations adopt either of two generic strategies to achieve their profit goals: a cost-leadership strategy or a differentiation strategy. In applying either of these strategies, a firm can either concentrate on serving a particular segment or they can serve an undifferentiated market. Most public sector organizations do not have these options; they cannot discriminate. As a result, creating public value is often a critical challenge to public sector organizations (Yang 2016).

The emphasis on competitive strategy to achieve profit maximization and the elements of Porter's generic strategies can be applied to government and public sector organizations for strategy design and operations. Akan, Allen, Helms and Spralls (2006) grouped a list of tactics in the generic strategies of a sample of 221 organizations. Selected strategies with potential application by public and non-profit sector organizations are shown in Table 4.3.

Public Sector Strategic Positioning

Clearly, when more than one option is available for prospective clients or customers, some public organizations must compete against like organizations for customers. The nine closely located seaports of northern Europe are an example (Haezendonck, Verbeke and Coeck 2006). Service at the European Union (EU) ports of Amsterdam, Antwerp, Bremen, Dunkirk, Ghent, Hamburg, Le Havre, Rotterdam and Zeebrugge is generally comparable and rates for services are non-competitive.

The researchers incorporated three analytical approaches to determine the competitive position of a port compared with other ports in the area. The

TABLE 4.3 Selected strategies applicable to government and nonprofit organizations

Selected Sample Public Sector Generic Strategies

Differentiation	Cost leadership	Service Cost Focus	Differentiation Focus
Extensive training of delivery personnel	Vigorous efforts on operation cost reduction	Provide best-case customer/client service	Provide specialty or high-cost service to needy groups
Develop new versions of core service	Achieving maximum control over overhead costs	Improve operational efficiency	Target a specific under-served clientele
Innovation in service and/or processes	Minimizing costs of service delivery processes	Devote maximum effort to assuring quality of the delivered good or service	Provide specially designed or special needs services to specific regions
Build strong relationships with network organizations		Extensive training of operational personnel	

Source: After material in Akan, Allen, Helms and Spralls (2006)

approaches were a product portfolio analysis, a shift-share analysis, and product diversification analysis. The product portfolio analysis (PPA) compared the range of services offered at each port; the shift-share analysis (SSA) covered the composition and evolution (growth or decline) of port traffic flows in the four 10-year periods from 1984 to 2004; the product diversification analysis (PDA) analyzed the diversification of the port's traffic (cargos, vessel classes, etc.) over a 20-year period. The study design did not require any confidential financial or marketing data, instead relying on easily attainable public information. For example, a previous study of 13 large European seaports concluded that all port authorities in the study considered cost recovery at all port activities a salient objective but did not consider profit maximization to be a critical goal for most of the ports. The portfolio analysis compared traffic volume for five cargo types: liquid bulk, dry bulk, containers, Ro-Ro (roll on, roll off), and conventional cargo. The growth rate for all categories was fast in all ports, but fastest in Rotterdam and Antwerp. Container traffic had the fastest individual growth rate in most seaports in the study. The research findings offer significant applicability to other semi-competitive public sector product/service "markets."

Public Sector Strategic Fit

Strategic fit describes the degree to which an organization matches its available resources and capabilities (its "organizational capital") to meet the mandated requirements of delivering its goods and services (Hill and Brown 2007). Sandra Miles and Mark Van Clieaf (2017, 55) defined organizational capital as "an intangible asset that is a continuous creator of value through generating above-normal ... growth, innovation, operational excellence, and stakeholder relationships." Achieving strategic fit results in ensuring that organizational strategies are aligned not only with internal environment, but also with the organization's external environment. The fit is institutionalized in the design of strategies for reaching an organization's goals and the operational strategies for achieving those goals through employing the organization's resources and capabilities in ways that enable the best possible outcomes under conditions mandated by events in the organization's external environment.

Pinning down the role of fit in the development of an organization's strategy has long been recognized. For example, Venkatraman (1989) identified six different applications of the concept. Focusing on studies describing fit in descriptions of structure and as strategy, he developed a conceptual framework for mapping six perspectives of fit: (1) fit as moderation; (2) fit as mediation; (3) fit as matching; (4) fit as gestalts; (5) fit as profile-deviation; and (6) fit as covariation. Subsequent research classified variables within the organization to determine whether the strategy design achieves a match with the organization's capabilities.

Hill and Brown (2007) saw the level of an organization's strategic fit is shaped by both internal and external variables. The three internal variables measures adjusted for application to the public sector are the level of consistency between the operational strategy and the overall strategy of the parent organization; the strategy's consistency with other functions in the organization; and its consistency with elements and processes of the organization's delivery system. The external environment consistency measurement is between the organization's position in the chain of government structure and mission delivery "market" and the operation processes and infrastructure in the levels of government participating in delivery of the mission goods and services. The following three tests help management assess whether an organization's strategic fit is appropriate for the environment and the organization's resources and capabilities (Hill and Brown 2007, 1355):

1. The importance of stakeholder criteria in the organization's position in the network of organizations that exist in the scope of the primary mission. Which performance criteria do clients and stakeholders consider important?
2. The strategies of operational functions. Are these strategies consistent and sustainable in scope and financial resources? Are performance measures and improvement incentives consistent across mission delivery levels?
3. The mission delivery system. Are different service levels across client categories consistent and sustainable? Are they aligned with each other? Does the strategy mesh with related strategies across different organizations at each of the level's partners and cooperating delivery organizations?

Public Sector Service Chain

The public sector is far more involved in providing services than producing and distributing products. This makes applying the value chain concept to government organizations difficult. Hence, a service chain model must overcome this applicability gap. The core concept in Porter's strategic positioning models is that an organization builds an advantage over its competitors that enables the firm to generate greater profits (Hansen and Ferlie 2016).

Addressing this strategy problem a decade earlier, Heintzman and Marson (2005) suggested that the primary activities in a public sector organization should include developing a service orientation and then begin procuring the resources needed to make it sustainable. This would require careful human resource selection and management and a mechanism for superior service creation and delivery. This approach posits adding three core components to the service value chain: employee satisfaction and commitment to the mission, the service recipient's satisfaction, and citizen/recipient's trust in specific government institutions and confidence in government in general (Figure 4.4).

Each of the core service chain components has its own set of drivers (Figure 4.4). In another approach to designing a public sector value chain, the support activities might include such processes as strategic planning, financial (budget) management, brand management, information and communications technology (ICT) management, accounting and management control (Rapcevičienė 2014).

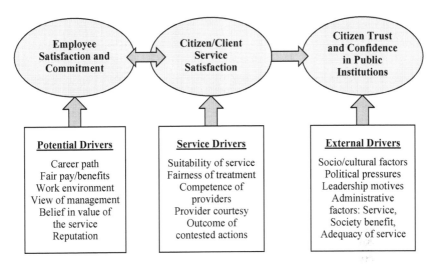

FIGURE 4.4 Public sector service satisfaction value chain.

Source: After Heintzman and Marson (2005).

Employee Link

Employee satisfaction and commitment to the process is necessary for the concept to function as envisioned. The link between employee job satisfaction is the only two-way link in the chain. A large body of human resources research in the United States and Europe has shown that customer/client/service recipient satisfaction is closely related to the job satisfaction of the employees performing the service. This link is particularly important for organization performance in the delivery of services, where customer satisfaction is the main measure of performance. Therefore, the "most appropriate criterion for organizational performance is customer satisfaction" (Ram, Bhargavi and Prabhakar 2011). The importance that agency managers and administrators give to this point is a key annual performance measurement mandated to all government agencies.

A measurement of customer satisfaction with government services has been published each year since 1999. The 2018 American Customer Satisfaction Index (ACSI) reported that customer/client satisfaction scores for government services is declining somewhat for all federal government organizations, with several agencies scoring among the lowest of all sectors measured. Declines occurred in all four major measurements: process, information, customer service and website effectiveness. The average for all government agencies was 68.9 on the 0 to 100-point scale, with the score for the Housing and Urban Development Departments scoring the lowest at 57. Although the government average declined from a peak in 2017, it was still the second highest score recorded since 2008 (Nextgov 2019).

Application Guide

Although it is no longer the sole guide, the competitive forces framework is the strategic management application most commonly addressed in discussions of strategic management. The seven steps for implementing the framework are included below:

Step 1: Conduct an external analysis to understand how macro-environmental factors might impact an organization.

- PEST analysis:
    - political factors (e.g., changes in government policy, legal requirements, and ownership);
    - economic factors (e.g., changes in the level of economic activity, wages and income distribution)
    - social factors (e.g., changes in demographics, attitudes, and social structure);
    - technological factors (e.g., development in science, technology, and innovation).

Step 2: Conduct a SWOT environmental analysis to identify potential strategies:

- SWOT Matrix
    - The layout of an analysis shown here illustrates the steps involved:

TABLE 4.4 Example opportunities and threats

	Strengths (S) List strengths	Weaknesses (W) List weaknesses
Opportunities (O) (List opportunities)	SO Strategies – Use strengths to take advantage of opportunities	WO Strategies – Overcoming weaknesses by taking advantage of opportunities
Threats (T) (List threats)	ST Strategies – Use strengths to avoid threats	WT Strategies – Minimize weaknesses and avoid threats

Step 3: Apply Porter's five forces framework to identify "competitive" forces that influence the operations of an organization:

- Threat of new entrants;
- Bargaining power of suppliers;
- Bargaining power of buyers;
- Threat of substitute;
- Rivalry among existing organizations or divisions.

Step 4: Formulate and implement public sector "generic strategies" to enhance the effectiveness of an organization:

- *cost leadership* (vigorous efforts on reducing costs of operations and service delivery processes through scale and scope economies, organization restructure and/or process improvement or redesign);
- *differentiation* (seek to create higher value by delivering services with unique features while keeping costs at the same levels).

Step 5: Focus on finding a "position" or a niche to achieve sustainability:

- Apply public sector value creation process to maximize value from the provision of public goods and/or services.
- Maximize the benefits accruing from the investments in public goods and services.

Step 6: Achieve "strategic fit" to ensure that organizational strategies are aligned not only with internal environment, but also with the organization's external environment.

Step 7: Continuous evaluation and control of factors that cause and influence strategies and changes.

Summary

Harvard professor Michael Porter made a significant contribution to management science beginning in the 1960s with a series of works on the influence of environmental factors on an organization's success in its chosen market. The benefits of environment analysis, value chain management, the influence of five competitive forces, generic competitive strategies and the organization's strategic fit, and an organization's competitive advantage were adopted early by public sector managers and researchers. This chapter described some of the key elements to what became known as *strategic management* and its application to management in the public sector.

The five forces framework, with its associated actions and processes, asserts that successful adoption of strategic management by public sector organizations is based on acceptance of four core principles: management decisions require a focus on long-term goals rather than short-term tactical objectives; goals and objectives must be designed as integrated; determining long-term objectives alone is not enough—their achievement must be designed and implemented; and management's attention priorities must be focused on the effects of forces in the external environment.

Two basic value chain strategies available to public sector organizations are (1) taking actions to maximize value from provision of a public service or (2) concentrating on maximizing the benefits accruing from investments in such public goods as transportation, defense, etc. Overall, the major factors that set the public and private value chain systems apart included the client-centered resources, management skills, comfort and technology of the private sector, and the regulatory actions and protection of the public interest of the public sector.

The extensive research on the competitive forces paradigm of Michael Porter for its applicability to the public sector found it to be applicable but limited in its use in total for government strategic design. This is because the concept focuses on adopting a strategy and position in an industrial setting that achieves success in the marketplace through exploitation in market imperfections (Hansen and Ferlie 2016). The elements of the management concept that are applicable in the public sector include strategic positioning, generic strategies that focus on superior performance, the five-step approach, and value chain and service chain analysis. Its greatest value is its emphasis on environment analysis and long-term focus.

5

THE RESOURCE-BASED FRAMEWORK

In the years following the seminal work of Porter, "an explosion of powerful frameworks" for evaluating performance and planning operational strategies followed (Cockburn, Henderson and Stern 2000, 1124). The common theme in all was agreement that competitive advantage is attained through a combination of access to resources, opportunities, management capabilities and thorough analysis of the organization's external environment.

The resource-based view of the organization (RBV) framework of strategy design was among the first to readily be adopted by public sector organizations. A possible reason for this is because the resource-based view of strategic management focuses on selecting strategies based on the organization's resources, capabilities and competencies rather than trying to acquire new skills and assets for each new focus or opportunity (Penrose 1959). Other researchers grouped resources with other factors as among the critical success factors that contribute to an organization's success (Bryson, Ackerman and Eden 2007).

Core Concepts

The resource-based view of the organization strategic management brings together a variety of factors that together are the competencies that enable organizations to implement strategies for developing and delivering the greatest possible value commensurate with the funds available (Bryson et al. 2007). Available competencies are necessary for achieving the organization's goals. These success factors include the organization's physical resources, its operational competencies, and the mission-critical competencies. Definitions for the success factors that are a part of the RBV framework follow.

Resources

An organization's resources are organization-specific

> assets that are difficult if not impossible to imitate. The secrets and certain specialized production facilities and engineering experience are examples. Such assets are difficult to transfer among firms because of transaction costs and transfer costs, and because the assets may contain tacit knowledge
> *(Teece, Pisano and Shuen 1997, 516)*

A definition was also suggested by Stadler, Helfat and Verona (2013, 1782): A resource is "a tangible, intangible, or human asset that a firm owns, controls, or has access to through other means on a semi-permanent basis."

Competencies

An organization's competencies are the "actions, technologies and processes that enable an organization to excel in the performance of achieving its goals.... Competencies are less flexible than resources and usually arise through learning by doing" (Bryson, Ackerman and Eden 2007, 703). They are the skills attained by service providers and managers and can be measured by how effectively and efficiently they employ their resources. Operational competencies include stakeholder and customer relations. As a result, they are often identified with knowledge building and knowledge management programs.

Core Competencies

These are the competencies built on the successful combination of resources and the management competencies that turn products or services to value for both the supplier and the recipient (Prahalad and Hamel 1990). Their character is found in the organization's strengths and weaknesses assessments. They are the application of the organization's core activities. Core competencies exist across the full range of the organization's family of services. In this way they become crucial to the success of the organization. The value of core competencies is amplified by combining staff and management's skills and knowledge with existing complementary resources. The degree to which a core competence is distinctive depends on how well endowed with both resources and capabilities the organization is relative to its mission strategies. Because public sector organizations seldom compete with other public sector organizations, the payoff for successful combinations of capabilities and resources is seldom measured in competitive advantage. Nor is success contingent on how difficult it is for competitors to replicate its competencies. Rather, success metrics are more likely to be client satisfaction, efficiency and effectiveness in meeting client and stakeholder needs, or assurance of sustainable operations.

Distinctive Competencies

Distinctive competencies are difficult for other organizations to emulate. They include the knowledge, operational experience, the skills of its managers, and the ability to implement selected strategies that exist within the organization. Together, the bundle of distinctive competencies make possible its long-term success. "What makes them distinctive is their uniqueness or lack of substitutability, [their] rarity ... difficulty of imitation, value for [the ability to] ward off competition or [exploit opportunities], and the resulting provision of competitive or collaborative advantage" (Bryson et al. 2007, 704).

Critical Success Factors

A core distinctive competency is a competency that the organization must have for sustainable operations. Critical success factors are the things an organization must have or do if it is to succeed in its mission. For government and nonprofit organizations, these include the rules and regulations they must abide by, the things they must do—and must not do—as they provide their services. They are the goals they must reach, the performance levels they are required to live up to, and the skills needed to survive in their rapidly changing political environments.

Resource-based Strategy

The resource-based view of the firm is thus an internally oriented way of strategic planning that is based primarily on the resources that exist within the organization. When applied to public sector strategic management, the resource-based view holds that public organizations should adopt a strategy or strategies based on their existing resources and the administrative and technological competencies they can strategize for achieving optimal success (Wernerfelt 1984; Prahalad and Hamel 1990; Barney 1991; Cockburn, Henderson and Stern 2000; Priem and Butler 2001). In short, strategic strategies must achieve a strategic fit with their available resources, capabilities and capacities in their environment.

Performance Measurement

Three types of organizational performance are common in strategic management research: objective financial performance, subjective financial performance, and subjective nonfinancial performance (Newbert 2008). Objective measurements include earnings and market share for individual firms. Subjective financial measurements include sales profitability and competitive advantage. Nonfinancial measurements can include customer/client satisfaction, mission effectiveness, efficiency, and objective and goal achievement, among others. Financial performance measurements are not applicable to public sector organizations. Hence, various metrics on subjective nonfinancial performance are more appropriate, with the catchall term "performance" used to imply nonfinancial data.

Organizational Assets

A resource is any asset that the organization has that can help it achieve its performance goals or perform well (Bryson, Ackermann and Eden 2007). Barney (1991) grouped resources into three categories: physical capital resources, human capital resources, and organizational capital resources. Physical capital assets include the type and degree of technology available, the organization's physical facilities (offices, laboratories, distribution facilities, etc.), the location of its facilities, and its access to the finished goods and services it provides. Human capital resources include the skilled personnel needed to provide clients the promised value, their training, experience and the level of service culture that guides performance. Barney also included individuals' judgment, intelligence, relationships with others, and the insight of managers and staff. Organizational capital resources are the operational characteristics of the organization. They include such processes and activities as a formal reporting structure, its skills in strategic planning, managerial controlling and coordinating operating systems, and the informal personal relations within the organization and their interchanges with the groups they were formed to serve.

Another way resources are grouped is on their character as assets. There are two types of asset: tangible and intangible. Tangible resources include land, buildings, vehicles, machinery, technology, equipment and capital. They are assets that an organization acquires over long periods of time, making them difficult to copy or purchase.

Intangible resources include human resources, processes, information, brands, trademarks and patents, intellectual property, networks, specialized knowledge and skills, and anything intangible that an internal analysis identifies as having client and organization value (Rumelt 1984; Wernerfelt 1984; Barney 1986, 1989, 1991). Because of their nature, they are things that cannot be easily acquired by other organizations and, as a result, contribute to an organization's sustainable performance.

Together, tangible and intangible assets shape the competencies of an organization. Those that are essential to the success and sustainability of the organization are its core competencies. A core competency is thus among an organization's major strengths that competitors cannot easily duplicate. While not necessarily unique, the core competencies and resources are the assets that are best for the organization, its management and staff, and the clients it serves. For sustainability, they should not be readily replicated and meet other VRIO (valuable, rare, easy to imitate, organized to implement) conditions (Rumelt 1984; Wernerfelt 1984).

In an RBV public sector study, Zhao and Fan (2018) included tangible and intangible resources with human resources in their resource-based view survey on the ability of municipal governments to acquire, retain and distribute open government data to the public. Tangible resources included the (1) financial resources that enable an organization's resilience and capacity for making needed investments and (2) physical resources that make it possible for the organization to perform its mission. Human resources were the services members of the organization must perform, including staff skills, knowledge, and management's decision-making ability. Intangible resources included technology intangibles, culture and reputation. An organization's resource base should undergo a VRIO analysis for determining whether it should be determined to be an asset that can contribute to an advantage for the organization (Figure 5.1).

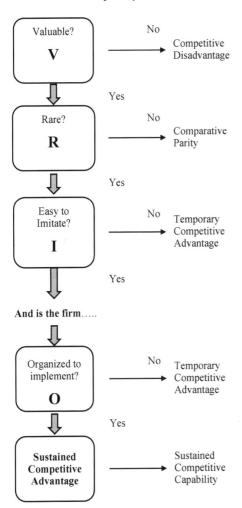

Is the resource or capability:

FIGURE 5.1 Steps in the VIRO analysis decision procedures.

Source: Adapted from Rothaermel (2015).

VRIO Resources

Public sector organizations' success in providing value to the recipients of their services depends upon the valuable, intangible, and not perfectly imitable (VRIO) resources that exist within the organization. To the extent that these resources enable management to develop strategies for delivering value, resources also enable them to cope with rapidly occurring and unpredictable changes (turbulence) in their political environment. (Szymaniec-Mlicka 2014). The ability to react quickly to meet changes in its environment is as important to public sector organizations as it is to private firms. The operational focus in public organizations is typically on its external environment by either maximizing public value with limited budget allocations or achieving more efficient delivery performance. However, because the RBV focus is on resources in the organization's internal environment, a VIRO analysis is doubly important.

Kraatz and Zajac's (2001, 632) interpretation of the insights to take away from a resource-based analysis is that "scarce, valuable, and imperfectly imitable resources are the only factors capable of creating sustained performance differences among competing firms, and that these resources should figure prominently in strategic making." Bryson, Ackermann and Eden (2007) add that distinctive competencies are an example of such a resource. The steps in the analysis are the asset's value, its rareness, imitability and usable by the organization (Rothaermel 2015). The advantage, sustainability or ability to meet all challenges to its mission occurs from firm-specific resources that are rare and superior in use, relative to others (Barney 1991, 1997; Peteraf and Barney 2003).

Superior resources are "more efficient" when they enable an organization to produce goods more economically or better satisfy customer needs and wants. The superior performance is attributable to resources of the organization that give it its efficiency. Organizations with superior resources are better able to deliver greater value to customers or clients or produce and deliver goods and more economically. Figure 5.1 lists the attributes that a resource must have for the organization to attain sustainable operations. The resource must be valuable to the organization, it must be rare enough to make it difficult for other organizations providing a similar service to employ, it must be very difficult to imitate, and other organizations cannot find effective substitutes. Barney's (1991) descriptions of these attributes follow.

Resource Value

A resource has value for the organization if it enables reductions in operating costs or aids the organization in responding to environmental threats or opportunities. For commercial organizations, this ability helps gain a competitive advantage. For public organizations, this enables the organization to function more efficiently and to achieve sustainability. Of course, the value of the resource is not attainable if the organization lacks the capability to take advantage of the resource's value (Newbert 2008). The value of a resource is not limited to its contribution to improving performance. Other sources can be the rareness of the resource (i.e., its heterogeneity), the difficulty of other organizations to copy the resource or to substitute others with similar characteristics. However, Barney warned that these attributes only become *resources* when they enable the organization to take advantage of the opportunities or neutralize threats in the organization's environment.

Rare Resources

Organizations need many types of resources. Those that contribute most to key goals and objectives should be rare, while the common resources that facilitate normal operations are also important (Barney 1989, 2007). Rare resources are not likely to contribute much to achieving core performance or sustainability goals. Resources easily adopted or widely copied by other organizations providing services have little value for creating an operational advantage or achieving sustainability.

To be truly valuable, resources should be rare and difficult if not impossible for other organizations to copy. However, achieving organizational objectives may be attainable with the contribution of common resources. One of the major benefits of participating in networks is often access to a combination of resources from sharing resources. A resource-based view framework analysis of the sustainability achievement goals of local municipal and regional associations in Italy by Barrutia and Echebarria (2015) are highlighted in Box 5.1.

BOX 5.1 RESOURCE-BASED VIEW STUDY OF SUSTAINABLE DEVELOPMENT PROGRAMS

Agenda 21 is a sustainability movement that emerged in the June 1992 Rio Declaration on Environment and Development and the Statement of Principles for the Sustainable Management of Forests. Both were adopted by more than 178 governments at the United Nations Conference on Environment and Development (UNCED) held in Rio de Janeiro, Brazil. Local Agenda 21 is the globally coordinated but local government led action plan to promote sustainable development (SD), social empowerment, environmental protection and economic prosperity in local jurisdictions or areas. Key success factors are full community participation, assessment of current conditions, specific goals, and progress monitoring and reporting (Xavier, Jacobi and Turra 2019).

Barrutia and Echebarria (2015) conducted a resource-based review of sustainable engagement by local communities in Italy. Two types of resources were included: municipal internal resources and relational resources that consisted of partnerships with a higher level of government and networks with municipal-level or higher government bodies. Earlier success studies found extensive public participation to be essential for achieving local sustainable development goals. They found that although local governments have necessary resources to make them suitable for designing and initiating sustainable development practices, they lacked the resources considered essential for implementing the programs in ways that satisfy local objectives and stakeholder expectations. To achieve success, Barrutia and Echebarria proposed that municipalities partner with resource-rich higher-level governments and gain access to shared resources by sponsorship of and participation in multilevel networks.

Source: From material in Xavier, Jacobi and Turra (2019)

Resources can also be shared in public sector strategic planning activities. Xavier, Jacobi and Turra illustrated this in their 2019 paper on sustainable development planning in São Paulo, Brazil. Cooperation and collaboration in regional planning follows a five-step process that begins with forming a partnership with multilevel governments, civil society organizations and other stakeholders for identification and sharing of common goals. This step involves forming a governance structure.

The second step is the analysis of the resources of the network and responsibilities for planning solutions needed for overcoming barriers. The setting of priorities, common goals and objectives, strategies and commitments for preparation of strategic plan follows. The fourth step is forming the structures and timetables for implementation of the activities. The final step is senior-level management evaluation and feedback to all interested parties.

RBV and Public Policy

The U.S. federal government affects nearly everything business firms do, ranging from the way they raise capital to assuring they have enough toilets for employees of both genders. From a macro point of view, decisions on the products make and sold are shaped by government rules and regulations pertaining to the environment and energy policies. On a micro scale, the "marketing practices, accounting rules, employee relations, equal opportunity regulation, and occupational health and safety standards are all within the realm of government policy" (Lehne 2005, 14). Public policies are looked upon by many business managers as the bane of their existence. However, others see these policies as resources to be exploited: resource-based view strategies. Strategic managers of public organizations are no different. The strategies adopted by agency managers at all levels and government policies are shaped by political forces and the influence of important stakeholders (such as crop growers organizations, hunting or fishing associations, police officers or fire fighters benevolent associations, etc.). Agency managers also exert open, and often subtle, efforts to influence decisions by legislative body on policies that limit or even eliminate the scope of their agency's mission. Anti-legislative decision pressures on legislators occur just as often as agency managers provide aid for legislation they support and policy decisions that enhance their sustainability.

Nicolas Dahan tested whether the resource-based view can apply to public policy studies in 2005. He questioned if and, if so, how political capital as an organizational resource may be used to influence corporate political behavior or to influence favorable policy decisions, to gain social capital for maintaining political power. Dahan defined a resource as something owned by an organization, and an asset as anything of public value that can be used by the organization. He then defined an organizational resource as "*any means of development controlled by* [an organization]" (Dahan 2005, 10—emphasis in the original). These concepts apply to public organizations, as they show that a resource can be anything of value to the organization that can be used to achieve positive goals. It did not have to be something owned by the organization, just something to which the organization has access.

Dahan added that previous research on political behavior using the resource-based view framework took two different emphases. One research stream focuses on how an organization can use its resources to influence a government decision. Examples include political participation or a fundraising activity to influence a policy (i.e., funding campaigns, supporting a political party, promoting demonstration, supporting adoption of a policy, etc.). The goal is to influence a change in an existing public policy.

The second stream of research focuses on the use of public policy to the advantage of a particular institution, an individual firm (at the expense of economic competitors), or a civic or nonprofit organization. In this second theme, public policy shifts from being an end to becoming a means for gaining a higher goal. In this second stream of research, public policy becomes a "strategic asset" used by the organization for its own goals. The relationship between education and political knowledge and skills, the level of interest and engagement in civic activities, is an example of a strategic asset. Citizens with more education tend to be more *advantaged* in the political arena (Mettler and Soss 2004, 56—emphasis in the original). In this way, a voter group with more knowledge can be considered a strategic asset.

Dahan concluded that the use of the resource-based framework is more relevant in the first approach than in the second. Yet, for political resources to be used to influence policy decisions, the organization must be able to access the resource. Access can be gained by any of four methods: legitimization, financial support, use of other sources, or the use of such recreational activities. Gaining legitimization can occur through knowledge or other expertise, or stakeholder support for the topic. Financial support through the funding of political campaigns, either directly or through contributing to special interest groups or funds, plays a large role in legitimization. The legitimization through the forming of coalitions or collaborations is increasingly common in the growing complexity of society's problems. Gaining access to a sympathetic ear can also occur through the gift of access to such recreational or entertainment activities as funding conferences in resort locations, providing legislators with paid issue indoctrination trips, gifts of tickets to sporting events, and other recreational or non-official events.

RBV and Strategic Alliances

A strategic alliance is a contractual arrangement between two or more organizations for the sharing of each organization's resources in ways that are beneficial to all the parties. Each organization maintains its autonomous position during the collaborative endeavor. The collaboration or support provides partners with the ability to perform their mission activities in a more effective and efficient manner. A partial list of motives for establishing strategic alliances include:

1. cost sharing;
2. risk sharing;
3. resource competency;
4. strategic motives;
5. access to influential stakeholders;
6. gain economies of scale;
7. enhance performance effectiveness;
8. access to new technology;
9. overcome political or social barriers;
10. acquire new skills.

Sharing costs and risks helps organizations continue to operate even under strictly limited funding conditions. Eisenhardt and Schoonhoven (1996, 137) used a resource-based view framework to determine why entrepreneurial organizations enter or form strategic alliances. They defined alliances as "cooperative relationships driven by a logic of strategic resource needs and social resource opportunities and capabilities." Strategic resources contributing to alliance activities include management skills and operational capabilities, and social resources and capabilities. Social capabilities are defined as the ability to leverage internal and external stakeholder relationships with the goal of reciprocal exchange. Exchanges can include information, products, workers, financial resources, and more intangible resources "such as compassion, education and care" (Tate and Bals 2018, 808). Social resources also include the organization's prior history with other alliance members.

Organizations decide to form alliances because they are in a vulnerable strategic position, as when another agency takes mission responsibility and part or the majority of the funding. They need access to the resources of other organizations to survive the challenge. Organizations also form or participate in alliances when they are assigned responsibility for overseeing emergent or competitive budget allocation situations, or because they are introducing new technology-related services.

The U.S. government supports engagement in strategic alliances as a way to improve efficiency and gain greater value for service recipients. The National Center for Advancing Translational Sciences (NCATS), an agency of the National Institute of Health (NIH), operates an office of strategic alliances to make it easier for firms and university research labs to interact and cooperate with government laboratories and to translate descriptions of research findings for greater understanding and use by other scientists, doctors, hospitals and biopharmaceutical companies. The alliances office reviews all their discovery reports and recommendations for filing of domestic and foreign patent applications. The office also manages licensing of all NCATS technologies (inventions made by NCATS researchers are owned by the federal government). The NCATS list of the benefits of its engaging in alliances with the agency or other researchers includes:

- exchange of research resources, competencies and materials under material transfer agreements;
- collaborative research conducted under cooperative research and development agreements;
- participation with others in and sharing results of clinical studies to determine the safety and efficacy of new agents under clinical trial agreements;
- exchange of confidential information under confidential disclosure agreements;
- informal collaborations that involve the transfer of tangible and intangible resources and data under a research collaboration agreement.

Despite their attractiveness, strategic alliances and other cooperative agreements with other government organizations are not without problems for participants. Problem examples include difficulty of partner sharing, lack of agreement over control or conflict resolution, lack of funding reciprocity, distrust, and disagreement over mission focus. Strategic alliances can have operational costs beyond an organization's budget, they can result in the organization failing to develop the long-term resources or capabilities it will need once the alliance ends, or an organization's technology or other competencies are lost to other alliance members.

RBV and Quality Cities

Intelligent cities, smart cities, happy cities, quality cities: How do they earn their reputations as highly desirable urban centers and, more importantly, how do they keep their favorable reputations? A 2018 study by a group of researchers in Portugal focused on the social and political capital as resources and capabilities that city managers and politicians use to accomplish their livability goals (Carvalho et al. 2018).

Adopting an extensive search of the literature on urban quality, the team grouped the large number of themes ("sub habitats") into five major categories and one omnibus category. The five major categories were political, economic, social, natural, and technology; they named the sixth general category an artificial group of resources. A list of possible resources for each of the six categories is shown in Table 5.1 (our review of the individual resources in each category led us to change the name of the artificial group to essential services, one of the single items originally included in this factor).

The objectives of the study were to list potential urban management resources and then to identify the conceptual connections between the resources and citizens' wellbeing, quality of life and happiness. The degree to which a city is considered a quality city was determined using the level of citizens' happiness and the level of controversy noted in the literature associated with each of the six dimensions. The researchers' review of the literature formed a composite human relations factor (family, friends, neighbors and society) as a resource and the possibility of contact with nature resource as the variable most often contributing to human happiness.

The Carvalho et al. (2018) RBV literature review closed with two resource hypotheses: (1) city residents base their decisions on the quality of a city on three

TABLE 5.1 Habitat resources with the potential to influence urban quality of life

Resource Categories	Resource Examples
Political capital	Policy forming participation, freedom, governance, identity, image, mission attraction (as they reflect decisions by legislative stakeholders)
Economic capital	Local and national economy, jobs, personal income, entrepreneurship (as they contribute to attracting and retaining people and businesses)
Social capital	Dominant culture (i.e., industrial, academic, cultural, etc.), entertainment, hospitality, tourism attractions, social cohesion, social support, work–life balance, security, demography (as aspects of society that contribute to citizens' happiness, well-being and life satisfaction)
Natural capital	Nature, green environment, landscape, natural parks, greenbelts (as perceived by citizens as essential to family well-being and happiness)
Technology assets	Availability of ICT, e-relationships, Internet, access to web-based open government (as related to availability and level of use and basic technological development and employment)
Essential services (the artificial dimension)	Physical space, affordable housing, mobility, education, justice, healthcare, energy, water, food (as related to city infrastructure and activities providing essential services)

Source: From concepts and content by Carvalho et al. (2018)

characteristics (sub-habitats), in descending importance order: social and natural factors, economic and essential services (the artificial composite factor), and finally on political and technological sub-habitats; (2) the level of controversy in the city, with the following factors again in descending order: political, economic, social, natural, essential services, and technological factors. These sub-habitats should be considered among a city's resources when designing strategies for attracting businesses, developers, and residents.

Applying the Framework

An organization's resources include tangible, intangible and human assets, organizational capacities and knowledge. When the organization controls or has access to the resources, it is likely to enjoy improved performance and achieve sustainability. The four steps to follow for applying the resource-based view framework are:

Step 1: Conduct an internal audit or assessment to identify the organization's core competencies—i.e., the unique strengths embedded deep within an organization:

- Core competencies are an organization's capacity to create new products or services by creatively combining core skills (e.g., 3M's core competencies are substrates, adhesives, and coatings; and Honda's core competencies are their capabilities to manufacture small but powerful and highly reliable fuel-efficient internal combustion engines).

Step 2: Identify the organization's resources, capabilities, and key activities:

- Resources: Any assets that an organization can draw on when formulating and implementing a strategy.
- Capabilities: Organizational and managerial/administrative skills necessary to orchestrate a diverse set of resources and deploy them strategically.
- Activities: Distinct organizational processes that enable an organization to add incremental value by transforming input into products and services.
- Core competencies are built through the interplay of resources and capabilities.
- Superior performance is achieved by leveraging core competencies through strategic choice of a set of specific firm activities.

Step 3: Apply the VIRO framework to assess the competitive implications of the organization's resources.

- Valuable (V): Resources that help an organization increase the perceived value of its products or service, either by adding attractive features or lowering costs;
- Rare (R): Resources that only one or a few organizations possess;

- Costly to imitate (I): Organizations that do not possess that resource are unable to develop or buy the resource at a comparable cost;
- Organize (O) to capture the value of the resource: Effective organizational structure, processes and systems to fully exploit the competitive potential of the organization's resources, capabilities, and core competencies.

Step 4: Leverage on the organization's VIRO resources to assist the organization in formulating and implementing strategies to create and sustain competitive advantage.

Summary

The resource-based view (RBV) of the organization framework for designing strategies in government organizations focuses on selecting strategies based on the organization's resources and the institutional capabilities and its competencies for putting these resources to work. Although it can sometimes mean trying to acquire new skills and assets for each new focus or opportunity, the foundation of the method is getting its existing resources in ways different from and better than other organizations (Penrose 1959). These resources are best identified following the traditional SWOT analysis processes. The combination of resources and institutional strengths can then become the critical success factors that enable the organization's mission delivery success and ultimately, its sustainability. The resource-based view of managing the organization's strategies cannot succeed without the competencies that enable organizations to implement strategies for developing and delivering the greatest possible value commensurate with the funds available.

Resources are organization-specific tangible and intangible assets that are difficult if not impossible to imitate. They include the secrets and specialized knowledge owned by the organization. Valuable assets are difficult to transfer from one organization to another because of transaction and transfer costs. A resource is a tangible, intangible, or human asset that the organization owns, controls, or has access to through such other means as collaborations, networks or strategic alliances.

The organization must also have the necessary competencies to put the asset to work if they are going to be employable. An organization's competencies are the actions, knowledge, technologies and processes that enable it to successfully meet its objectives and accomplish its goals. Competencies are the skills attained by service providers and managers that can be deemed valuable by how effectively and efficiently they employ their resources. In addition to internal abilities, operational competencies also include favorable relations with stakeholders and customers/clients. As a result, they are often identified with knowledge building and knowledge management programs.

An organization's core competencies are the competencies that make it possible for an organization to conduct its operations. The organization's strategy is built on a solid foundation of its core competencies. They are a reflection of the successful combination of resources and management competencies that result in value for both the supplier and the recipient (Prahalad and Hamel 1990). The character of the organization's strategy is developed after a thorough understanding of its strengths and weaknesses and opportunities and threats. Core competencies exist across the full range of the organization's family of services. In this way they become crucial to the success of the organization. The value of core competencies is amplified by combining staff and management's skills and knowledge with existing complementary resources. Success is maintained only to the degree to which a core competency is distinctive and cannot be easily replicated by other organizations.

6

THE DYNAMIC CAPABILITIES FRAMEWORK

Both the resource-based view of the organization and the dynamic capabilities (DC) framework for guiding strategic implementation of the firm's resources were originally developed as management tools for business firms; both soon found acceptance in applications of strategic management in government operations. However, before common agreement could be reached as to its suggested public sector applicability, a number of challenges had to be overcome and common agreement on how the framework could fit the dynamic capabilities framework into strategic management. Augier and Teece (2009, 411) described some of the challenges public sector managers had to surmount:

> strategic, organizational, and human resource decisions made by management lie at the heart of enterprise performance … in today's [fast-changing environment] success requires that managers behave in an intensely entrepreneurial manner and build into their organization the capacity to sense and seize opportunities, and then transform and reconfigure as opportunities and competitive forces dictate. Such capabilities, if built, constitute what we call the dynamic capabilities of the enterprise. Not many [public sector managers] have the necessary skills, and fewer still succeed in building them into their [organizations].

Since the model was introduced by Teece in the 1990s, a large body of management research has looked at what the framework is, what it should involve, and when and how it can contribute to an organization's success. The DC approach advises organization leaders to support development of strategic management capabilities and cross training in organizational, functional and technological skills. In doing so, the knowledge and skills thus attained could build on the "theoretical functions" of earlier frameworks. In this way, the organization would receive the benefits from improved skills and knowledge in such management disciplines as research and development, product and process development, intellectual property, and human resources. By investing in and rewarding development of enhanced management knowledge and operational skills, these enhanced management capabilities can contribute to gaining a firm-specific and difficult-to-imitate competitive advantage.

The dynamic capabilities (DC) framework is related to the resource-based model in that it is also based on employing efficiencies and resources in the organization. However, rather than focusing exclusively on the organization's resources, the DC model holds that organization-specific capabilities are fundamental to an organization's employment of its resources in ways that best lead to achieving its goals. Achieving and retaining service delivery competence and sustainable mission performance depends upon both the organization's resources and the ability to put those resources to work in the best possible way. The DC approach thus focuses on methods for developing and implementing combinations of competencies and firm-specific resources (other than assets acquired off the shelf from suppliers or copied from competitors). Teece, Pisano and Shuen (1997, 515) describe this approach as "a coherent framework which can both integrate and facilitate prescription." The ability to react quickly to rapidly occurring changes in the external environment is manifested in rapid adoption of new and innovative products and services, together with the processes of their production and delivery.

Core Concepts

Although the work of Teece et al. (1997) and Teece (2000, 2007, 2012 and 2014) serves as the leading papers on the dynamic capabilities framework, many others have adopted the concept, some with Teece as a secondary author. For example, in the introductory study by Katkalo, Pitelis and Teece (2010), the three-section classification scheme for dynamic capabilities was described (Figure 6.1).

Sensing and seizing capabilities included requisite resources and organizational infrastructure for supporting an opportunity. Transforming capabilities are necessary for supporting sustainable operations (a competitive advantage in a business organization). Objectives for the three classes are further defined according to whether they create value or capture value from such other sources as lower operating costs.

The dynamic capabilities framework is seen as an extension of the resource-based view strategic framework. Its core concepts include the management of competencies as they relate to application of the organization's resources in its operational strategies (Eisenhardt and Martin 2000). Eisenhardt and Martin's (2000) review of the literature on the dynamic capabilities framework led them to conclude that little agreement exists on definitions of capabilities and dynamic

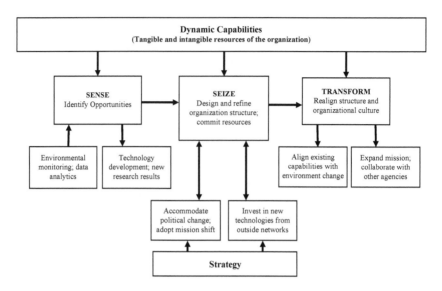

FIGURE 6.1 The dynamic capabilities model of the organization.

Source: Teece (2018, 44), modified to apply concept to public sector organizations.

capabilities. Therefore, the definitions included here were proposed, among others, by Teece and Pisano (1994); Teece, Pisano and Shuen (1997); Teece (2000); Eden and Ackerman (2000); Winter (2003); Bryson, Ackerman and Eden (2007); Helfat and Martin (2015); and Albort-Morant et al. (2018).

Capabilities

An organization's capabilities are defined as a *"high-level routine (or collection) of routines that, together with its implementing input flows, confers upon an organization's management a set of decision options for producing significant outputs of a particular type"* (Winter 2003, 991—emphasis in the original). Organizational capabilities are the human side of an organization's resources. They are the internal organizational processes, routines and activities that affect the ability of an organization to employ its research in ways that best improve its performance. When put to use, they constitute the set of problem-solving patterns that the organization's leadership follow in designing and implementing the tactics necessary for accomplishing its goals (Andrews, Beynon and McDermott 2016).

Dynamic Capabilities

Dynamic capabilities were defined by Teece et al. (1997) as an organization's "ability to integrate, build, and reconfigure internal and external competences to address rapidly changing environments." The concept was described as pertaining to enhanced management capabilities, which were then labelled as "dynamic capabilities." *Dynamic* refers to the organization management's ability to use and renew capabilities to meet changes in the organization's environment. The modification and reuse of these capabilities enable an organization to change in ways that make it possible to sustain operations while adjusting to the changes that will occur in the operating environment. The external environment and skills needed to adjust to the changes never stand still and neither should organizations. Often, the ability to rapidly meet and react to changing external conditions can be critical.

Seeing the ability of dynamic capabilities to alter the scope of an organization's capabilities, Teece believed they should reflect the ability of the organization's management to "adapt, integrate, and reconfigure" their organizational skills and functional competences. Moreover, the changes should result in rapid refocusing of the organization's resources to coincide with the changes in the environment.

Dynamic capabilities thus reflect "an organization's ability to achieve new and innovative forms of competitive advantage given path dependencies and market positions" (Teece, Pisano and Shuen 1997, 516). Albort-Morant et al. (2018, 43) defined dynamic capabilities as "the capacity that enables [an organization] to integrate, build, and reconfigure internal and external competencies to address rapidly changing environments."

Capability Lifecycles

Following the product lifecycle of introduction, growth, maturity and decline popularized by Theodore Levitt in 1965, the capabilities associated with resource-based strategies also vary with time and changes in an organization's environment (Helfat and Peteraf 2003). The package of capabilities that enable success at each stage in the lifecycle are not always the same for operations in other stages. It is possible for capabilities to be applicable in more than one stage before they lose their effectiveness. Equally important, the capability may also be applied with other products or services and may even be successfully adopted by other organizations.

Dynamic Capabilities Processes

Restructuring of an organization and transformation of its governance systems force managers and staff to learn quickly while they embrace the new thinking. Changes in technology often require reconfiguration of the organization's assets. To achieve and maintain sustainability under these and related forces, an organization's managers and staff need to embrace newness and the incumbent need to transform. This can happen only when managers adopt the following three operational processes (Teece 2007, 2018b):

- *Sensing*: The capacity to sense the effects of change and to reshape the organization's assets to better function in the new environment; employing analytical systems for scanning, concept search and exploration on clientele/customer needs and wants.

- *Seizing*: The commitment to proactively seek and accept new operational opportunities; seizing new opportunities through organization model design and strategic innovation in service deliveries.

- *Transforming*: Achieve and maintain sustainable operations through building on new ideas, combining existing assets through networking, and reconfiguring the organization's existing capabilities and tangible assets to meet the new operational challenges; transforming or reconfiguring existing operations models and strategies.

Sensing New Opportunities

Sensing is the capability of being able to recognize the need for a change or to restructure one's resources to take advantage of new opportunities. Sensing describes the ability of an organization's management and staff to spot, interpret and pursue opportunities for enabling the organization to modify its operational capabilities to accommodate changes in the environment (Pavlou and El Sawy 2011). Simply sensing the impact of environmental change alone is seldom sufficient. Rather, Teece, Pisano and Shuen (1997) urged honing sensing abilities by regular environmental scanning and enhanced management's interpretative and creative abilities for development of dynamic capabilities.

Other researchers have slightly different views of this activity. In their comparative study of dynamic capabilities and the adoption of innovation in three large water and wastewater utilities, Lieberherr and Truffer (2015) saw sensing as being related to the ability of managers of an organization to project the innovation that will be needed for restructuring or other innovative actions that will be required for sustainability as they are seen occurring in the operating environment. In addition to their existing capacities for detecting and creating opportunities by such programs as formal research and development activities, public sector organizations such as public utilities often draw on the competencies of other organizations through collaborations and exchanges with experts in the field, trade associations and their own distinctive formal and informal networks.

In their study of front-line sensing abilities, Hallin, Anderson and Tveterås (2017) considered an organization's managers' and/or employees' capability to sense the possible need for changes in both the external environment and its dynamic capabilities. They found these capabilities to be strong predictors of a service organization's ability to turn capabilities into dynamic capabilities for future performance strategies.

Seizing Opportunities

Seizing is the process that describes an organization's reaction to dramatic changes in its operating environment by investing in new technologies and new management practices. The process includes designing innovative organizational models and gaining access to deploying capital and resources (Wong 2016). Seizing opportunities involves the ability to design and deploy an organization's resources to efficiently and effectively deal with environmental challenges and take advantage of opportunities.

Lieberherr and Truffer (2015) described this step as senior managers' capacity to transform strategies into new products or services and implement the changes when they are needed. The adoption of certain types of innovations were based on findings from environmental scanning and other analytic capabilities. Incremental innovations as well as substantially new processes were of particular importance to the large water utilities they studied. Example innovations identified included adopting solar technologies, preparing plans for sustainability during drought conditions, installing new water treatment processes, and installing smart meters as a mechanism for identifying leaks and excessive water use.

Restructuring Capabilities

Restructuring of the organization by recombining existing physical assets and intangible knowledge and skills to contend with changes in an organization's external environment consists of evaluating distribution of resources and reconfiguring the evaluation of resources to projects that promise great success in meeting critical goals. Together or alone, these changes may give managers a high-efficiency means of turning existing capabilities into dynamic capabilities. Alternative definitions of reconfiguring are shown in Table 6.1.

In a large-scale study of the forces influencing capabilities in central government departments in the United Kingdom, Andrews, Beynon and McDermott (2016) found that the two organizational attributes most associated with high-value capabilities were low structural complexity for greater efficiency and personnel stability (low turnover) for knowledge retention. Configurations associated most strongly in departments with low measurements of capabilities were personnel instability and a combination of structural complexity and department agencification (*agencification* is the transfer of government activities from one department or agency to another, often newly established unit, to perform specific regulatory or administrative tasks. In some instances, political pressures result in the new unit moving from a central government location to a distant area).

The nature of elected oversight of public sector operations restricts the opportunity for managers to extensively restructure to transform their operations. Providing public goods and services under mandate makes extensive change difficult to bring about. One way of getting around such barriers that may be possible is to initiate a digital transformation. There is as yet little agreement of a definition for this process. Warner and Wäger (2019) proposed the partial list of existing attempts at defining the process shown in Table 6.2.

TABLE 6.1 Alternative definitions of reconfiguring through digital transformation

Authors and Dates	Definitions
Fitzgerald, Kruschwitz, Bonnet and Welch (2014)	The use of new digital technologies such as social media, mobile telephones, analytics or creating new business models.
Liu, Chen and Chou (2011)	An organizational transformation that integrates digital technologies and processes in a digital economy.
Singh, Klarner and Hess (2019)	Substituting transformation for change, the process goes beyond functional thinking and considers the "comprehensiveness of actions" that must be taken to exploit the opportunities or avoid the threats that stem from digital technologies.
Rogers (2016)	Digital transformation is fundamentally not about technology, but about strategy … that senior leaders must find ways to capitalize on new and unexpected [organizational] innovations that optimize [client/constituent] needs and experiences … improving the tactical or implemental skill set on how fast, how customer centric, how agile these decisions are put into practice.
Vial (2019)	At the organizational level, it has been argued that firms must find ways to innovate with these technologies by devising strategies that embrace the implications of digital transformation and drive better operational performance
Warner and Wäger (2019)	Digital transformation is an ongoing process of strategic renewal that uses advances in digital technologies to build capabilities that refresh or replace an organization's business model, collaborative approach, and culture.
Warner and Wäger's collection of responses provided by un-named study participants (2019)	1 Digital transformation is not about technology or about acquiring new technological skills. It is in fact about getting new awareness and bringing new ideas on how to think and how to act in a classical organization. 2 Digital transformation describes a journey of a company trying to be equipped in for the digital age … different capabilities needed to survive and succeed as a company in the digital age.

Source: From Warner and Wäger (2019) and others

Core Concept Themes

The large body of strategic management research has shown that several common themes in successful private sector organizations also apply to organizational performance and strategic management in government organizations. In her introductory review of David Teece's contributions to the dynamic capabilities framework, Veselina Stoyanova (2017) identified four core themes incumbent in three fundamental dynamic capabilities processes.

The first theme was that the framework has a definite role in and importance to strategic management and organizational performance in the management of organizations in all sectors. Second, in addition to managers within existing organizations, the emphasis on managerial competencies shows that the knowledge and practical contributions of entrepreneurs and individuals outside the organization also contribute to development of newer and more effective management models and organizational forms. Third, management decision-making effectiveness is enhanced by appropriate organizational structures and performance incentive programs. Fourth, the dynamic capabilities framework regards strategic processes as evolutionary and reflective of the ever-changing external environment.

Examples of public sector strategic management activities in which high capabilities influence the organization's effectiveness fall into the four broad categories shown in Table 6.2: internal operations, stakeholder relations, program planning and services delivery processes, and core strategic management activities (Poister and Streib 1999). The process is common in many nations and larger political bodies. Over a several-decade period, for example, 30 such new agencies were formed in the European Union and more were being planned (Ospina, Kersh and Trondal 2014). As might be expected, moving the unit and its staff was found to have a strong negative effect on the capabilities of the parent organization.

TABLE 6.2 Examples of core strategic capabilities

Internal Operations	Stakeholder Relations	Planning and Delivery	Strategic Management
Human resources development	Client/constituent relations	Program planning and evaluation	Organizational structure
Organizational culture	Community relations	Asset management	Budgeting/financial management
Internal communications	Intergovernmental relations	Program and project management	Performance management
Labor relations	Legislative agenda	Service delivery systems	Administrative processes

Source: After concepts in Poister and Streib (1999)

Federal Restructuring Efforts

Restructuring—redesigning, reforming and revitalizing—U.S. federal government agencies is a transformation outcome promoted by the Partnership for Public Service (PPS), an industry-supported nonprofit organization. The mission of the organization is to "revitalize the federal government by inspiring a new generation to serve and by transforming the way the government works." It does this by teaming "with federal agencies and other stakeholders to make ... government more effective and efficient" (PPS 2018, 1). Transformation programs at three federal agencies—the Department of Agriculture (USDA), the Federal Insurance and Mitigation Administration FIMA), and the Department of Veterans Affairs (VA)—were described in a 12-page 2018 PPS report.

Restructuring at the USDA

The USDA transformational, restructuring program is a department-wide strategy designed to improve the experiences and expectations of individual customers and organizations served by the department. With more than 105,000 employees, the USDA is one of the larger departments. The department has 17 separate agencies with more than 385 separate programs. Close to 90% of its employees live and work outside of Washington, DC.

A new centralized Office of Customer Experience was established in 2017 to solicit reports from department staff, front-line employees and customers. The plan was designed to be an employee-led, bottom–up approach for identifying, addressing and improving the agency's customer experience efforts. The focus was "on making the department faster, friendlier and easier to interact with, including speeding up service delivery, simplifying access to USDA programs and people, and creating a culture of courteous and helpful employees."

Focus Restructuring at FIMA

The Federal Insurance and Mitigation Administration (FIMA) manages the National Flood Insurance Program (NFIP) and a range of programs designed to reduce future losses to homes, businesses, schools, public buildings, and critical facilities from floods, earthquakes, tornadoes, and other natural disasters. Mitigation focuses on breaking the cycle of disaster damage, reconstruction, and repeated damage. The transformation began with reorienting employees' perceptions of the purchasers of its services as the agency's primary customers.

FIMA partners with private insurance providers by subsidizing policies. In the past, the staff focused on the needs of these private insurance company partners, not on the needs of the purchasers of the insurance. The transformation involved changing its organizational culture by adopting a customer-centric culture. The goal was to expand employees' perceptions of the customers of its services and, in turn, implement plans for improving the experiences that matter most to them. The change meant focusing on improving their interactions with customers and established a customer experience office to collect customer experience data, coordinate improvement programs and ensure the change functions as designed by annually measuring how well the culture change "sticks."

Unfinished Restructuring at the VA

Not all transformations result in measuring up to the targets underlying the change initiatives (Bozeman and Straussman 1990). Transformations fail to accomplish the goals for which they were designed. The experiences at the U.S. Department of Veterans Affairs (VA) are an example. The VA provides benefits, healthcare and cemetery services to military veterans. The VA is the federal government's second largest department after the Department of Defense, employing nearly 280,000 people at VA medical facilities, clinics, and benefits offices, and is responsible for administering benefits programs for veterans, their families and survivors. In 2015, the VA started a refocusing of its services, beginning with the establishment of a Veterans Experience office. The purpose was to better measure its performance through collecting the experiences of veterans being served. This information was passed to secretary and senior management for improving veterans' interactions with VA healthcare, veterans' benefits and memorial services.

The VA's transformation described in the PPS study was placed on hold when a period of leadership instability followed the election of a new administration in 2016. The General Accountability Office's (GAO) 2017 and 2019 high-risk reports on the VA's operations found a number of problem areas yet to be resolved. The 2019 report highlighted a large number of unfinished improvements. Selected segments of the 2019 high-risk report follow (GAO 2019):

- **Leadership commitment still only partially met.** Since this area of concern's 2015 designation, VA has made organizational changes, including establishing the Office of Integrity, to standardize and streamline the agency's oversight of its programs and personnel. However, since 2017, the lack of stability in the Under Secretary for Health position has hindered its ability to demonstrate sustained commitment to improving this area of concern.
- **Capacity not met.** Plans to implement capacity-building initiatives directed at improving oversight and accountability started but not complete. For example, VHA's Office of Internal Audit and Risk Assessment, a key component of the department's oversight and accountability model, began conducting audits in 2018, but as of 2019, the department had yet to allocate resources for this office, such as sufficient staff to carry out its activities.
- *Action plan requirement only partially met.* In 2018, VA conducted an analysis of the root causes contributing to findings of inadequate oversight and accountability, an important step in identifying the underlying factors contributing to

this area of concern. However, the resulting action plan lacked key elements, including clear metrics to monitor and assess progress. The VA's March 2018 action plan lacked specific metrics and mechanisms for assessing and reporting progress in this area.

- *Demonstrated restructuring progress not met.* GAP's work continues to indicate VA is not demonstrating progress in this area. Since its 2015 designation, GAO made 85 new recommendations in this area of concern, 50 of which were made since our 2017 report was issued. For example, in June 2018, it reported that VHA could not systematically monitor the timeliness of veterans' access to Veterans Choice Program care because it lacked complete, reliable data to do so. As a result, it was recommended that VA take steps to improve its oversight of the future consolidated community care program that will replace the Veterans Choice Program when authority ends (scheduled for June 6, 2019). VA concurred with this recommendation.

- **Inadequate training capacity:** VA has created working groups and task forces—such as the Learning Organization Transformation Subcommittee in the National Leadership Council—with specific responsibilities. However, VA's ability to demonstrate capacity is limited because, according to VA's March 2018 action plan, the department relies on external contractor support services to meet training goals, and that funding has not been allocated.

Conceptual Differences

Teece, Pisano and Shuen are usually credited with introducing the most-often cited version of dynamic capabilities in 1994 and 1997, along with the first core concepts that make up the dynamic capabilities framework. However, there remains some differences in what dynamic capabilities are and what their role is in strategic management. Eisenhardt and Martin (2000), while in general agreement with the core DC management themes, proposed a somewhat different interpretation of its concepts. Easterby-Smith, Lyles and Peteraf (2009) and Peteraf, Stefano and Verona (2013) both proposed models that included the importance of management skills and processes in the organization, and both saw the DC framework as an extension of the resource-based view concept. Their salient disagreement on the popular definition was on the question of whether possession of dynamic capabilities contributes to achieving competitive advantage in environments characterized by rapid change. The Teece model supports the view that the DC framework works in environments in which technological change is rapid. The Eisenhardt and Martin model disagrees, believing that the DC can succeed under certain resource and environmental conditions. Achieving competitive advantage is sustainable when change occurs at a moderate pace but cannot be sustained under conditions of rapid technological change. Thus, "dynamic capabilities can be a source of only limited competitive advantage" (Eisenhardt and Martin 2000, 1394).

In their study of the role of dynamic capabilities for water systems transitions, Hartman, Gliedt, Widener and Loraamm (2017) described five areas where conflicting interpretations exist:

1. The level at which dynamic capabilities are considered varies from lower-level routines and tacit knowledge to capabilities that must be created from combinations of resources and capabilities.
2. Concentration on different sources that range from organizational structures and routines to the role of individuals who contribute to innovations.
3. Some researchers follow the Teece view that to be considered dynamic, capabilities must contribute to competitive advantage or greater earnings, while others contend that dynamic capabilities contribute to but alone are an insufficient factor in creating competitive advantage.
4. Disagreement over the contention whether organizations attain competitive advantage by leveraging existing capabilities or whether they are created from acquisition of new resources and capabilities.
5. Disagreement on whether dynamic capabilities are equally important in organizations operating only in highly dynamic, in relatively stable external environments, or both.

Finally, Stoyanova (2017) concluded a divergence existed in what is the right determination of what dynamic capabilities really are. Scanning the dynamic capabilities research literature from Teece and Pisano's 1994 introduction of the concept through the first decade of the 2000s, agreement could be reached on three main propositions. First, dynamic capabilities may be composed of either organizational or managerial process. Second, they are more often higher-level organizational routines. Third, they are a combination of both organizational processes and routines. Which is right depends on the researcher.

Applying the Dynamic Capabilities Framework

Dynamic capabilities are defined as the organization's ability to integrate, build, and reconfigure internal and external competencies to address rapidly changing environments. Applying the dynamic capabilities framework takes place through the following four steps:

Step 1: Identify and differentiate the organization's resource stocks and resource flows, and decide which investments to make over time:

*   *Resource stocks*: The organization's current level of intangible resources, i.e., culture, knowledge, reputation, and intellectual property.
*   *Resource flows*: The organization's level of investments to maintain or build a resource, i.e., investments in building an innovation capability.

Step 2: Identify the organization's administrative or managerial processes, the position of its assets, and the paths ahead for opportunities and growth:

- *Processes*:
    - Use search processes, decision-making processes, change management processes, and others to coordinate and integrate available resources and to identify the need or opportunity for change.
    - Implement processes for organizational learning and the reconfiguration of resources.
- *Positions*: Specific set of resources (both tangible and intangible assets) available in an organization.
- *Paths*:
    - The current position of an organization is shaped by the patterns evolved from the past. Hence an organization's previous investments and its repertoire of routines constrain its future behavior (i.e., path dependence).
    - An organization's VIRO resources and capabilities must be built and organized effectively over time.

Step 3: Adopt dynamic capabilities processes to restructure and transform the organization to achieve and maintain sustainability in a fast-changing environment:

- *Sensing (i.e., identification and assessment of new opportunities)*: Employ analytical systems for scanning, concept search and exploration on clientele/customer needs.
- *Seizing (i.e., mobilization of resources to address an opportunity and to capture value from doing so)*:
    - Design and refine organization structure to accommodate political, economic, and social changes and proactively seek and accept new opportunities.
    - Capitalize on new opportunities to invest in new technology and commit resources to strategic innovation in (public) service design, development, and deliveries.
- *Transforming (i.e. continued renewal)*:
    - Realign organizational structure and culture to achieve the best "strategic fit," i.e., to ensure organizational strategy and structure are aligned with internal and external environments.
    - Build on new ideas, combine existing assets through networking, and reconfigure the organization's capabilities to transform the organization to meet the new challenges.

Step 4: Continuous innovation and change:

- Returns on investment or "profit gains" tend to flow not just from the asset structure of the organization and the degree of its rareness or imitability (i.e., VIRO framework), but also by the organization's ability to reconfigure and transform.

Summary

Similar to the resource-based view framework for strategy design, the dynamic capabilities framework focuses on environment changes and redirecting assets and capabilities for organizational success. In business, success means higher earnings and competitive advantage in the chosen market. In government organizations, it can mean maintaining exceptional performance and sustainability under dramatic shifts in governance, strategic focus, and justification of the budget negotiations for financial resources. Hartman et al. (2017) connect an organization's success to regular environmental scanning and adoption of strategic innovation to changes in the environment. Accordingly, they suggest that adopting dynamic capabilities processes can go far to reverse what they consider the "innovation deficit" in public utilities. They see the Teece three-phase DC process of restructuring resources and capabilities to dynamic capabilities that prepares an organization for success in dynamically changing environments.

The dynamic capabilities framework appeared as a companion framework to the resource-based view of the organization. The organization's resources can be tangible or intangible. Capabilities themselves are the knowledge and skills that exist in an organization that enables its managers to shape, re-shape and reconfigure its tangible and intangible resources in order to respond successfully and rapidly to changes in its operating environment. Dynamic capabilities are not the operational capabilities and learned processes that are common in similar organizations anywhere. Dynamic capabilities are the ability to rapidly and relevantly put these resources to work within the changing environment.

The combination of the dynamic capabilities framework managing resource-based view strategies enables government organizations to transform the way they deliver their public goods and services. An example described briefly in this chapter illustrated the way three federal organizations were transforming the culture and service delivery processes to become more customer centered.

In their introductory paper in a 2009 special *British Academy of Management* issue on dynamic capabilities, Easterby-Smith, Lyles and Peteraf address one of the early unresolved criticisms of the dynamic capabilities concept. They were still difficult to measure in practice. Moreover, because the routines and practices in an organization are often idiosyncratic, it is also difficult to generalize the routines and process capabilities of the one to other organizations. Another difficulty is the dynamic nature of the salient capabilities as they vary with changes in the environment.

7

THE NETWORK MANAGEMENT FRAMEWORK

Government has for many nations come to rely on a vast complex of agencies at all levels, nongovernmental organizations and specialized business forms in what has become known as network governance. To understand how governments work today, it is necessary to know what networks are and how they work. In this chapter we introduce a discussion on the concept of network governance and how the network framework is a necessary alternative to public sector strategic planning. In public management, governance usually refers to the funding and oversight roles of government agencies working in concert on developing and delivering public services. Although no longer possible to consider government or governance as single sector systems, the elements of leadership and management performance continue to be as critical for performance as they have in the past. Government organizations are increasingly including members of the partnership team; cooperation and collaboration from private and civil society organizations are necessary for providing public goods and services. Therefore, private sector strategy selection and planning must be considered when planning a government organization strategy (Goldsmith and Eggers 2004; Hill and Lynn 2005).

A variety terms are used by researchers examining the connection between networks and government performance. Some include network governance (Agranoff 2006), network management (Herranz 2006), metagovernance (Sørensen and Torfing 2005), public value management (Stoker 2006), collaborative public management (McGuire 2006), and new public service (Denhardt and Denhardt 2002), among others. Although there are no doubt shades of difference between these terms, from a practical perspective, they all refer to pretty much the same phenomenon. Although there were often slight differences in what the term referenced, it seems apparent that there was enough commonality for a general consensus. Despite the large number of options, we include the following as common enough to serve as that consensus. The definition used by Ansell and Gash is: "A governing arrangement when one or more public agencies directly engage non-state stakeholders in a collective decision-making process that is formal, consensus-oriented, and deliberative and that aims to make or implement public policy or manage public programs or assets" (Ansell and Gash 2008, 544).

The idea of network government is as relevant to state and local government agencies as it is for the many departments and agencies of the national government. This point was stressed in an annual progress report on the United Nations Human Development:

> Government [and governing] is not only about the political system and institutional structures and processes at the national level. Yet most discussion of governance and its major ingredient—participation is often confined to the national level. It is understandable why the national or central level is the main focus of interest and analysis. Not only is most power located and exercised at this level but most of the resources are concentrated there as well. Yet the most immediate level of governance for most citizens relates to their experiences at the community, village, ward and district level. It is at this level where they encounter the effects of economic and social policies, and the various laws and programs. This is the level where their rights are enjoyed or frustrated, where their basic rights are attained or denied. This is where their participation in the running of local or community affairs can be meaningful and productive or frustrated. In short, local governance is a level which affects the daily lives of citizens.
>
> (UNDP 2000, 16)

The network framework for designing strategy focuses on the contributions gained through collaboration and cooperation with like-minded organizations for accomplishing organizational mission tasks (Kamensky and Burlin 2004; Johanson 2009). This model was defined as (emphasis in the original):

> *a dynamic process of the creation and implementation of policy, politics, and administration, that is animated by the endeavour of manifold social and economic groups with different interests, but also by the search for a sustainable development orientation and social contract(s), that could counterbalance these interests in a way that will be compatible with the long-term interests of the whole society— including its future generations.*
>
> (Potůček 2006, 1)

The Network Management Framework

Having achieved widespread acceptance only in the 1980s, the network management framework (NMF) is a relatively recent addition to a long-standing practice of public administration. More important, it is one that is considered to be particularly well suited to public sector management (O'Flynn and Wanna 2008). It supports both the management and governance requirements of public sector controls. It is, therefore, applicable for organizations in all levels of the public sector. NMF is also appropriate for management of a collection of more than one agency or organization and the way that collective authority in the collection is exercised (Radin 1996; Starling 2005). In this application, it is referred to as either collaborative strategic governance or simply strategic collaboration. In practice it includes elements of earlier strategy design frameworks, including game theory, the competitive forces, resource-based view, and dynamic capabilities frameworks.

The adoption of network management is a product of critical changes in the operational environment of government. Public administrators can no longer achieve desired performance levels in many if not most of the primary responsibilities of governing with only their own human resources. They must work with others. A single public organization is unlikely to have access to the full supply of resources and capabilities it needs for the tasks at hand. Therefore, public sector management is no longer a one-organization process of meeting the public goods and services needed by its internal and external publics. This no longer means a large number of individual organizations working individually for the resolution of a problem faced by all. Rather, it now means a group of similarly interested and capable partners working together on resolution of common problems. A variety of different actors in the team often includes a combination of public, private and civil society contributors. The tactics involved in agency performance are less the practices of compliance enforcement than one of more "soft" activities such as negotiations, forming alliances and networks, and coordinating collaborative approaches (Johanson 2009).

Governance of Public Sector Networks

The collaborative strategic management models such as networks and other joint activities are tools for organizational guidance and are, therefore, now one of the chief means of attaining effectiveness and high performance in the management of government organizations. As these strategic frameworks are increasingly adopted, management of cooperative teams becomes a task for which governance is an issue. The governance of collaborative teams is defined as "cooperative agreements that lead to the allocation of resources and skills by two or more organizations for the achievement of common goals, as well as goals unique to individual partners" (Nakos 2013, 197). These collaborative teams are common in multilevel and multinational public organizations.

The cooperative governance of state and local administration of federal health services is an example of a multilevel alliance; the North Atlantic Treaty Organization (NATO) is another, larger example of a multinational alliance in which governance is an ongoing issue.

Example of a Federal–State–Local Network

Transportation planning in the United States is an example of a cross-agency and cross-level network. The FHWA and FTA cross-agency example provides guidance, planning, regulatory assistance and technical support to cross-level state departments of transportation, metropolitan planning organizations (MPOs), and providers of public transportation.

Rules for federal administration of public transportation planning require cooperation among state, region, and community government agencies and consideration of alternative strategies. Also required are evaluation of alternative solution viewpoints; the collaborative participation of multilevel transportation-related agencies and organizations; and open, timely, and meaningful public involvement. According to the Federal Transit Administration (FTA) (2020), "transportation planning is a cooperative process designed to foster involvement by all users of the system, such as businesses, community groups, environmental organizations, the traveling public, freight operators, and the general public, through a proactive public participation process."

In large urban areas, the transportation planning process is typically conducted by a metropolitan planning organization (MPO) that cooperates with the state department of transportation and public and private transit providers. In rural areas, transportation planning processes are usually carried out by a state transportation department, again cooperating with local officials. In rural or non-metropolitan areas, members of all organizations may work with the region's transit agency to plan for meeting community public transportation and highway needs. In all these collaborative partnerships, the governance system is led by a network of all level administrators supported by federal agencies and federal grant specialists. The FTA and the Federal Highway Administration (FHWA) are the lead organizations, jointly administering the federally required transportation planning processes in metropolitan and rural areas statewide. Local transportation operations have their own problems and operate in different internal and external environments. Although not uncommon, major governance conflicts seldom arise when federal and local organizations meet. Instead, the source of conflict more often exists between the transportation provider and its collection of diverse stakeholders. The current rule on transportation planning adopted in May 2016 included the following requirements:

- A performance-based approach to planning.
- A new emphasis on the nonmetropolitan transportation planning process, by requiring states to have a higher level of involvement with nonmetropolitan local officials and providing a process for creating regional transportation planning organizations.
- A structural change to the membership of large metropolitan planning organizations (MPOs) to include transit provider representation.
- A framework for voluntary scenario planning.
- A new authority for integrating the planning and environmental review processes as well as programmatic mitigation plans.

Network Governance Issues

Network governance issues are common in the management of teams with different values and under different collaborative relationships consisting of the government agencies, private companies and nongovernment organizations responsible for programs that extend across interstate boundaries (Forrer, Kee and Boyer 2014). Governance arrangements for collaborative natural resource management, for example, may be viewed as a network with a set of nodes (agencies, stakeholder groups) and relational ties (collaborative relationships, possibly of various types). Issues emerge at any one of these points. The teamwork arrangements may also include municipal and/or special districts. It is not uncommon for the teams to include members representing diametrically opposing values or special issue organizations.

Robins, Bates and Pattison (2011) point out that some of the problems of the governance of collaborative arrangements might include: difficulties in hierarchical coordination in the face of fragmentation; the occurrence of uncontrolled or unexpected changes and the complexity of group collaborations; issues with market-based outcomes where public goods are involved; inadequate collection or adoption of existing innovation; ineffective collective action; and slow cultural change. Some of the collaborative systems where governance might be an issue include a marine system coalition and a professional system teamwork.

California implemented a collaborative system of 124 marine protected areas (MPAs) in 2012, beginning in San Mateo, San Diego, and Santa Barbara. The networks allow civil societies, fishermen, tribal representatives, government staff, municipalities, academic institutions, scientists, teachers, and aquariums to work together to enhance understanding and compliance of MPAs. System staff work to enable local experts to partner with the state, strengthening connections and facilitating the flow of information between these local MPA professionals and managing agencies, and California's Department of Fish and Wildlife, State Parks, Ocean Protection Council and Ocean Science Trust. Such collaboratives are considered "a key part of the Ocean Protection Council's guiding principles for governing California's MPA network, allowing the state to engage in meaningful partnerships at the local level, leverage resources, and ensure transparency" (MPA Collaborative Networks 2018).

Measuring Network Performance

Performance measurement is an integral process in network management. How to assess the effectiveness of a collaborative arrangement of diverse participant organizations with different values and points of view remains difficult to achieve effectively (Provan and Milward 1995; Milward and Provan 1998). Robins, Bates and Pattison (2011) reported that a network group's performance may reflect outcomes across such factors as community reaction to costs or individual client outcomes. Therefore, performance effectiveness means that positive outcomes may not be achievable by isolated or independent action alone. A collaborative group such as a network

> represents a structured social system, and understanding the structure helps illuminate the potential functioning of the network. Accordingly, an assessment of multilevel outcomes that does not consider structural issues cannot address the question of whether an inadequacy in network structure underpins governance failure or success.... [this includes] simple network measures such as density and centralization in their assessment of a network. In this paper we propose structural patterns that go beyond these simple measures and examine theoretical arguments for the structural features of a network that are likely to enable effective network governance.
>
> *(Robins, Bates and Pattison 2011, 1294)*

Network Governance Foundations

Two network management models have largely replaced traditional governance systems in multi-agency government. The first is a performance-based, highly structured model that requires adherence to codified cross-agency behaviors. The management of such activities as education, defense, and health topics generally fit this mode. The second is more focused on maintaining relationships through collaborative ties between multilevel and multi-sector partners. In this second model, the governance model changes to fit the needs of the partners and the issues at hand. Performance goals are achieved through the collaborative efforts of more than one agency or sector participant. In both, participant organizations may include resources and capabilities spread across public and private sector partners. Both models are more collaborative than were the top–down or donor–recipient models common in government for more than a hundred years. Multiple independent government and nongovernment organizations pursuing similar goals characterize network strategies. This strategic approach is found in situations where a group of different participants, none of whom has the power to shape the strategies of others in the group, form a loose network to accomplish some specific goal. Under this scenario, the boundaries between public and private operations are often blurred.

Blended Network Versions

Four blended versions of governance models dominate government efforts at sharing power and responsibility today: partnering, collaboration between government agencies and one or more private organizations, collaboration between government agencies at different levels (federal–state, state–local, etc.), and total outsourcing of delivery of government services to private firms. Working with others to deliver government services is referred to as *third party government* (Berry and Brower 2005).

Program/Project Partner Networks

Partnering refers to a type of agreement between contractual parties to share management. Two types of partnering agreements are (1) longer-term (lasting as long as 10 years or more) strategic partnering similar to joint ventures in the private sector and (2) shorter-term, specific project or program partnering. The State of Maine provides the following suggestions for local government administrators considering partnering with other private sector agencies or public organizations:

- Before approaching providers and agencies with whom you've not worked previously, there is value in preparing. No matter what your job function, consider the other agency's "culture" and how to approach it, and how to be prepared to demonstrate to those organizations or providers why they, too, can benefit from collaborating with you.
- Learn more about the agency and its staff. What are the definitions and cultural beliefs around causation, strategies for intervention, sources of funding, policies and procedures, role of staff, including families in the child welfare system?
- Conduct cross-training with staff of both agencies (including administrators and supervisors).
- Learn about the terms, procedures, and forms that the other agency uses.
- Allow additional time to hear staff concerns, priorities, and resources and to determine the next steps in the partnering process. Remember that rapport-building may take considerable time, but it is critical to achieving positive outcomes for families and children.
- Recognize the power differentials that many families experience between agency representatives and themselves; be aware of the larger sociopolitical climate that is influencing agencies' decision-making.

Cross-sector Networks

Private/public cross-sector networks have become an increasingly common governance model in the public sector (Agranoff 2006). This approach to problem-solving and service delivery often emerges after some national or regional emergency, such as terrorist attacks, natural disasters, threats of a pandemic, or crises in such national programs as defense, health and education (Cooke 2012). Responding to the crisis brings participants from both sectors together to solve a problem. These arrangements can be informal collaborations or formal cooperative arrangements.

Two official definitions have been offered for network cross-sector collaboration arrangements. The National Association of State Chief Information Officers (NASCIO) has adopted a definition in which these partnerships are defined as relationships among government agencies and private or civil society contractors formed for dealing with services or products of high complexity. In comparison with traditional contractor–customer relationships, they require radical changes in the roles played by all partners. This means that the governance of such collaborative relationships must also be special. Collaborative partnerships are non- or semi-legal working relationships that bring members of both the public and private sector together to achieve a common purpose or solve a common problem. Often, the glue holding the network partnership is enlightened self-interest mixed with goodwill, commitment to meeting public need, and a desire to collectively leverage resources for a common purpose. Self-interest is the anathema of collaboration. It is not a zero-sum game. Partnerships do not require unwillingness to express an opinion or to support a point of view. Rather, it means a willingness to compromise when the final decision is best for all participants. Examples of such arrangements abounded during the response to the devastation resulting from hurricanes Katrina and Rita.

Cooperative partnership networks, on the other hand, are usually more or less formal systems held together by contractual agreement. They are a form of collaboration that can be either public/private or public/nonprofit. They may require a formal governance agreement, with rules and responsibilities—and penalties, if necessary. A co-operative (co-op) is thus an organization that is owned entirely by its members, and in which all members have an equal say in how the partnership will be run.

Most co-operatives are small, local organizations owned by their customers/clients, with all decisions made by locally elected board members (Burr 2004). This local control is seen by some to have been one of the strengths of the co-operative system. However, local control often limits a co-op's ability to achieve its primary mission, that of providing its customers reliable service at the lowest possible price.

Cross-level Networks

The third blended model considers "network" a new form of organization, and multiple cooperative relationships of with other-level government organizations can be the source of important resources and capabilities for strengthening the operational activities.

Blended Networks for Outsourced Services Delivery

Outsourcing is the practice of contracting with other sector organizations for the supply of one or more services. The network thus formed may also include members from other same-level agencies. What may be a controversial condition of networks with more than a few non-government memberships is the loss of control of the services delivered. An example is the U.S. military networking with outside agencies for delivery of security services in Afghanistan and Iraq. During the long wars in the region, contracts for such non-traditional items as prisoner interrogation and management of prisons were added to the long-standing tradition of logistics, housing, meal service and other non-combat functions. Contracts with what became essential private sector soldiers was a new and ultimately controversial phenomenon.

The Downside of Services Delivery Networks

Some problems do exist with cross-sector and cross-level networks. One is the problem of maintaining voluntary adherence to established governance responsibilities and collaborative contributions. Many network actions require management skills that are different from the skills managers in business or nonprofit organizations customarily employ. Clearly, effective network collaboration among diverse organizations can contribute significantly to the delivery of public goods and services. However, studies over many years of networks in business, health services and other sectors show that, taken together, approximately half of networks, alliances, coalitions and other partnerships that involve two or more independent organizations coming together voluntarily do not succeed. In a jointly sponsored study for the New York Academy of Medicine, the American Medical Association and the American Public Health Association, Prybil, Jarria and Montero (2015) listed the following recommendations for improving the success of these networks:

- Avoid conflicting mission, vision and values.
- Support a culture of collaboration.
- Harmonize goals and objectives.
- Commit to a durable program organizational structure.
- Jointly designate a well-qualified and dedicated leadership.
- Conduct regular performance evaluation and improvement activities.

Collaborative Networks

In one of three definitions for provided by IGI Global, collaborative networks are:

> an alliance constituted by a variety of entities (e.g., organizations and people) that are largely autonomous, geographically distributed, and heterogeneous in terms of their operating environment, culture, social capital and goals, but that collaborate to better achieve common or compatible goals.
> *(IGI Global 2020)*

The other two, which are essentially identical, include electronic (computer) ties between partners. However, while electronic communications methods are indeed increasingly the communication tools of choice between cross-sector and cross-government-level organizations and individuals, face-to-face communication is still possible and, in some cases, the preferred means of communication between partners.

Robert Agranoff (2006), productive researcher on public sector collaboration and networks, saw that it was well known by the early 21st century that managers and administrators of public sector organizations were already involved in collaborative and vertical networks, and that networks needed "to be taken seriously in public administration."

Three years earlier, Agranoff and McGuire defined collaborative networks as "the process of facilitating and operating in multi-organizational arrangements to solve problems that cannot be solved, or solved easily, by single organizations" (2003, 4). Agranoff added that collaborative networks are similar to but should not be seen identical to social networks. Social networks focus on ties linked by social relationships, whereas collaborative networks are collaborations for solving government's difficult problems (Agranoff 2006, 56). From data collected in his study of 14 public management networks in federal, state, regional and local government and managers of nongovernmental organizations, Agranoff listed 10

TABLE 7.1 Points to consider in forming a collaborative network

Point	Discussion
Not the only management tool	In cross-organization relationships, most of the networks are only one of several collaborative networks.
Do most work in the hierarchy	More network arrangements are occurring; most public sector managers report they still spend the majority of their time working in the traditional hierarchy.
Network activity keeps you involved	Most networks have existed for a long period and are considered to be worth the commitment they require; participating managers feel they benefit from them.
Networks are similar to but are not organizations	Networks are different; they are not hierarchical; participants begin as equals. But networks still require rules, organization.
They don't make policy or programs	Not all the successes reported really occur. Yet, most have benefits, but must be taken with an open mind.
Decisions are from mutual learning	Networks do not make decisions; they enable collaboration and discussion. Decisions are still made by managers.
Most activity comes from public sector knowledge management	Knowledge management is the most common product of collaborative network activity; knowledge and best practices are communicated and shared.
Conflicts and issues will arise	Many of the challenges encountered are the result of conflicts and disagreements over values and goals among participants within the network.
Collaboration has costs	For some, the highest cost is giving up authority and sharing resources. Members must give up time, energy, power-sharing, dealing with risks, and legislation.
Networks are not replacing public bureaucracies in any way	Networks enable collaborative activity toward achieving common goals; they do not replace governance.

Source: From concepts in Agranoff (2006)

concepts that managers considering starting or participating in a collaborative network should keep in mind. Elements of the lessons are included in Table 7.1.

The points and caveats of collaborative networks that are listed in Table 7.1 are reinforced by many advocates of this management tool. These networks are recognized as complex systems needing multi-disciplinary contributions and a combination of different perspectives; they are not the same as social networks. Nor can electronic communication systems assure their success (Camarinha-Matos 2009; Durugbo 2016). That will require a new way of thinking about governance. Members must be able to communicate, to share ideas and values, and to understand and appreciate other members' perspectives, boundaries and demands. The rationale for forming and participating in a collaborative network, "instead of being on securing resources while protecting organizational boundaries, is on breaking down boundaries through enhancing trusting relationships and realizing that each organization is only one piece of a new entity" (Mandell, Keast and Chamberlain 2017, 328). The new collaborative administration entity is formed for supporting joint effort for the collective benefit. In the public sector, the collective benefit extends far beyond the success of the organization. The policy of the public sector organizations is designed for assuring the benefit of the electorate (Cristofoli, Meneguzzo and Riccuci 2017).

Implementing the Network Framework

This model considers "network" as a new form of organization, and multiple cooperative relationships of an organization can be the source of values and its competitive strengths. To implement the strategy design framework, follow this six-step process:

Step 1: Identify the goals and purposes of establishing a strategic alliance or forming a strategic network:

- Efficiency: Networks can achieve efficiencies via scale and scope economies (i.e., through specialization, focus and size), and via the reduction of transactional inefficiency in the open market.
- Synergy: Networks can be formed to link and exploit the different competencies of a group of organizations.
- Power and influence: Networks can be established for organizations to expand the ability to influence the (political) decisions or actions of others.
- Cost- or risk-sharing: Organizations can share the cost and/or risk of technology and product/service development as well as logistics and distribution.

Step 2: Identify and select alliance or network partners:

- Evaluate potential partners' attributes, such as prior cooperative history, compatibility of management styles and organizational culture, potential learning opportunities, and complementarity of resources and competencies.

- A detailed agreement that lays out the specific responsibilities and obligations/expectations of all members must be in place before establishing an alliance or strategic network.

Step 3: Determine the governance structure and mode of the network:

- Choose between equity arrangement for more control (i.e., create new equity or institutions, such as joint venture or new government agencies) or contractual agreement among network of organizations for flexibility (e.g., collaborative network strategies).
- Select either intergovernmental cooperation or public–private collaboration, or strategic outsourcing service and delivery, to implement the alliance or network strategy.

Step 4: Design and implement mechanisms to prevent, manage, and resolve conflicts and disputes among network members:

- Design and implement a collaboration governance structure for the strategic network.
- Build trust and reciprocal relationship among partners.
- Cultivate a collaborative culture and develop a sense of strategic interdependence.
- Avoid or restrain shortsighted and opportunistic behavior.
- Ensure mutual forbearance with network partners and a desire to seek common ground.

Step 5: Evaluate network stability and performance:

- Develop specific plans and measurements for assessing the network performance to ensure the stability and continued progress toward the strategic goals.
- Periodically collect data and gather information, including stakeholders' feedback, to ensure the continuous improvement of performance.

Step 6: Terminate or dissolve the strategic alliance and network structure and relationship when internal conflict restricts the network's performance:

- Strategic alliances or networks can be terminated or dissolved when the strategic goals or objectives have been accomplished.
- The process of dissolving a strategic network must be open and transparent to ensure a proper reallocation of resources and competencies.

Summary

Public sector networks have been classified based on whether they are governed by the organizations that make up the network or if they are governed by an external office or an individual not a member of the network. There are two types of brokered networks: governance by a central lead agency (lead organization governed), or governance by an external network administrative organization (NAO), which can be a separate agency, an un-associated group, or an individual "network facilitator" appointed to provide governance without participating in the mission of the network. In non-brokered participant-governance networks, all members of the network share equally in shared governance.

The network framework focuses on strategy planning based on resources and capabilities enabled by collaboration and cooperation that include the contributions of a network of like-minded organizations. The network governance framework supports broad-based acceptance and adoption of all public sector levels and external stakeholders. The model requires management of a collection of more than one agency or organization in the way that collective authority is exercised (Radin 1996; Starling 2005). Referred to as either the multi-agency approach to strategic governance or simply network governance, it includes elements of the competitive forces, resource-based, and dynamic capabilities frameworks. The network governance model assumes that government strategies are no longer the product of a single public policy organization, but is more often a governing structure shaped through accommodating the influences of internal and external stakeholders. Strategy design thus involves a variety of different actors that include a combination of public, private and civil society contributors.

Two collaborative governance models are reshaping the traditional hierarchical governance systems. The first is a performance-based model that requires cross-agency cooperation. The second is a multilevel network model. In both, the contributions of participant organizations may include resources and capabilities spread across public and private sector partners. Both models are more collaborative than were the top–down or donor–recipient models common in government for more than a hundred years. Multiple independent government and nongovernment organizations pursuing similar goals characterize network strategies. This strategic approach is found in situations where a group of different participants, none of whom has the power to shape the strategies of others in the group, form a loose network to accomplish some specific goal. Under this scenario, the boundaries between public and private operations are often blurred.

8

THE GAME THEORY FRAMEWORK

The game theory framework describes a set of mathematics-based methods for making strategy decisions based on the utility (payoffs or benefits) expected to accrue with each optional strategy. A "game" is thus a decision-making event. "Players" can be an individual such as the manager of a government agency, or a group of players "competing" for a winning outcome. Game theory is widely known as a procedure for achieving optimal decision outcomes between two or more options, competing individuals, or organizations in zero-sum games. The outcome for any decision made is dependent on the decision made by the player and decisions made by all other participants. Only one player wins.

In non-zero-sum games, outcomes are utilities accruing from a selection of each option in a set of two or more options. Players select a strategy deemed best able to produce the best option as determined by the greatest sum of benefits. In this version, game theory is a valuable tool for helping managers select the "best" strategy from a set of possible strategies.

There are many different versions of game theory, although the defining characteristic is whether the game is cooperative or non-cooperative. In cooperative games, a set of players can form a coalition to achieve a common goal. Players negotiate agreement on the best combination to adopt. This model may be used during the formation of a network, collaborative group or a strategic alliance. Cooperative game theory assumes that groups of players, called coalitions, are the primary units of decision-making, and may encourage or even require cooperative behavior. In the public sector strategy selection, cooperative games are more likely to be seen as "competition" between a group of different strategies, rather than a choice of a single strategy. In addition, in the increasing presence of collaborative networks, the choices will be between combinations of players. As shown in the reuse of water example shown in this chapter:

> The basic assumption in cooperative game theory is that the grand coalition, that is the group consisting of all players, will form. One of the main research questions in cooperative game theory is how to allocate in some fair way the payoff of the grand coalition among the players.
>
> *(Coalition Theory Network n.d.)*

Non-cooperative games are games in which the players decide their own strategy with no collaboration. Non-cooperative games are used in strategic planning in which each player's decision is based on what that player perceives is the best personal outcome. Decisions are typically made on the Nash equilibrium solution. A game in which the payoffs and strategies of a game are listed in a table is considered a *normal form*. Games in which the expected payoffs are determined in the form of a decision tree are considered *extensive form games*.

Important Game Theory Terms

Mary Jane Sterling (n/d), author of a series of important game theory concepts, offered this list of important game theory terms:

- Payoff matrix: A matrix whose elements represent all the amounts won or lost by the row player.
- Payoff: An amount showing as an element in the payoff matrix, which indicates the amount gained or lost by the row player.
- Saddle point: The element in a payoff matrix that is the smallest in a particular row while, at the same time, the largest in its column. Not all matrices have saddle points.
- Strictly determined game: A game that has a saddle point.
- Strategy: A move or moves chosen by a player.
- Optimal strategy: The strategy that most benefits a player.
- Value (expected value) of game: The amount representing the result when the best possible strategy is played by each player.
- Zero-sum game: A game where what one player wins, the other loses; no money comes in from the outside or leaves.
- Fair game: A game with a value of 0.
- Pure strategy: A player always chooses the same row or column.
- Mixed strategy: A player changes the choice of row or column with different plays or turns.
- Dominated strategy: A strategy that is never considered because another play is always better. For the row player, a row is dominated by another row if all the corresponding elements are all larger. For the column player, a column is dominated by another column if all the corresponding elements are all smaller.

Game Theory for Decisions

Brandenburger and Nalebuff (1996, 7) believed the value of game theory emerges from its ability to help managers focus "directly on the most pressing [management and planning] issues of all: Finding the right strategies and making the right decisions." They further describe it as a systematic way to develop strategies when one organization's success depends upon what actions its internal and external stakeholders and service recipients take. The framework is also valuable as a means of sharing the rationale behind selection of an organization's strategy by making it easier to explain the need for a particular activity. Accordingly, these characteristics justify identifying game theory as a strategy science.

Applying this mathematics and economics-developed game theory framework to the design of public sector strategies begins with an evaluation of the expected benefits that can result from a thorough analysis of each potential strategy and comparing these with the probable outcome costs of each. The actions and choices of all players affect the outcome of each competitive decision (Von Neumann and Oskar Morgenstern 1944). Mathematician John Nash contributed to the theory in 1951 with the concept that an equilibrium point in a decision outcome will eventually arise between all choices. From the equilibrium point on, no player (organization) can increase the value of a payoff by unilaterally making game decisions.

Game theory research and application to decision-making emerged in military and defense planning from the 1950s to the 1960s. Researchers at the Rand Corporation used the method to game (i.e., estimate) the likelihood of a nuclear warfare exchange with the Soviet Union. However, with the slow decline of the USSR as a potential aggressor in the 1980s, the gaming of nuclear exchange faded. This resulted in growth of the framework's use in other disciplines.

Normal Form Game Theory Applications

Public sector game theory applications tend to focus on alternative strategic decisions of a single player. Game theory in now common in business and government research. It has also become a standard analysis tool in political science, where it is applied in such applications as international relations analysis, behaviors of political parties and the electorate, legislative decisions, lobbying and other fields (McCarty and Meirowitz 2007; Samuelson 2016). With no decisions by competitors with which to compare, public sector game theory often focuses on alternative strategic decisions of a single player. Ouenniche, Boukouras and Rajabi (2016) chronicled an example of its use in this way. They applied game theory in a study on public sector organizations' selection of non-public sector partners in public–private partnership projects. Such partnerships are often used for infrastructure projects and the supplying of goods or services to special-needs populations. Provision of the good or services in this way has the advantage of little or no increase in already stressed public debt limits. The five commonly employed types of partnership are:

1 subcontracting management of a project, activity or public entity;
2 turnkey (design and build) infrastructure construction;
3 subcontracting facility or project management to a private sector organization;
4 private sector concession for operating a project or facility;
5 private ownership with private sector finance for design, build and operation with public sector leasing of the facility.

In game theory strategy selection, the organization's added value projected as emerging from an alternative decision evolves from the combination of service provider performance and recipients' perceptions of the payoff or utility resulting from the decision. Two types of analysis models are used in evaluating the potential added value: cardinal or interval utilities (Ross 2011). Cardinal utility functions are finite returns, such as the prices charged for services, per diem expenses involved in stakeholder participation, percentages of risk-sharing agreements with service delivery partners, allocations for resource pricing and claims, and quality incentives. Easier to understand and evaluate, in game theory strategy planning, cardinal utility functions are used more often than ordinal utilities.

Bidding Proposals Game Theory Example

Ordinal utility functions in game theory are numbers assigned for identifying the position of a set of utilities in the order of all utility functions. They are not measurements of the quantity of any "thing." Using an ordinal game theory-based framework, Ouenniche, Boukouras and Rajabi (2016) showed how the game theory could be used for examining any set of proposals for analyzing competing bidding strategies, alternative contractual terms and performance measures. Advantages for the ordinal-based analysis identified for the ordinal utility design included ability to include any number of private sector players and any number of contractual terms and related performance criteria, ease of ranking proposals or bidders, and it can be used to identify salient terms and performance measures.

The study project was bidding on a fixed price contract for a transportation infrastructure project. Three contract terms included in the game theory analysis: price, delivery time, and risk. Price was the amount the private sector bidder was willing to accept for the completed project; delivery time was the number of years specified for completion of the project and ownership transferred to the city; risk referred to the percentage of the operational, financial and technical risk that the bidder was willing to accept.

The study included bids comprising amounts for two bidders, as shown in Table 8.1. The optimal bid combination for each of the two bidders would be

TABLE 8.1 Bidder selection game theory example data

Utility	Bidder 1	Bidder 2
Price		
Option 1	510 million	480 million
Option 2	560 million	560 million
Option 3	630 million	610 million
Risk		
Option 1	55%	55%
Option 2	60%	65%
Years		
Option 1	3 years	4 years
Option 2	4 years	6 years

Source: Ouenniche, Boukouras and Rajabi (2016)

Bidder 1: 630 million, 55% risk and three years; Bidder 2: 480 million, 65% risk and six years. The optimal bid for the public sector organization would be that of Bidder 2—except for the six-year time factor. The PPP contract would most likely be awarded to Bidder 2, with the probable likelihood of negotiating the time period.

Game Theory and Data Security Example

Game theory was used in a study of cybersecurity in cloud computing described in a 2019 conference paper by India's Petroleum University researchers Kakka, Shah, Patel and Doshi. Cloud computing allows users to store files and applications on remote servers and then access all the data via the Internet. Security is a major concern with the cloud, particularly so with defense and financial data. The *Cybersecurity Framework* provides security guidelines collected and managed since 2014 by the National Institute of Standards and Technology (NIST), an agency of the U.S. Department of Commerce. NIST describes the cloud as an on-demand network with access to a shared pool of computing resources. NIST's guidelines help organizations be better prepared for identifying, detecting, and responding to cyber-attacks. The best practices and standards distributed by the agency framework help an organization improve its cybersecurity measures and prepare protections for fighting hackers, data pirates, and ransomware. Defenses against two types of problems common in cloud computing were evaluated with game theory analysis in the cybersecurity study: cloud cyber space security and pricing strategies for different cloud services

Solid Waste Disposal Example

Game theory has also been used in decision option analysis for many local governments. An example is the study conducted in Vancouver, Canada to determine the comparative advantages of disposing the city's large solid waste problem. The two options were using the collected waste as fuel to generate electricity or selling the waste material as a fuel needed to produce cement. The U.S. EPA defines solid waste as "any garbage or refuse, sludge from a wastewater treatment plant, water supply treatment plant, or air pollution control facility and other discarded material, resulting from industrial, commercial, mining, and agricultural operations, and from community activities." Box 8.1 is a brief description of the study.

BOX 8.1 EVALUATING SOLID WASTE DISPOSAL OPTIONS WITH GAME THEORY

Game theory was used to evaluate best outcomes for an efficient waste treatment strategy in Vancouver, Canada. The successful solution was to have been cost-effective and minimize potential impacts on various stakeholders and the environment. This study proposed a decision framework that can model the stakeholders' conflicting priorities over the sustainability criteria, when selecting a municipal solid waste treatment option. Converting waste to energy by incineration was the chief treatment.

> The proposed framework compared lifecycle sustainability impacts of selected options and [applied] a weighing scheme for combining impacts based on stakeholders' preferences. It then [used] game theory to help the stakeholders fairly share the costs and benefits and guide the stakeholders to reach an agreement on a mutually sustainable and pragmatic solution.

In this study, the application of the framework was to select a waste-to-energy technology for Vancouver, Canada. The study compared the prospect of producing refuse-derived fuel by the cement industry against energy for the municipality. Results show that the cement industry and the municipality may mutually benefit from the refuse-derived fuel, if the industry pays a tipping fee of US$1.048 per 2.2 pounds of waste to access the required amount of solid waste from the municipality. The outcome of the framework can help in the approval and application of an overall sustainable option by both stakeholders and in making the negotiation more efficient and timelier.

Source: Soltani, Sadiq and Hewage (2016)

Water Reuse Cooperative Example

A 2018 study of citizens' willingness to accept a variety of applications of recycled or reused water included a cooperative game theory study (Chhipi-Shrestha, Rodriquez and Sadiq 2019). Game theory was used in evaluating eight water reuse options and three participants or stakeholders: a municipality, citizens, and the region's farmers. Scores for three dimensions affecting all dimensions contributed to the game theory solution: the environment, economic costs, and social costs. These resulted in utility functions for the eight alternatives (Table 8.2). A section of the game theory payoff matrix for the three water uses is shown in Table 8.2.

The optimal solution for the three-player combination was a mix of uses for lawn, golf course, and public park irrigation and toilet flushing. This combination provided equal sharing of benefits to be shared by a municipality, private citizens, and farm irrigation water users. Using the described option was estimated to gain yearly savings of $35 per household. Plumbing of residential toilets and lawn irrigation was estimated to cost an additional $100 per year, an amount within earlier survey results of the public's willingness to pay for recycling and reusing water.

Because water reuse is a decision that affects all levels of society in the community, the study design was considered a cooperative game with all players having full information. The solution sought in the game was a Pareto optimal equilibrium (the 2008 OECD glossary of terms notes that the Pareto optimum is also referred to as Pareto efficiency and as allocative efficiency; it occurs when resources are so allocated that it is not possible to make anyone better off without making someone else worse off). The Pareto optimal equilibrium is a game theory solution in which there is no way of improving any player's score without reducing the utility of at least one other player's objective; the Pareto optimal outcome is the maximum payoff for all players. Table 8.3 shows just a few examples of scores for all players in the following order—municipality, and economic and social—with the optimal decision of A5 for all players shown in boldface.

TABLE 8.2 Alternative water reuse applications

Alternative	Description
A1	Toilet flushing only
A2	Golf course and public park irrigation
A3	Lawn irrigation and toilet flushing
A4	Agricultural irrigation
A5	Lawn, golf course, public park irrigation, and toilet flushing
A6	Golf course irrigation only
A7	Potable reuse only
A8	No reuse of water

Source: Chhipi-Shrestha, Rodriquez and Sadiq (2018)

TABLE 8.3 Selected portions of a payoff matrix for three players and strategies

Player 3 Farm operators (data not included)
Player 2 Citizens (data not included)

Player 1	A1	A2	A3	A4	A5	A6	A7	A8
A1								
A2								
A3			0.16, 0.19, 0.33					
A4			0.16, 0.08, 0.67					0.16, 0.18, 0.67
A5					0.17, 0.17, 0.33			
A6								
A7							0.12, 0.19, 0.33	
A8								

Source: Selected data from Chhipi–Shrestha, Rodriquez and Sadiq (2018).

Note
Only winning values shown; 0.37 value substituted for missing farm operators' alternatives.

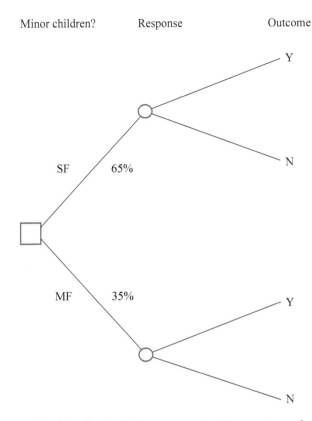

Minor children?   Response   Outcome

SF   65%

MF   35%

FIGURE 8.1 Simple decision tree, one decision, two states of nature (S/F).

Source: Data and drawings by the authors.

Extensive Form Game Theory Applications

Statistical decision-tree decision analysis approaches are tools for assisting managers to make strategic decisions based on the likely payoff of a decision (Southorn 2016). The key to these models is probabilities that the utilities will occur or not for each relevant variable in the model. For example, a decision-tree model can be used for determining what percentage of dwelling units in a large city are likely to have a problem with lead in the water supply. The municipal water department has a dataset consisting of information about every dwelling unit in the city. An algorithm based on selected probabilities is prepared for the analysis.

The decision tree consists of a root, nodes, branches, and leaves. The root is the base variable (characteristic) of interest. For example, the root characteristic in a lead-in-domestic-water study could be: Is the structure a single-family residence? If so, are there minor children present? The two branches are single-family (SF)

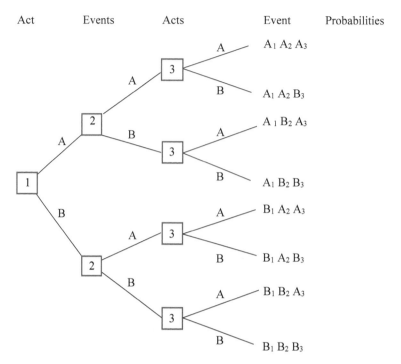

FIGURE 8.2 Decision tree with three decision points and eight possible outcomes.

Source: The authors.

and multifamily (MF). A node consists of a question regarding minor children are present in the residence. Branches represent answers to the node question that are established based on the answer of its corresponding question. The node will have two branches: A "yes" branch and a "no" branch.

A leaf is an endpoint in the tree. The decision tree uses the leaf to predict the class of given data by utilizing several predictor functions. The decision tree grows on the characteristic data, grouping people into subgroups. The final result is probabilities that individuals in the group will respond in one way or another, based on the collection of the probabilities of characteristics of past behaviors.

Implementing a Game Theory Project

Game theory is the study of mathematical models of strategic interaction among rational decision-makers where the outcome of a participant's choice of action depends critically on the actions of other participants. By combining business strategy and game theory, Brandenburger and Nalebuff (1996) argue that it is better for competitors to cooperate while competing (also referred to as co-opetition).

The method is used for almost any decision; examples have been used in banking, marketing, medical, legal, government, economic, industrial, and other applications. Figure 8.2 is an example of a complicated decision tree. As the tree notes, the best series of decisions indicates following the top sequence of decisions.

There are two models of the framework: the competitive forces model and the value net model. The competitive forces framework focuses exclusively on competition but fails to include the collaborative potential in an industry or family of cross-sector public service organizations. When working together, organizations can create a much larger and more rewarding market or other performance payoff than they could by working individually. The new value net model combines the advantages of both competition and cooperation into a new dynamic approach for strategy formulation, thereby improving the possibility of reward.

At heart, game theory is a superior decision tool. The standard model calls for a set of rules and all players' freedom to choose any strategy. In a perfect game, players have complete information, where they all know all the rules, the possible choices, and the record of previous choices. In another a version of the game, game theory without perfect information, a problem in choosing a strategy comes up; the players are challenged because there is no pure strategy that ensures a win. In the standard game, the Nash equilibrium is an important concept in game theory. The equilibrium is the point in a game when no player can improve their payoff. This is also known as a "stable game." The Nash equilibrium provides the solution concept in a non-cooperative game.

Implementing the Game Theory Framework

Game theory is the study of mathematical models of *strategic interaction* among *rational decision-makers* where the *outcome* of a participant's *choice of action* depends critically on the actions of other participants. By combining business strategy and game theory, Brandenburger and Nalebuff (1996) argue that it is better for competitors to cooperate while competing—known as co-opetition. The new *value net model* combines the advantages of both competition and cooperation into a new dynamic approach for strategy formulation. *The competitive forces framework* focuses exclusively on competition but fails to include the collaborative potential in an industry. Organizations when working together can create a much larger and more valuable market than they ever could by working individually. Strategy planners desiring to implement the game theory framework can follow these seven steps:

Step 1: Identify types of player in the *value net* that every organization faces and could directly influence your organization:

- *Customers/clients:* The people or parties that pay for your product or service.
- *Suppliers:* The parties that provide your organization with the resources needed to produce or sell your final products or services.
- *Competitors:* The parties that fight over the same pieces of market share as your organization by targeting similar customers with similar products or services.
- *Complementors:* Organizations that offer (complementary) products or services that could work well together with your own products or services to make the end result more attractive to consumers or clients.

Step 2: View your organization's strategy formulation process as a game and identify all the elements of the game—known as *the PARTS approach*:

- *Players:* What are the opportunities for cooperation and competition with each of the various players? Are there any parties you could potentially form a strategic alliance or network with?
- *Added value:* Apply *the VIRO framework* and value chain analysis to identify the organization's sources of value. Added value measures what each player, in each role, brings to the table. Are there any ways in which your organization could combine forces in order to add value for your customers?
- *Rules:* Each industry and market has both written and implicit rules and regulations. Identify which rules are helping or hurting your organization. Who has the power to create, enforce and overturn rules? Perhaps there are certain rules of the game that can be changed in your favor by collaborating with the right parties.
- *Tactics:* What actions can one player take to shape the strategies, actions and perceptions of other players? How can you deliberately send signals and messages that influence the perception of other players, which in turn may influence their actions?
- *Scope:* Identify what industries could potentially be linked, how your organization could create added value from linking your products and services to that industry, and how that may affect the perceptions and actions of other players.

Step 3: Formulate and implement strategy through the application of the *value net model* and the *PARTS approach*:

- *The value net* and *the PARTS approach* may help to identify possible players to cooperate with.
- It is possible to cooperate while competing and achieve mutually beneficial results for all players in the game, i.e., shifting from a zero-sum game to a win-win situation.
- *The value net model* is an extension to Porter's *competitive forces framework* that includes the complementors component. *The VIRO framework* can also help organizations identify the sources of added value.

- It is becoming more important for organizations to remain flexible and innovative by establishing strategic alliances and networks to create and sustain competitive advantage.

Step 4: Apply a game theory mindset to make better decisions and strategies:

- Are the players in the situation rational?
- Are we able to reach Nash equilibrium (i.e., an "equilibrium" where no side would benefit by changing its course)?
- Do players act according to their self-interest?
- Do players understand the rules of the game?
- Are players' dominant strategies really that dominant? (Dominant strategy refers to strategies that are better than other strategies for one player, no matter how the opponent may play.)

Summary

As described in this chapter, the game theory framework is a method for evaluating choices with alternative payoffs (utilities or preferences) accruing between two or more strategies by two or more "players" (Ross 2019). The goal of the game is to achieve the most preferred utility. *Utility* refers to "some ranking, on some specified scale, of the subjective welfare or change in subjective welfare that an agent (player) derives from an object or an event" (Ross 2019, Sect 2.1). In a competitive zero-sum situation, the goal is for at least one player to maximize the available utility. In a cooperative game, the goal is for all players to achieve the maximum possible utility that does not result in taking some utility from another player—an equilibrium.

Games can be displayed in two different ways. Matrix games are referred to as "normal-form" or *strategic-form* games, and tree games are extensive-form games. An example of a matrix game is a two by two matrix in which the horizontal boxes represent decisions of one player and the vertical alternatives as decisions of the second player. Matrix games show the different utilities accruing from a selection. The other way is as a decision tree. A decision tree is a set of lines to connected points in a graph. The lines between points illustrate a sequential representation. Trees are *sequential* games; the nodes show the order in which actions are taken by the players. Outcomes following each note are also included.

Game theory may also be used in association with any one or more of the other main strategic planning frameworks by the use of a game for deciding how best to use the other management tools for planning the intricacies of the strategy deemed to have the best possible outcome.

PART III

Public Sector Strategies

9
STRATEGY DESIGN AND STRATEGIC ORIENTATION

An organization's strategic orientation is the guiding principle that underlies all strategic decisions. It shapes the direction that a public sector organization takes in planning to perform its mission and the way it plans to continue to function over the foreseeable time period. It therefore influences both current operational plans and schedules and the proposed human and administrative capital investments that must be available. There are two major components to this idea. The first is the sense that an organization has a plan that delineates its strategic goals and for the tasks and performance objectives for achieving its long-term goals. In government organizations, the time period established for strategic plans can range from two to four years, beginning and ending with a new administration's term of office. The orientation adopted is based upon and further shaped not only by its available resources, management strengths and mandated actions, but also by the influence of one or more newly elected officials.

The second is the regular monitoring and measuring performance progress gained toward achieving its short-term objectives and longer-term goals. Only by measuring its performance can the organization gauge how well it is moving along its chosen strategic path. These two components together enable the strategy and form the strategic orientation for the organization.

Shaping a Strategic Orientation

Public sector organizations tend to follow either one of three basic strategic orientations: a focus on the needs of its "customers" (as in the Veteran Administration's patient orientation), a focus on the process (as in the Army's Corps of Engineers' focus on installing dams for improving flood control), or a transformation position (as in an agency's openness to changing its service system to e-government).

Adopting a strategic management approach implies an openness to change and acceptance of new and innovative processes and actions. If the subsequent actions reflect guidance indicated in the strategic plan and are to achieve the objectives for specified priority goals, managing the process must be guided by an all-embracing strategic orientation that provides a rationale for acceptance of the change. This organization's orientation becomes "a vision of how the changes are to be made, over what time period, and by whom" in the organization (Baker 2007, 1). Strategic orientations in the public sector are often designed to focus on meeting the needs of the client/customer/group or individual recipient of the service, expanding value of, or public acceptance of the service provided, or to focus on achieving sustainability through improving efficiency of the agency's operations through participating in governance networks and strategic alliances. Example descriptions and operational goals are shown in Table 9.1. Studies of the

TABLE 9.1 Strategic orientations and core strategies for public sector organizations

Strategic Orientation Missions

Strategic Orientation Focus	Example Operational Missions	Example Management's Tactical Role Objectives
Client/stakeholder (customer orientation)	The role of the agency is to continue to invest on improving its resources and capabilities for meeting all needs of a focused clientele.	The role of management is to guide use of resources to build its capability to meet or exceed all performance goals and objectives for providing services.
Mission positioning/ value chain/ (service orientation)	The most effective way for the agency to achieve maximum value from a limited budget is by emphasizing detailed strategic planning and asset management.	The role of the agency is to continuously improve in order to become the best, most efficient and most trustworthy provider of public goods and services.
Transformation/ technology/ innovation (change orientation)	The best way for the agency to maximize its budget allocations is to replace inefficient operational "stovepipes" by combining its assets, knowledge and skills with other institutions and levels of government through cooperative membership in individual, organizational and mission networks.	The role of management is to network with other agencies and non-government firms for maximizing service quality and efficiency and achieve sustainable operations with cooperative governance and participate in networks and strategic alliances.

Source: The authors

strategies of firms in the industrial and commercial sectors often include learning (knowledge) as additional orientation—a concept that could also apply to some government organizations. Still others claim that innovation is a contributing factor shaping all strategic orientations, regardless of which sector is being considered.

Following Igor Ansoff's 1980 proposals for a system of strategic issues management (SIM), Norwegian professors Brønn and Brønn (2002) suggested issue management as a tool in the process of adopting a given strategic orientation. Ansoff saw a strategic issue as "a forthcoming development, either inside or outside of the organization, which is likely to have an important impact on the ability of the enterprise to meet its objectives" (Ansoff 1980). An issue can be interpreted either as an emerging opportunity in the organization's environment, as an internal strength for dealing with threats, or as the external threat or an internal weakness. What and how the organization functions under these conditions can be considered its orientation.

Public Sector Orientation

The limited but growing research on strategic orientation in the public sector suggests that operational success in the public sector is closely associated with its decision to develop and follow a consistent orientation that focuses on service to one or more bodies of citizenry (Berry 1994; Bryson, Ackermann and Eden 2007; Bloch and Bugge 2013). Table 9.2 shows examples of salient research on the topic. It is for this reason that the men and women who toil in the public sector are referred to as public servants. The relationship between strategic orientation and performance was supported by studies such as these.

TABLE 9.2 Representative strategic orientation research

Authors	Year	Theme
Gatignon and Xuereb	1997	Strategic orientation and new product performance
Noble, Sinha and Kumar	2002	Market orientation and alternative orientations
Bhuian, Mengue and Bell	2005	Fit of entrepreneurial orientation with performance
Ruokonen and Saarenketo	2009	Strategic orientations of software firms
Johnson, Martin and Saini	2012	Strategic orientation's dimensions and market
Sen	2014	Multiple strategic orientations
Ejdys	2015	Strategic orientation and innovativeness
Deutscher, Zapkau, Schwens, Baum and Kabst	2016	Strategic orientation influence of firm performance
Lee, Chan and McNabb	2017	Strategic orientation and innovation
Adams, Freitas and Fontana	2019	Strategic orientation and innovation performance

Defining Strategic Orientation

Bader Obeidat (2016) provides an important rationale for government organizations' attention to adopt a strategic orientation. The following paragraph, modified for public sector relevance, explains his contribution: Adopting the best strategy available requires organizations to coordinate their approaches in establishing public service positions and/or by relying on their resources, competences, and capabilities in an effort to achieve a fit with their internal and external environments and in turn achieve a sustained operational advantage, improved performance, and greater efficiency. To achieve these goals, organizations should give serious consideration to what will be their strategic orientation. The chosen strategic orientation will guide the direction that an organization will follow in monitoring its activities for better performance. The strategic orientation of the organization reflects its operational, promotional and innovation positions and enables the organization to achieve its goals in delivery of client value by taking risks and embracing innovation (Obeidat 2016, 479–80). Box 9.1 is a description of the disagreements as to what a strategic orientation really is.

BOX 9.1 SEARCHING FOR A DEFINITION OF STRATEGIC ORIENTATION

"Strategic orientation has received widespread attention from management, marketing, and entrepreneurship scholars. However, no universally accepted definition of strategic orientation exists. The very nature of orientation is a matter of debate, and different streams of literature have developed diverse concepts. Orientation refers to the general or lasting direction of thought, inclination, or interest. Strategic orientation refers to the manner in which a firm adapts to its external environment. In other words, it refers to the pattern of responses that an organization makes to its operating environment in an effort to enhance performance and gain competitive advantage. Other scholars see strategic orientation as an aspect of organizational culture. Organizational culture is a form of intangible resources and the deployment of those resources, i.e. orientations, will have different impacts on the organization."

"Strategic orientation focuses resources to achieve desired outcomes. This is supported by Balodi (2014), who stated that strategic orientation manifests in the firm's culture and serves as antecedents to organizational practices and decisions associated with resources allocation and pursuing opportunities. In this paper, strategic orientation is viewed as principles that direct and influence the activities of a firm and generate the behaviors intended to ensure the viability and performance of the firm. These principles can also be used to guide the organization."

"Previous studies have specifically advocated the use of behaviors associated with the organization wide generation, dissemination, and use of market intelligence as being the key ingredients of strategic orientation. A growing stream of studies today endorse the adoption of different strategic orientations such as innovation orientation, technology orientation, entrepreneurial orientation, quality orientation, and productivity orientation."

Source: Obeidat (2016, 480)

Different Approaches

Four different approaches to the adoption of a strategic orientation option are followed in government: the narrative approach, the classificatory approach, the innovative approach, and a collaborative approach. One, the narrative approach tends to be a verbal description of the strategy followed by an individual firm. Two, the classificatory approach seeks to establish a typology of strategies and classifies a range of organization strategies according to this typology. Three, innovative or policy approach focuses on strategic management. It is based on cross-level and cross-sector strategies that require collaborative efforts. Four, the comparative approach, evaluates different strategies by some trait or dimension common to all firms.

Public service providers typically serve a captive market and are restrained from change by limited access to investment capital. Their "customers" are typically limited in their choices of providers to a single source. For example, urban residents desiring water and electricity service must connect to the one municipal water utility and the one wastewater supplier that serves their community. Their only options are to purchase bottled water in small quantities at local retail outlets and generate their own electricity. Rural dwellers, however, can dig their own wells, withdraw water from streams and lakes, and install their own septic systems. Similar supplier choice limitations exist for electricity, solid waste disposal and urban public transportation. Therefore, a new classification system for strategic options for public service providers is necessary. Some of these are suggested in the following pages.

An organization's strategic orientation is the direction and focus the organization follows as it directs and employs its assets for designing and implementing present and future operations. In addition to the more commonly used term of strategic orientation, it has been described in a variety of ways, including strategic fit, strategic disposition, strategic thrust, and strategic choice (Morgan and Strong 2003; Lee, Chan, McNabb and Khalifa 2019). A strategic orientation reflects the operational and competitive paths that an organization plans to follow in its drive to success in achieving its comprehensive strategic goal. Central to an adopted orientation are the concepts of differentiation and innovation (Cheng, Yang and

Sheu 2017). There are two major components to this concept. The first is that an organization prepares and follows a strategic plan that identifies future operations for achieving its long-term goals. Second is that the organization has and implements a system for measuring progress in gauging how well it is moving along that path. These two components together establish the strategic orientation for that company.

The strategic orientation of an organization is rooted in the internal and external environment in which it operates (Tutar, Nart and Bingöl 2015). Once established, the strategies and orientations adopted by businesses are then influenced by market uncertainty, technological change and competitive intensity. The accelerating pace of economic and technological change has left public organizations in a difficult spot, hobbled by ambiguous authorizing legislation, expansive missions, inflexible workforces and decision-making procedures, all of which make them vulnerable. Adept use of evaluation and performance measurement has lessened the risk of sudden strategic failure, but it continues to be a significant fear of those leading public organizations.

Having been a widely evaluated management theory for more than 50 years, the influence of an organization's strategic orientation upon its performance has been thoroughly documented (Slater, Olson and Hult 2006). The degree to which that orientation influences its performance is commonly referred to as how well the chosen strategies fit with an organization's resources and capabilities and with the extant environmental conditions, such as the four components of strategy suggested by Andrews in 1971 and many following investigators: market opportunity, corporate competence and available resources, management's personal values and aspirations, and obligations to society as well as to stockholders (Andrews 1971; Venkatraman and Camillus 1984; Morgan and Strong 2003). The concept has been applied in both public and private organizations, ranging globally from hospitals (Heatwole 1980), retail furniture markets (Tutar, Nart and Bingöl 2015), the U.S. defense industry (Arbaugh and Sexton 1997) and many others.

Strategic Fit and Performance

Strategic orientation is the approach that an organization follows in its performance-related decisions. It has been described in a variety of different ways: strategic fit, strategic disposition, strategic thrust, strategic choice and the more commonly used term, strategic orientation. Porter (1980) grouped all business strategic orientations into three generic groups: cost leadership, differentiation, and focus. Cost leadership strategies emphasize low cost relative to competitors; differentiation strategies focus on developing products or services different from competitors'; focus orientations refer to focusing on a special group of customers, geographic markets or product line segments. Porter then classified industries as falling in one of five generic industrial categories: fragmented, emerging, mature, declining, or global.

The concept of an organization's strategic orientation fit and its operational implementation was described in the seminal work on a theory of strategy (Porter 1991, 102):

> A firm's strategy defines its configuration of activities and how they interrelate. Competitive advantage results from a firm's ability to perform the required activities at a collectively lower cost than rivals or perform some activities in unique ways that create buyer value and hence allow the firm to command a premium price. The required mix and configuration of activities in turn is altered by competitive scope.

The association of strategic fit and performance was further established by such studies as that of Bhuian, Mengue and Bell (2005) in their study of the fit of entrepreneurial orientation with performance; by Ruokonen and Saarenketo (2009) in their evaluations of a variety of strategic orientations of software firms. Strategic orientations are believed to influence market performance of high technology firms. Managers and administrators in all private and public sector organizations see different conditions, threats and opportunities in their external environments and their capabilities to defend against or take advantage of those conditions. In the competitive private sector, three common strategic orientations identified for private sector organizations are: a market orientation, technological orientation, or an entrepreneurial orientation (Koli and Jaworski 1990).

Underlying Principles

Strategic orientation is the underlying beliefs and principles that shape the way in which an organization interacts with the people and institutions of society it serves. It shapes the path that the organization's managers follow in directing actions for providing the goods and services that meet the needs and expectations of the organization's customers and for achieving its goals. The success of the organization's mix of strategic options, capabilities and assets necessary for creating value and sustaining competitive advantage depends on the strategic orientation of the top managers of the business. Five underlying constraints shape the strategic orientation of organizations:

1. the concept, service or field for which the department, agency or unit operates;
2. citizen demand for the product, service or idea;
3. the level of governance within which the organization operates (federal, state or local);
4. the operating funds (budget allocation) available to sustain or to grow existing services;
5. the resources, competencies and capabilities needed to achieve sustainability in the operational environment.

Strategic Orientation Planning

The need for planning a strategic orientation was an early addition to the strategic management concept. For example, the three basic strategic orientations identified for private sector organizations are market orientation, entrepreneurial orientation and technology orientation. An organization with a market orientation is one where the focus is on customers or on competitors. An entrepreneurial orientation is one where the focus is on product or market innovation, risk and being first with new products or services (Miller 1983). A technological orientation is one in which a capability and performance relationship reflects a multidimensional mix of top management capability, technological capability, commitment to learning and commitment to change (Gatignon and Xuereb 1997; Helac 2015). These three basic strategic orientations needed to be modified and expanded for application to public sector organizations. For example, a study of strategic orientations in public libraries included a community orientation to a list of private sector orientations that included market, learning, innovation, brand, entrepreneurial, and service innovations. The community orientation appeared to be synonymous with market orientation, while the service orientation included activities associated with sustainability—also sometimes included as a public sector strategic orientation.

Importance of Strategic Fit

The literature has long shown agreement that the fit of business operations with strategic orientation is critical to successful business performance. The early work of strategy theorists such as Venkatraman and Camillus in 1984 and Michael Porter in the 1980s and 1990s saw the connection of strategic orientation to innovation firmly established. The concept of strategic fit described in Porter's seminal paper on a theory of strategy (Porter 1991) is:

> A firm's strategy defines its configuration of activities and how they interrelate. Competitive advantage results from a firm's ability to perform the required activities at a collectively lower cost than rivals or perform some activities in unique ways that create buyer value and hence allow the firm to command a premium price. The required mix and configuration of activities in turn is altered by competitive scope.

In the process of formulating their strategy, managers and administrators must decide on what levels of major strategic elements best fit the capabilities of the organization and its managers. For private sector organizations, these dimensions include market aggressiveness, market analysis, defensiveness, future orientation, proactive orientation, and a tendency to accept risk. For public sector organizations, these dimensions might include willingness to accept political discontinuity, periodic transformation, innovation proclivity, resource restrictions, and a commitment to collaborative problem-solving. Possible strategic orientations include but are not limited to a public service orientation, an innovation orientation, a knowledge-based orientation, and a sustainability orientation. Individual chapters are devoted to each of these public sector strategic orientations. In the process of preparing the best strategic orientation to follow, managers must also take care to avoid these potentially catastrophic mistakes (Lee, Chan, McNabb and Khalifa 2019):

1. committing resources to a losing cause;
2. repeatedly dividing the market and driving up costs;
3. missing opportunities to create new markets; and
4. failing to capitalize on emerging technologies and innovations that may revolutionize the market and industry.

Example Public Sector Orientations

In their study of the influence of a firm's strategic orientation on new product performance, Gatignon and Xuereb (1997) focused on just three generic strategic orientations: customer, competitive, and technology. Alternative categories of principle strategic orientations are customer orientation, competitor orientation, and product orientation. All categorizations agree that an organization seeking to create superior value while striving for achieving sustainability must have a strong customer focus, whereas in high-growth environments, a competitive orientation is preferred. In markets where high uncertainty of success is extant, a combined consumer and technological orientation is deemed better. The research was introduced by Day and Wensley in 1983, with a focus on the influence of market performance of customer orientation versus competitor orientation.

With modifications to reflect the service rather than commercial focus, these same three orientations can be applied to public sector organizations. The customer orientation may be changed to recipient or customer. Broadly, the orientation could be based on who benefits from a government service: individuals, sectors of society, organizations or institutions, and the like.

The competitive orientation is more difficult to transfer, although it may be shifted to a mission-focus orientation. Realistically, there is no "market" for a government service; there is only demand. There is, therefore, a value orientation. The "demand" can be thus categorized by those who value the product or service and those who don't. The technology orientation can stand as it is. E-government is growing rapidly in many nations, including the United States. The technology orientation may describe organizations that focus on electronic delivery of government services and those that do not.

Canada Revenue Agency

The Canada Revenue Agency (CRA) is an agency of the Canadian government that regulates tax laws for the federal government and for most provinces and territories. All employee tax deductions withheld from an employee's gross pay are sent to the CRA and then dispersed to the appropriate government department. The CRA also monitors compliance on behalf of governments at all levels across Canada. Located in Ottawa, the CRA is divided up into five regions: Atlantic, Quebec, Ontario, Prairie, and Pacific. Each region contains tax services offices which carry out a variety of duties, such as audits and collections (CRA 2016, 2019). The agency defines its strategic orientation as "acting in accordance with the organizational priorities, strategies or vision." The direction of the agency's strategic orientation is based on these three concepts:

1. A course of action that leads to the achievement of the goals and the vision through organizational strategies.
2. A point that the organization wants to get to in its operations and what path it will take to get there.
3. The means to make strategic decisions, allocate resources effectively, align employees' efforts, and measure performance and progress against identified targets.

Government of British Columbia

The Indigenous Relations program of the province of British Columbia, Canada defines its strategic orientation as providing:

> [the] link between the long-range vision of Indigenous citizens' self-determination and daily work. The orientation may range from a simple understanding to a sophisticated awareness of the full impact of thinking and actions. It is the ability to think and operate broadly, with the goal of sustainability, to further the goals of Indigenous peoples in a way that meets the collective public interest. This also means taking responsibility to collaboratively design and implement steps to redress past harms and set frameworks in place to prevent their recurrence.
>
> *(BC, n/d)*

Horizon Europe Strategic Orientations

Horizon Europe (EC 2019) is a multinational program for economic development and sustainability. Its purpose is to

> generate knowledge, strengthen the impact of research and innovation in developing, supporting and implementing Union policies and support the access to and uptake of innovative solutions in European industry, notably in SMEs (small and mid-sized enterprises), and society to address global challenges, including climate change and the Sustainable Development Goals.
>
> *(emphasis in the original)*

In their 2019 first strategic plan, Horizon Europe grouped organization strategic orientations as targets for funding further research by the key strategic orientations shown in Table 9.3.

TABLE 9.3 Horizon Europe sustainability strategic orientations

EC Orientation	Core Orientation Focus
Health	Promote and protect human health and well-being, prevent diseases and decrease the burden of diseases and disabilities on people and communities, support the transformation of healthcare systems in their efforts towards fair access to innovative, sustainable and high-quality healthcare for everyone, and foster an innovative, sustainable and globally competitive European health industry.
Culture and creativity	Meet EU goals on enhancing democratic governance and citizens' participation, and on the safeguarding and promotion of cultural heritage; respond to multifaceted social, economic, technological and cultural transformations; expanding civic engagement, boosting transparency, accountability, inclusiveness and legitimacy of governance, improving levels of trust and tackling political extremism.
Civil security	Contribute to protecting the EU and its citizens from threats posed by crime and terrorism (including in the cyber environment) and from the impacts of natural and man-made disasters.
Digital industry and space	Advance key enabling, digital and space technologies, underpinning the transformation of our economy and society, support the digitization and transformation of European industry and contribute to securing global industrial leadership and autonomy in technologies and resources; growing a low-carbon, circular and clean industry respecting planetary boundaries and foster inclusiveness in the form of high-quality jobs and societal engagement in the use of technologies.
Climate, energy and mobility	Fight climate change while improving the competitiveness of the energy and transport industries as well as the quality of the services that these sectors bring to society. This entails establishing a better understanding of the causes, evolution, risks, impacts and opportunities of climate change, as well as making energy and mobility systems more climate- and environment-friendly, smarter, safer, and more resilient, inclusive, competitive and efficient.
Food, bioeconomy, natural resources, the environment	Advance knowledge, expand capacities, and deliver innovative solutions to accelerate the transition towards the sustainable management of natural resources. Includes measures for: climate adaptation and climate neutrality of sustainable primary production (agriculture, forestry, fisheries and aquaculture), value chains, food systems and bio-based industries; optimizing ecosystem services including for climate mitigation; reversing biodiversity decline; and reducing environmental degradation and pollution.

Source: EC (2019)

Political Party Strategic Orientation

With the 2019 India re-election of Narendra Modi, his party, the Bharatiya Janata Party (BJP), won a total of 303 seats in the election, 21 more than it did in 2014 (Ranjan 2019). The BJP became the first party in 35 years to return to power with absolute majority, also garnering a record increase of 6% in its share of the vote. Return of the incumbent BJP means that the country's strategic orientation will probably continue in the same vein and possibly even increase its focus on the country's strategic presence in the Indo-Pacific region. At the same time, India will simultaneously ensure that it attains a credible strategic deterrence against both China and Pakistan. The new government is likely to retain this strategic orientation as a part of its Grand Strategy without altering the existing civil–military relationships. Key points are:

- It is expected that the new government's strategic orientation will focus on expanding its strategic presence in the Indo-Pacific, while simultaneously attaining a credible strategic deterrence against both China's and Pakistan's conventional and nuclear threats.
- India is likely to strengthen its capacity to engage in limited warfare against both China and Pakistan.
- India's maritime strategic outlook will be a major element in its conception of the Indo-Pacific and that will constitute a part of its Grand Strategic outlook.
- The new government will appoint a Permanent Chairman of the Chief of Staff Committee as an interim measure to creating the office of Chief of Defense Staff (CDS).

Wisconsin Utility Strategic Orientation

The water supply for the City of Janesville, Wisconsin distributes freshwater from eight wells, three booster stations, two water storage reservoirs and one elevated tower. Its strategic orientation focuses on assuring no gap exists between the disinfection and chemical treatment procedures and the health and safety of all who are served by the water distribution system. Like all freshwater distribution organizations, the Janesville utility collects and tests water samples daily. The utility must then manage a distribution network of over 371 miles of water mains. Delivered water must meet all customer service performance standards. The mission of the Janesville water utility, therefore, is to provide a high-quality water supply for domestic, commercial, industrial, and fire protection purposes at an adequate pressure and in abundant supply to all customers. This is its strategic orientation.

Customer services activities include responding to low water pressure complaints, raising and lowering stop boxes, installing new water meters, and thawing frozen services and meters. Other services include shutting off water to allow plumbing repairs and making seasonal water service connections. Emergency maintenance service is provided 24 hours a day, seven days a week. Each quarter water meter readers record readings from over 22,900 meters. The consumption recorded on the water meters is used to establish water and wastewater charges for the majority of the customers. As part of its customer orientation, the water utility gives tours of its facilities to interested groups or organizations.

Adopting the Strategic Orientation

An organization's strategic orientation is the guiding principle that underlines all strategic decisions to achieve organizational goals. It shapes the path that the organization's managers follow in directing actions for providing the goods and services that meet the needs and expectations of the organization's customers. The following six steps guide you through the process of analyzing and adopting the best strategic orientation for your organization.

Step 1: Understand the two major elements that together form the strategic orientation for the organization:

- An organization prepares and follows a strategic plan that delineates its future operations and performance objectives for achieving the long-term goals.
- Regular monitoring and measuring performance progress gained toward achieving its short-term goals and objectives.

Step 2: Select basic strategic orientations and core strategies for public sector organizations:

- customer orientation (client or stakeholder);
- service orientation (mission positioning/value chain);
- change orientation (transformation/technology/innovation).

Step 3: Identify the relationship between strategic fit and performance:

- Strategic orientations are believed to influence market performance of organizations in the private sector.
- Five underlying constraints shape the strategic orientation of public organizations:
  - the concept, service or field for which the department, agency or unit operates;
  - citizen demand for the product, service or idea;
  - the level of governance within which the organization operates (i.e., federal, state or local);
  - the operating funds (budget allocation) available to sustain or to grow existing services; and
  - the resources, competencies and capabilities needed to achieve sustainability in the operational environment.

Step 4: Initiate and implement a strategic orientation:

- Determine the level of major strategic elements that best fit the external environment and the resources and capabilities of the organization;
- Three basic private sector strategic orientations that can be modified for public sector organizations:
    - *market orientation*, which focuses on customers or competitors;
    - *entrepreneurial orientation*, which focuses on being the first to innovate in new products, services, and/or markets; and
    - *technological orientation*, a multidimensional structure composed of top management capability, technological capability, learning and unlearning.
- Strategic orientations for the public sector include but are not limited to: *public service orientation, innovation orientation, knowledge-based orientation,* and *sustainability orientation.*

Step 5: Avoid potential catastrophic mistakes in the process of preparing for the best strategic orientation:

- committing resources to a losing cause;
- repeatedly dividing the market and driving up costs;
- missing opportunities to create new markets; and
- failing to capitalize on emerging technologies and innovations that may revolutionize the market and industry.

Step 6: Implement strategy evaluation and control for continuous improvement:

- Determine whether the chosen strategy is achieving the organization's objectives.
- Review internal and external factors that are the bases for current strategies, measuring performance, and taking corrective actions.

Summary

An organization's strategic orientation can be as complex as necessary when applied to the operation of a major division or arm of a regional or national government, or it can be focused on the performance of a single objective for any level or agency of a larger government. An example of how it can be applied to a local program of the government of Canada's province of British Columbia, which provided the following description of why strategizing according to a specific program's strategic orientation is important to the society it serves, and particularly to the province's native population: The BC government described the program's strategic orientation as focusing on the ability to link the long-range vision of Indigenous self-determination to daily work, ranging from a simple understanding to a sophisticated awareness of the full impact of thinking and actions.

An organization's strategic orientation is the guiding principle that underlies all strategic decisions. For a government organization, it is the focus of its commitment to serve its clients to the best of its ability, given its existing resources and capabilities. The orientation is shaped by many internal and external factors, including the abilities and skills of its leaders. The scope of the mission and the resources allotted toward solution of the social conflict at the time of its delivery of services also contribute to the orientation of the direction that a public sector organization will take in planning, performing and strategic functioning and it will continue to function in the future. The organization's strategic orientation, therefore, influences both current operational plans and schedules plus the proposed human and administrative capital investments that is believed will be available for future budgetary decisions.

Two major components underlie the organization's strategic orientation. The first is the sense that an organization does indeed have a plan that delineates its strategic goals and for the tasks and performance objectives related to the long-term goals. In the federal government, the time period established for strategic plans is four years, beginning and ending with the elected stakeholders' term of office. The second is the stakeholders' monitoring and measuring the organization's staff performance on efforts to progress in achieving its short-term objectives and longer-term goals. These two components together enable the strategy and form the strategic orientation for the organization.

Adopting a strategic management approach also implies an openness to change and acceptance of new and innovative processes and actions. Public sector organizations may be said to follow either one of two basic strategic orientations: openness to change or resistance to change. If the actions reflect progress gained on achieving objectives and goals indicated in the strategic plan, managing the process must be guided by an all-embracing strategy that provides a rationale for the change. This strategy is thus "a vision of how the changes are to be made, over what time period, and by whom" in the organization (Baker 2007, 1).

Like their fellow managers in businesses and nongovernmental organizations, governments and their operational divisions adopt different strategies to adapt to changes in their environments, or for designing strategies that will enable them to function in a more favorable environment. The orientation is not something that changes with the advent of new staff personnel, but often may change significantly with the advent of a major political change. This is because the strategic orientation of the organization plays a key role in how the organization defines and structures its goals, and its activities for achieving operational objectives.

In sum, an organization's strategic orientation is a description of the organization's overall vision and direction. The success of the organization depends on the top management's ability to make the right choices and guide it to success. The strategic orientation is the direction that the government organization's leaders want it to go. Its strategic plan describes how it plans to get there in the future. An analysis of its orientation will help the organization's managers determine how well its assets and capabilities and the organization is staffed and organized to do what it is mandated to accomplish. There are two major components to this idea, the first of which is the sense that an organization has a current strategic plan with clear and achievable goals for operations in its predicted environment. The second is regular performance analysis to identify how well it is performing along that chosen path. Together, these components establish the strategic orientation for the organization.

10

INNOVATION STRATEGIES

Many public service organizations face a daunting confluence of the challenges of increasing operating costs, and the need to replace failing infrastructure, improve the quality of their services in a timely fashion, offer new and innovative services to "customers," and adopt new technologies, all while delivering their services through a variety of new channels and media. As they seek to overcome these challenges, public organizations are often constrained in their limited budgets, lack of organizational capabilities, the absence of an entrepreneurial culture, insufficient knowledge of market and technological changes, and an outdated managerial mindset. In this chapter we discuss the role that a commitment to a strategy of innovation plays in government operational strategy. Also discussed are aspects of innovation in planning frameworks used to assist public administrators in the development of the right strategies for their organization, service, their client/customer base, and timeframe. The goal is to formulate strategies that create the maximum possible value for their constituents and society as a whole. These are the strategies of innovation in goods or services and process, or in all.

Public Sector Differences

The public sector consists of organizations that provide public goods and services to a variety of publics without reference to a profit motive. Hence, until recently, the issue of innovation never came up. This does not mean that public services were given away. Rather, most services provided by public organizations come with a cost. A more detailed definition compiled by contributions of many researchers might be: The public sector includes organizations owned and operated by some level of government that exists for providing a service for its citizens and is usually funded through taxes, fees for service, or by financial transfers from other levels of government.

The public sector has long been considered different from the private sector in many ways, and almost to be entirely different in terms of innovation. That perception may be based on the belief that the open administrative climate in which they must operate and make decisions render public organizations limited to being only static recipients of innovations imported from the private sector. Too often, public sector organizations have also been considered to be conservative, risk-averse, and bureaucratic rather than innovative and change-oriented. However, many years of research have shown that administrators and managers in modern public sector organizations are often very far from resembling this perception of passivity. These leaders and the governments enabling their operations are more often eager adopters of innovation and of transformational changes (McNabb 2009; Borins 2014; Demircioglu and Audretsch 2017).

In the way they run their operations, many public service providers have had to shift from what has long been described as a bureaucratic focus to what is coming to be known as a strategic orientation that embraces innovation in the way they provide their services. Both private and public organizations make many changes during their operational life. Most of those changes are easy to manage, informal and ad hoc adjustments to existing operations. Others, however, are transformational. They are deliberate, sometimes radical, often difficult to manage, and are the result of adopting an innovation in some way. However, when innovations result in the need for a transformational change, research suggests that successful innovations occur most often when five organizational conditions and management practices are in place (Sahni, Wessel and Christensen 2013; Demircioglu and Audretsch 2017; Grotenbreg and Van Buuren 2018). The first two of these are rooted in the organization's abilities: the ability of the organization to experiment and innovate, and the organization's ability to improve performance by changing outdated methods and structures. The second group of three conditions are motivational factors. They include the existence of relations with stakeholders, feedback that includes acceptance of investments in change, the existence of incentives and trust for employee willingness to search for and accept service and organizational improvements, and the existence of budget constraints that in some organizations may result in a culture of internal searches for new and improved performance to compensate for missing funds.

Types of Strategies

In their seminal text on strategic management, Wheelen, Hunger, Hoffman and Bamford (2017, 17) described a strategy as a "comprehensive master approach that states how the corporation will achieve its mission and objectives." In this role, strategies fall into three categories: At the first level are strategies for the master-level political organization, as for a new president's term of office, a new

Congress or a state governor. Each provides direction the elected office will take in its funding capital improvements or controlling infrastructure repair and replacement. In the private sector, Wheelen et al. identified these as corporate-level strategies.

The second level of strategies are strategies that identify the way activities in the master-level strategies are to be implemented. At the federal level, these are generally the strategies for actions of each of the major departments, such as Education, Labor, Agriculture and Interior. The strategies are specifically designed to address a problem or issue of importance to the constituents affected by a program managed by the department. Similar responsibility-based strategies exist for state and municipal governments. The third or functional level are the strategies pertaining to specific programs. For the Department of the Interior it would include, among many others, programs for Native Americans. An example of a strategy for a program for improving nutrition for disadvantaged school-aged children would be a functional strategy of both the Department of Agriculture and the Department of Education. At the state level, an example is a program for allowing the use of reclaimed or recycled water for augmenting potable water supplies. At the city or town level, an example would be a program for patching and resurfacing roads in town.

Strategic Innovation

Since its early introduction, the innovation concept has long been accepted as an important source of competitive advantage in the private sector. The following official definition of innovation clearly associates it exclusively with business organizations: "An innovation is the implementation of a new or significantly improved product (good or service), or process, a new marketing method, or a new organizational method in business practices, workplace organization or external relations" (OECD 2005; Gault 2018).

However, this exclusivity of focus is no longer a dominant management philosophy. Innovation is today also recognized as a spur to greater efficiency and effectiveness in the public sector. The definition also merits further expansion. Professor Kenneth Kahn (2018), commenting on the global acceptance and popularity of the innovation concept, suggests that although its pervasiveness is indeed widespread, many business and public organizations are still not sure of what it fully implies, or whether a relatively minor change should be considered an innovation. Too often, managers and administrators who would adopt an innovation policy are unaware that to "really reap its benefits," innovation must be transformative and recognized as more than just a new product or a new process; it is three different things. It is an outcome, a process and a mindset. As an outcome in business, innovation is the result of a transformative change in something. The something can be innovation in products, processes, organization structure, markets, supply chain, business model or leadership. In the public sector, examples of innovation as an outcome may be implementation of a new drug for treating a disease, a public–private collaboration in solid waste collection and disposal, a shift in regulatory focus, different organizational configuration, such as the 2003 combining of 22 different federal departments and agencies into the U.S. Department of Homeland Security.

Innovation as a process is a new way of doing things and the capability to bring new ideas to fruition. It can include such examples as new production or distribution methods. Examples can be a new quality control process for a production line, more efficient way of processing product returns, new ways of electronically counting votes, or new internal techniques for administering insurance claims. The process of combining government security and safety agencies under a new Cabinet department is an example.

Innovation as a mindset involves a transformational change in the organizational culture and attitudes toward innovation, collaboration, and experiment. Successful innovation requires both a learning environment and a "supportive culture throughout the organization" (Kahn 2018, 458).

Public Sector Innovation Defined

De Vries, Bekkers and Tummers (2014) defined innovation in the public sector as "the introduction of new elements into a public service—in the form of new knowledge, a new organization, and/or new management or procedural skills, which represents discontinuity with the past." This definition emphasizes the notion that the innovation is not just a new way of looking at or describing the mission of an organization or a routine change. To be truly innovative the change must be strategic, accepted, and put to use. To really understand what innovation is, Kahn (2018) pointed out that three definitions of an innovation are more appropriate: one for each of its three different scopes of application. Innovation is an outcome, it is a process, and it is a state of mind. Because of this, there are many places in a public sector organization where an innovation can improve operations and the effectiveness of operations. Samples of the types of innovations generated by public agencies are included in Table 10.1.

In all its many types and objectives, it can follow many levels or degrees of pathways, the most commonly identified poles of which are: incremental innovation to radical innovation, disruptive innovation to merging innovation, top–down or bottom-up innovation.

Many public organizations are facing the challenges of a need to expand operations, improve the quality of their services in a timely fashion, offer new and innovative services for their "customers," invest in and adopt new technologies, and deliver their services through a variety of channels and media. All these and other challenges are made more difficult by their rapidly increasing operating costs with growing budget constraints, the lack of organizational capabilities, the absence of an entrepreneurial culture, insufficient knowledge of market and

TABLE 10.1 Some areas where innovation is found in public sector organizations

Concept	Examples
Service Innovation	New or innovative changes in the services provided to the public.
Process Innovation	A new method of processing or a significant change to the service or product provided by the organization.
Administrative Innovation	New administrative methods or a change in the way a regulated policy is administered, monitored or recorded.
Delivery Innovation	New ways of delivering services or interacting with users of the service and relevant stakeholders.
Organizational Innovation	Redirection in the organization's primary mission, its management structure, operating principles and governance models.
Policy Innovation	Implementation of new policy orientations required by shifts in political orientations of governance changes.
Systemic Innovation	Innovations associated with a new system or improved methods of interacting with other agencies, as required for multi-agency solutions to societal needs, extreme weather events and similar cooperative operations.
Conceptual Innovation	A change or redirection in the way of thinking about a traditional service that results in new concepts and attitudes.

Sources: Arundel and Hollanders (2011); Koch and Hauknes (2005); Bloch and Bugge (2013); Alpkan and Gemici (2016).

technological changes, and an outdated managerial mindset. To overcome these challenges while complying with the mandate to contain operating costs, organization leaders find themselves forced to employ new knowledge, skills and strategies in order meet the demand to create value for their constituents and society. A strategic orientation that fits with an organization's mission capabilities can serve as an aid for managers and administrators to design clear and attainable strategies for achieving goals and overcoming challenges. The wrong strategic orientation makes it impossible to form strategies that will guide their organizations safely through the social, technical and administrative jungles in years to come.

Technology Issues

Technology-driven issues such as cybersecurity requirements, big data analytics, machine learning and data-based decision-making have forced governments to adopt innovation as a core strategic orientation. Resource-based views of strategic management have brought about formation of different innovation strategies based on their differences in mission, funding, organizational, and technological capabilities. Effective strategy formulation and implementation must take into consideration the strategic vision, mindset, and intent of senior elected leaders, appointed agency heads and elected members of principal oversight bodies.

Technological innovation continues to become more complex and integrated into decision-making processes. This accelerated pace of technological change presents new challenges to managers. In the increasingly globalized economic and political world of today, technology-dependent government organizations need proficient strategic management practices and a commitment to innovation and collaboration to maintain their operational sustainability. Technology-dependent government (or "digital-era governance") refers to the what Dunleavy et al. (2006, 468) have described as the "central role that IT and information system changes now play in a wide-ranging series of alterations to how public services are organized as business processes and delivered to citizens or customers."

Researchers have identified four broad categories of generic public sector innovation strategy. The categories were adopted after an informal rating of selected agencies and other government organizations on two performance axes: operational performance in their dominant mission (observable output and outcome) and estimation of their capacities to succeed in their intended mission focus (resource sustainability). The categories are mission-related strategies, service delivery strategies, personnel strategies and sustainability strategies.

Overall Mission Strategies

The two intended strategies and mission focus categories are (1) strategies that focus on a mission and (2) strategies that grow their budget requests by an emphasis on a need for adopting new problems to solve or new processes to use in solving the problems. Public agencies seldom try to encourage citizens to consume a larger amount of an existing public sector good or service. Instead, they grow by applying innovation for identifying and serving untapped societal needs or problems, by identifying innovative and better delivery methods for their services, or by increasing their application of innovative technology. Mission innovation strategies such as these allow political leaders and the general public to compare and contrast agencies from two perspectives based on an analysis of their key capabilities.

Service Delivery Innovation

Performance is the sum of the existing strategy followed by the organization and is measured by the degree to which the organization accomplishes its specific objectives. A scale of 1 to 10 is used on the two poles of "struggling" and "succeeding." Typical satisfactory strategies are focused on gaining scores of more than 8 on the scale; a show of consistently improving performance typically results in greater funding support. Typical struggling strategies are often followed by reductions in allocated funding or shifting to new services; continuously low performance scores seldom result in adoption of new or innovative practices or processes.

Organizational capacity in public sector organizations is defined as "a set of attributes that help or enable an organization to fulfill its missions" (Eisenger 2002). The underlying assumption is that agencies can do the "most with less" if they can identify specific areas of organizational capacity where resources should be targeted, that is, where they should target their limited resources to achieve the most good (White et al. 2005, 4). Moreover, the offices charged with allocating funds may decide which agencies to support based on their assessments of how organizations have employed their previous budget allocations.

Acquiring Personnel with Innovative Skills

There has long been a growing concern about government's ability to compete with the private sector and other public sectors for efficient and economic delivery of public goods and services. To remain competitive in an environment where private sector employers often offer higher salaries, governments must employ innovative recruitment approaches that meet their mission needs and also address the needs of the workforce and market the Government's strengths as an employer (McPhie 2004, 1). Other examples of personnel strategies are the public health workforce shortage, the declining number of new schoolteachers, and the armed forces personnel shortage. These and other public sector organizations are looking for innovative ways to overcome these shortages of critical personnel.

The federal government downsized its workforce dramatically during the administrations of President Ronald Reagan (1981–1989) and George Bush (1989–1995). The result essentially eliminated most new hiring. At the same time, many federal and state agencies downsized their staffs and reduced or eliminated their recruitment programs. Since then, however, federal agencies have begun to increase hiring and rebuild recruitment programs. They have done this for a variety of reasons, including preparing for increased retirements and replacing skills lost during downsizing. At the same time, greater emphasis is placed on changing skill sets and staff size to meet evolving mission requirements, to increase diversity, and to target hard-to-fill occupations.

Innovation and Strategic Orientation

Strategic orientation is the underlying beliefs and principles that shape the way in which an organization interacts with the people and institutions of the society it serves. It shapes the path that the organization's managers follow in directing actions to provide the goods and services that meet the needs and expectations of the organization's customers and for achieving its goals. It also influences the degree to which an organization adopts and implements innovation of all types. The four strategy orientations identified for private sector organizations were market, entrepreneurial, learning and technology. The lack of the profit motive in public sector organizations requires modifying these categories to reflect what might be logical for public sector organizations. However, the orientations included here as examples of a class of strategies are conceptual only. The four categories we have used for discussion purposes are shadow, missionary, magician and bright star. Table 10.2 employs these four management orientations as a basis for identifying innovation-related operational strategies.

TABLE 10.2 Hypothetical public sector management of innovation-related strategies

Orientation	Description	Operational Strategies
Shadow	Strategies intended to avoid redistributing the existing budget allocations by avoiding allowing public interest in the mission to be replaced by attention to other more newsworthy programs.	Little interest in innovation of any kind; unlikely to forge or participate in networks; employ "don't rock the boat" strategies; focus on existing clientele and small government.
Missionary	Strategies that focus on increasing public awareness of the agency's progress on mission performance and collaboration with nongovernment stakeholders, thereby stimulating oversight support for retaining and reinvesting in the agency.	Support for mission innovation; open to managed networks with state and local service distributors; open to shifting service delivery functions to lower levels of government.
Magician	Strategies that reflect a policy of low-cost but highly visible programs that exist mostly for a political base; avoiding high-price programs with distant payoffs; force to comply with demands to "do it with less."	Support for process innovation; tendency to forge internal department mission-centered best practices networks; employ strong collaboration "let's do it together" strategies.
Bright Star	Strategies that focus on research for greater benefits to society through investment in innovation; willing to adopt radically different distribution of benefits and/or networks that focus on and support investing in long-term improvements in both service and process innovation.	Strongly support innovation in all mission and process opportunities; open to both other agency and/ or external nongovernment networks; employ "best team for the task" strategies.

Source: The authors

Shadow Agency Strategies

Shadow agencies are public organizations that follow strategies designed to retain their existing niche in the mix of government-provided goods and services; they are uninterested in securing a greater share in the overall mission network of providers. Organizations in this category fall into what we call "don't rock the boat" or zero-sum category of strategies.

Satisfactory shadow strategies may also be agencies that are quickly approaching an end to their original missions or for programs that have been reduced to a static or greatly reduced existence by a new administration. In limbo situations, agency management has little interest in investing the time, effort and already reduced allocation on either a product or process innovation strategy or adopting new or improved operational processes. Under their reduced mission support, there is no way of enlarging the potential budget allocation.

Government agencies in struggling or failing operating environments are common in organizations whose management is reluctant to innovate or shift out of an existing mission for which they have invested years of energy developing special competence but demand for is in limbo or for which the administration has simply moved on to other, newer products or services. The strategies of shadow agencies focus on retaining a place in public service from which there might be promise of resurrection once a new administration is elected.

Missionary Agency Strategies

Struggling strategies can also exist in very high-cost product purchases and services such as the Department of Defense and extreme story recovery services of the Federal Emergency Management Administration (FEMA). These are the strategies wedded to investing large sums in research to advance innovation in technology, weapons, security and large story recovery projects. These organizations tend to be large and growing stronger—the leviathans of government spending.

Magician Agency Strategies

Magician agencies appear to be more concerned with survival strategies than innovation strategies. A small portion of the many examples of the new 2016 administration's decision for eliminating programs that were arbitrarily chosen to be included here are:

- the Education Department's $2.4 billion Supporting Effective Instruction State Grants Program;
- the Corporation for Public Broadcasting, which had a budget of $485 million;
- the $221 million budget of the Department of Commerce's Economic Development Administration;

- the Department of Energy's $3.4 billion Low-Income Home Energy Assistance Program; and
- the $715 million Community Services Block Grants, an innovative anti-poverty grant program.

Bright Star Innovation Strategies

The U.S. government has often been a significant supporter of product innovation and, in doing so, became an adopter of process innovation as well. Examples of agencies that support innovation through grants and low-interest loans are the National Institute of Health with a 2019 budget of $39 billion, the CIA's In-Q-Tel, which is funded from the government's $50 billion secret funds, the Defense Department's Defense Advanced Research Projects Agency (DARPA) with a 2019 budget of $3.44 billion, and the Small Business Innovation Research program with a budget of $2.5 billion. These agents and others strongly support innovation research.

Technological innovations are dynamic and fast moving. Market situations are also constantly changing. Strategic orientations are not fixed but can—and need to—change as the environment changes. It implies consistent analysis of the market conditions and organizational capabilities. It is critical for business executives to understand how strategic alignment shapes and sustains a firm's competitive advantage over time.

Generic Strategy Examples

For this book, we identified four broad categories of generic strategy. The categories were identified after rating government organizations on two performance axes: mission achievement under their dominant operations model and our perception of their intended strategic orientation and action focus. Individual ratings were subjectively determined. The categories, their descriptions and examples are shown in Table 10.1.

Adopting an Innovation Strategy

Adopting an innovation strategy implies an openness to change. If the objectives for making the change are to be achieved, managing the process must be guided by an all-embracing strategy that provides a rationale for the change. This strategy includes estimating how the changes are to be made, when they should be made, and who in the organization should initiate and monitor the change (Baker 2007, 1).

Strategies for innovation in the public sector are designed to include such categories as technology development, enhancements to public safety, emergency disaster repairs, and the improvement of services delivery methods. Studies of these strategies include a focus on technology innovation and learning as study orientations. Other researchers see innovation as a contributing factor shaping strategic management in all sectors. These generic strategy classifications are not always ideal for a public service organization, however. A few examples include organizational factors where innovation is less often adopted, including services delivery, who shall be served and sustainability. Performance is a reflection of the existing strategy followed by the firm or common in the specific industry.

Intended Constituency Focus

The two intended strategies and market focus categories are (1) strategies that focus on serving existing clients with existing public goods or services, or *shadow* organizations, and (2) strategies that grow with an emphasis on new markets or new products, or *missionary* organizations. Shadow government bodies try to outperform their rivals by gathering a greater share of the existing demand for its goods or services, whereas missionary organizations grow by identifying and serving untapped demand and by educating their clientele on the benefits of their services.

Sustainability Focus Strategies

Governments following strategies designed to retain an existing or secure a greater share of a declining demand for their services fall into a zero-sum class of strategies that focus on sustainability rather than innovation. Leadership in the *magician* orientation focus on retaining the status quo. Their performance reports play with mirrors by focusing on fringe development. The *bright start* orientation exists in an organization in which the prevailing philosophy of innovation in services and process is desired, as is continuing collaboration with partners in other sectors and other levels of government (Lee, Chan, McNabb and Khalifa 2019).

Implications

A government commitment to an innovation strategy is not fixed; it can change as the environment changes. It must perform regular analysis of operational environment conditions and organizational assets and capabilities. Both private and public organizations make many strategy changes during their operational life. Most of those changes are easy-to-manage, informal and ad hoc adjustments to existing operations. Others, however, are transformational. They are deliberate, sometimes radical, often difficult to manage, and are the result of adopting an innovation in some way. However, when innovations result in the need for a transformational change, research suggests that successful innovations occur most often when five organizational conditions and management practices are in place (Sahni, Wessel and Christensen 2013; Demircioglu and Audretsch 2017; Grotenbreg and Van Buuren 2018).

The first two of these orientations are rooted in the organization's abilities, the capacity of the organization to experiment and innovate, and the organization's ability to improve performance by changing outdated methods and structures. The second group of three conditions are motivational factors: (1) existence of relations with stakeholders' feedback that includes acceptance of investments in change, (2) the existence of incentives and trust for employee willingness to search for and accept service and organizational improvements, and (3) the existence of budget constraints in some organizations. Budget constraint may result in a culture of internal searches for new and improved performance to compensate for missing funds.

Adopting Strategic Innovation Strategies

Innovation is the use of new knowledge to offer a new product or service that customers want. It is the outcome of the innovation process, which is the combined activities leading to new services and/or new delivery systems. Innovation in the public sector is defined as "the introduction of new elements into a public service—in the form of new knowledge, a new organization, and/or new management or processual skills, which represents discontinuity with the past" (De Vries et al. 2014). An innovation strategy may be designed and implemented through the following seven steps:

Step 1: Understand the four basic types of innovation approach:

- *Product innovation* is the introduction of a good or service that is new or significantly improved with respect to its characteristics or intended uses.
- *Process innovation* is the implementation of a new or significantly improved production or delivery method.
- *Incremental innovation*: The knowledge required to offer a product builds on existing knowledge.
- *Radical innovation*: Technological knowledge required to exploit it is very different from existing knowledge.

Step 2: Choose the initial type of innovation approach to engage in creating value for customers.

Step 3: Identify types of innovation generated by public agencies:

- *Governance innovations*: New forms of citizen engagement and democratic institutions, new public and user participation in service design and delivery, and the use of public boards to govern particular choices (Hartley, 2005).
- *Administrative innovation*: New administrative methods or a change in the way a regulated policy is administered, monitored or recorded.

	Incremental	**Radical**
Product or Service Innovation (*What we offer the society or community*)	New features New versions New improvements	• Adopt new radical or disruptive technologies; • Require new competencies and capabilities
Process Innovation (*How we create and deliver that offering*)	Improve efficiency, quality, and/or the speed of delivery (using the existing manufacturing and delivery processes)	Implement radically different processes of manufacturing or delivering the products or services

FIGURE 10.1   Types of innovation: product or service, incremental or radical.

- *Organizational innovation*: Redirection in the organization's primary mission, its management structure, operating principles and governance models.
- *Policy innovation*: Implementation of new policy orientations required by shifts in political orientations of governance changes.
- *Systemic innovation*: Innovations associated with a new system or methods of interacting with other agencies.
- *Conceptual innovation*: A change or redirection in the way of thinking about a traditional service that results in new concepts and attitudes.

Step 4: Design and implement public innovation strategies:

- *Shadow*: Strategies intended to avoid redistributing the existing budget allocations by allowing public interest in the mission to be replaced by attention to other more newsworthy programs.
- *Missionary*: Strategies that focus on increasing public awareness of the agency's progress on mission performance and collaboration with nongovernment stakeholders.

- *Magician*: Strategies that reflect a policy of low-cost but highly visible programs that exist mostly for a political base.
- *Bright star*: Strategies that promote greater benefits to society through investment in innovation.

Step 5: Review the (public sector) innovation process for continuous improvement and renewal:

- Select targets for innovation.
- Identify and choose the types of innovation.
- Formulate and implement strategies for innovation.
- Identify which organizations create value and which parties capture the value.
- Create a culture that is conducive to innovation.
- Exploit strategic networks for sources of innovation.
- Develop a solid financial strategy and build a strong case to support innovations.
- Promote the adoption and diffusion of innovations.

Summary

Designing and carrying out a strategic transformation involves establishing or reviewing the vision and mission of the organization, analyzing internal and external environmental factors, forming both long-term and short-term objectives, and selecting, implementing, and evaluating a strategy to accomplish those objectives. The transformation occurs over three separate related stages: (1) during environmental analysis and development of a vision and mission for the organization; (2) while identifying and planning the organizational components and processes that enable the agency to accomplish its mission; and (3) when crafting, selecting and prioritizing strategies, and implementing performance measurement systems, and controls. During the first stage, the organization engages in environmental analysis and determining how the change will affect its vision, mission and values. In the second stage, activities and decisions for enabling changes in organizational resources and organizational systems are assembled. These facilitate the functioning of the agency and provide the resources from which organizational objectives and strategies may be identified, prioritized, and implemented. In the third stage, management uses the product of the two earlier levels of analysis to set realistic and attainable agency objectives. It then identifies, selects and prioritizes strategies for the agency to follow in order to accomplish those objectives.

Organizations go through different types of change depending on changes in their internal or external environments. The organization can make the small incremental adjustments associated with maintaining stability in its operational environment, or it can suffer through the larger discontinuous changes necessary to adjust to instability or uncertainty in its environment. It can then employ a planned adaptation to meet an anticipated shift in the external environment, or it can be an unplanned transformation requiring a fundamental re-creation brought on by a threat to the organization's very existence.

Transformational change to a strategic management structure occurs in response to, or in anticipation of, significant changes in an organization's environment, technology or by a major disruption of its organizational structure. These changes often result in a significant revision of an organization's mission and its core strategy. This, in turn, may require modifying the way the organization's members perceive, think and behave at work, as well as its corporate culture to support the new direction and target service recipients.

A model for developing and implementing an organization transformation includes three transformation pillars which combined transformation strategies, organization capacity and organization outputs and outcomes to form a general model of transformation. Two of the four core components were context-based and two were sustainability related. Strategic change can also include elements of historical strategy change in what is called strategic restoration.

11

PUBLIC SECTOR SUSTAINABILITY STRATEGIES

The public sector has long been considered to be different from the private sector in many ways, and almost to be entirely different in terms of long-term planning. That perception may be based on the belief that the open administrative climate in which government managers must operate often renders public organizations being restricted to political aims and budgetary limitations. Too often, public sector organizations have been considered to be conservative, risk-averse, and bureaucratic rather than innovative and change-oriented. However, many years of research have shown that administrators and managers in modern public sector organizations are often very far from resembling this perception of passivity. These leaders and the governments enabling their operations are often eager adopters of innovative practices and of transformational changes (McNabb 2009; Borins 2014; Demircioglu and Audretsch 2017). Strategic (long-term) management is one of the latest management frameworks to be adopted by the public sector. For strategic management to be effective, organizational transformation is often called for. This chapter discusses the transformation process.

When government organizations fail to integrate sustainability into their processes, strategies and long-term vision for their service delivery activities, they risk generating negative impacts on their clientele, stakeholders, policy controllers, the environment and society in general. Stakeholders become increasingly aware of the role of strategic management in the transition to sustainable operations. Together, societies served and stakeholders "have the power to make choices that reward organizations demonstrating true commitment to sustainability" (Calabrese, Costa, Levialdi and Menichini 2019, 155). This is when a strategic design for transforming the organization is called for.

Sustainability Strategy Challenges

In addition to their strategic challenges, public organizations are increasingly encouraged to develop a sustainability strategy and plan for implementing the plan. The plan includes three components or tools: a self-assessment, development of a strategy for accomplishing goals and rectifying problems, and an action plan for how to accomplish its sustainability goals. An example of a public organization's definition of a sustainability strategy was released in 2014 by Penn State University:

> Sustainability is often likened to democracy, in that it is not a problem to be solved, but a challenge that requires constant innovation, commitment, vigilance, and learning. Thus, it is not another thing to do, or another box to be checked. It asks us to discern our contribution to this challenge of our time, delivered in the context of our passion and purposes. When sustainability is understood and "owned" at the unit level, and when it is strongly linked to the unit's mission and unique expertise, innovation takes place.
>
> *(PSU 2014)*

Sustainability is a government-wide initiative for the federal government agencies. The Office of Federal Sustainability (OFS) was established in 1993 as a unit of the White House Council on Environmental Quality. The OFS assists federal agencies, departments and other government organizations in implementing statutory requirements and meeting sustainability goals that include vehicle fleet efficiency rules, adoption of efficient technologies such as heating and air conditioning, and in the modernization of federal facilities and operations. For example, like other agencies, the General Services Administration (GSA) has appointed a Chief Sustainability Officer to guide sustainability programs within the organization. Under what it terms its "Strategic Sustainable" program, it defines sustainability as meaning "strong finances, a clean environment and healthy employees and communities. At GSA, sustainability is helping federal agencies meet their missions today without sacrificing their ability to serve future generations" (GSA n/d).

Changes in the external and internal environments that have occurred since the beginning of the 21st century have forced large and small, federal, state and local government agencies to adopt strategic management processes that embrace innovation and interagency collaboration on provision of services and how they are structured (Andrews et al. 2012). A strategic management orientation is expected to help organization leaders employ their limited assets in accordance with a strategy designed to ensure resilience and sustainability. Their focus has expanded from their traditional budget-based operations to a propensity to innovate so as to gain greater benefits from current assets and capacities. The orientation also influences the decisions for which tasks will be taken for achieving the organization's short-term operational objectives and, ultimately, its long-term goals.

Increasingly, the tasks, objectives and goals of government agencies are required to be spelled out in a strategic sustainability plan that includes objectives and goals and the strategies for overcoming the increasing severity of obstacles. Long-term goals must also reflect external challenges that are amplified by climate change, population growth and unbridled urbanization. The adopted strategic orientation serves as a roadmap for the agency to follow in maneuvering through the environmental and operational challenges they will face over the period of the plan. Moreover, the strategy must identify the internal changes the organization will have to make during that same period, for a "strategy that does not drive and facilitate change and improvement is of little use" (Baker 2007, 149). The degree to which the organization's leaders remain committed to their strategic orientation and employees buy into the plan plays a big role in determining whether the agency will succeed in accomplishing its objectives and its long-term goals.

Sustainability is now a multilevel objective of the strategic goals of many nations' public sector organizations. For some, the sustainability goal is to maintain economic development. For others, the concept refers to government programs designed to increase their ability to survive through the growing number of extreme environmental crises. And for others, the sustainability goal is to be able to continue to serve their constituencies under conditions of extreme population growth, climate change and failing infrastructure. In all of these and other circumstances, governments' concerns are with acquiring sufficient funds for meeting all their growing needs.

Defining Sustainability

Trying to come up with an all-inclusive definition for sustainability is difficult, if not impossible. Sustainability is both the ability to continue government service missions while continuing to provide the economic growth necessary for maintaining adequate standards of living and doing so in ways that protect the environment and sustain access to resources for future generations. The definition of sustainability adopted by the Forum for the Future, a UK sustainability charity, comes close to describing this concept: Sustainability is "a dynamic process which enables all people to realize their potential and improve their quality of life in ways which simultaneously protect and enhance the Earth's live support systems" (UK Forum for the Future 2006). The following brief sampling of sustainability and sustainability development definitions were collected from various sources, including the UN and the US federal government:

1. Sustainability is the ability to meet the needs of the present without compromising the ability of future generations to meet their own needs (United Nations World Commission on Environment and Development).
2. Sustainability is the capacity to improve the quality of human life while living within the carrying capacity of the Earth's supporting eco-systems (International Union for Conservation of Nature (IUCN)).

3. "Sustainable development is development that meets the needs of the present without compromising the ability of future generations to meet their own needs" (United Nations).

4. "Sustainability has often been defined as how biological systems endure and remain diverse and productive. But, the 21st-century definition of sustainability goes far beyond these narrow parameters. Today, it refers to the need to develop the sustainable models necessary for both the human race and planet Earth to survive" (sustainablilitydegrees.com).

5. "Sustainability means strong finances, a clean environment, and healthy employees and communities. At GSA, sustainability is helping federal agencies meet their missions today, without sacrificing their ability to serve future generations" (GSA).

Strategic sustainability should not be confused with the concept of *strategic stability*, a defense strategy developed during the Cold War to avoid competition between the United States and the Soviet Union to escalate into a nuclear war. Strategic stability can be understood to mean

> a situation in which no party has an incentive to use nuclear weapons save for vindication of its vital interests in extreme circumstances … the essence of the concept is that the only reason a nation should see sufficient reason to use nuclear weapons is in response to major aggression against its established, well-understood, and reasonably conceived vital interests. In a strategically stable situation, then, a nation would see neither need nor incentive to use nuclear weapons except to make clear to an opponent that he had crossed a most vital red line with the probability that he would suffer further—and perhaps catastrophic—loss if he continued his aggression…. In a stable situation, then, major war would only come about because one party truly sought it, not because of miscalculation.
>
> *(Colby 2013, 54)*

Defining Strategic Sustainability

The sustainability concept has two meanings for government administrators. The first is government control of economic development to meet the needs of the current population without compromising the needs of future generations. This results in the three-part inclusion of service to humanity, economic growth, and protection and preservation of the biosphere. A second approach is centered on longevity, seeing sustainability as referring to actions that assure maintenance of a sustainable government and agencies that provide public service, particularly with respect to human health and safety. Thoughtful planning that includes consideration of the future of the natural environment is necessary for meeting the demands of both of these meanings of sustainability.

Strategic Sustainability Planning

Strategic sustainability planning (SSP) has been adopted by government agencies to help them plan for meeting such crises as natural disasters and the effects of climate change on agriculture. SSP consists of a combination of elements from three planning models: (1) the combination adopts elements of strategic planning, (2) asset management planning, and (3) financial planning. There is no one best way to combine these tools, or which section or tool to emphasize. They all begin with making sure that you know who you are, where you want to go, and how you plan to get there. This situation analysis step of strategic management is defined as a systematic analysis of the internal and external factors that shape an organization, the capabilities, customers, competitors within the organization's current and projected environment and its financial viability.

EPA Sustainability Research

The EPA has undertaken a series of studies that encourage utilities to plan for sustainability. One of those studies, the 2012 report on Planning for Sustainability, was developed to serve as a step-by-step guide for leading water and wastewater utilities through the planning process. The importance of planning was clearly spelled out in the report's introduction (Box 11.1).

BOX 11.1 PUBLIC UTILITY PLANNING FOR SUSTAINABILITY

"Utilities typically have a long-term planning horizon and long-term infrastructure operation and maintenance commitments. The costs and potential benefits of investment decisions will be realized over a long period of time. Accordingly, the EPA's Sustainability Policy calls for drinking water and wastewater systems to undertake 'robust and comprehensive' planning to ensure that water infrastructure investments are cost-effective over their lifecycle, resource efficient, and consistent with other relevant community goals. Throughout this Policy, EPA emphasizes the important relationship between utility and community sustainability. The core mission of water sector utilities is to provide clean and safe water in compliance with all applicable standards and requirements at an affordable price in order to protect public health and enhance the economic, environmental, and social sustainability of the communities they serve."

Source: U.S. EPA (2012, 3)

Preparing for Sustainability

Functioning as a prelude to preparation of a strategic plan are a comprehensive asset management plan and a policy and practice of engagement with customers and the community served by the water system. The asset management plan described in the previous chapter provides an inventory, condition and criticality of the utility's infrastructure, a risk-based schedule for maintenance and repair or replacement, and access to a financial plan for assuring the capital for these activities. Without the support of ratepayers and the community, necessary rate increases are difficult to achieve—making sustainability nearly impossible. The many published success stories available on the Internet reveal that while large utilities are more likely to use the strategic planning process as a vehicle for engaging the community and their ratepayers, smaller and rural water systems with as few as 50 connections have also begun to do so.

Planning to ensure supply and service sustainability in a public service organization such as a municipal utility begins with an internal analysis to ascertain the readiness of the utility's ratepayers to accept—and pay for—change. At the same time, an analysis is needed to determine whether the staff is ready and willing to invest the considerable time and effort a change to sustainable operations can entail. Willingness to accept and pay for change is not a widespread characteristic among many ratepayers. Workers in any organization can often have very different attitudes toward change than those of elected commissioners, and senior administrators charged with implementing and overseeing the transition may balk at the idea. The philosophy of "if it works, don't change it," exists everywhere.

Federal and state agencies and local municipalities and special service districts such as public utilities in many parts of the United States are confronted with formidable challenges as they maintain and expand their infrastructure systems for acquiring, treating and supplying clean and safe freshwater to their customers, collect and treat all wastewater, and, for many, to manage stormwater runoff. These problems have intensified as pressure from population growth and development have increased along with more and more severe infrastructure failures. New challenges to utility operations have also emerged: The effects of climate change and escalating costs of energy, labor and supplies are among the newest challenges faced by utilities in their commitment to providing safe and reliable water supplies and treatment services. As these challenges converge, it has become clear to many utilities that their operations must focus not just on meeting current needs, but instead are such that they must now plan for ensuring a sustainable ability for meeting continuously increasing demands under rapidly changing environmental conditions. In planning for sustainability, they also remember that changing operations must not curtail their responsibility for acting as stewards of the environment.

Before beginning planning for the sustainability transformation process, administrators must identify and adjust for any disparity between governance goals and persistent attitudes against change. Transformational change cannot begin until the causes of the disparity are identified, and a strategy designed for bringing everyone's attitudes to a point where the new policy and new way of operating will be accepted.

The causes of this disparity can usually be found in the culture of the organization and/or its operating climate. Agency leadership must assess these facets of the organization to identify factors affecting commitment to the organization and its current and projected mission. Successful reshaping of the organizational culture and climate can then become the foundation for building increased levels of commitment to the strategy of organizational transformation. Transformation requires a change in the culture in which public agencies function (Lau, Kilbourne and Woodman 2003).

Sustainable Operations

A good place to begin planning for sustainable operations is to ensure there is internal organization agreement and external stakeholder awareness of what the organization does and what it stands for. Planning for sustainable operations may begin with a review of the organization' mission, the external environment in which it performs its mission, and the perceived support it has from major stakeholder groups.

Changing the Organization's Culture

Public agency administrators are aware of the difficulties associated with attempts to initiate a long-term change in the culture that exists within their organizations. Organizational cultures are self-perpetuating; they preclude major alterations that are, on the surface, intuitively correct. That is, a particular culture "works" for the members of the organization at the time, and the place it exists. Without a culture that brings people in the organization together, working to achieve a common goal, the organization ends up spinning its wheels, accomplishing nothing. This fact is emphasized in this definition by Edgar Schein, a pioneer in the study of organizational culture:

> Culture is the pattern of basic assumptions … a group has invented, discovered, or developed in learning how to cope with its problems of external adaptation and internal integration, and that have worked well enough to … be taught to new members as the correct way to perceive, think and feel in relation to these problems.
>
> *(Schein 1985, 9)*

Organizational culture can also be defined as a system of shared values that are exhibited through the organization's different cultural and behavioral patterns and preferences that reflect the shared beliefs, values, and assumptions of the members of a specific group or organization. Often, change efforts in organizations achieve only partial results or fail to achieve desired results. Most of the change-adoption failures should not be looked upon predominantly as failures of the administrators who oversaw the change effort. Rather, it may be more appropriate to attribute them to a deeper, more critical source: the fundamental, all-pervasive, bureaucratic culture of traditional government organizations and the operating climate that results in inertia. This unwillingness to accept change has long been considered to be a reflection of bureaucratic thinking that often characterizes bureaucratic organizations. Public managers become victims of that culture, just as change initiatives become victims of poor or sloppy implementation of a change.

An organization's culture and the operating climate it generates have a direct influence on the *state of readiness* required for a renewal or other organizational change to take place. If the organization's culture and climate make it impossible to achieve change, the transformation initiative and other change programs will most likely fail, regardless of the desires and plans of the organization's leadership. Therefore, to improve the odds of success when attempting to introduce any change into an organization, public managers should first conduct a comprehensive examination of the underlying values and beliefs shared by members of the organization.

Components of a Strategic Sustainability Plan

The sustainability planning process begins with the utility setting the sustainability goals that emerge from an internal analysis of the barriers to sustainability in the community it serves and the strengths and weaknesses that emerge from an operating environment analysis. A selected list of typical sustainability goals included in the EPA's planning for sustainability guide is presented in Table 11.1. There are three key components in a sustainability plan: (1) goal-setting, (2) objective-setting and attainment strategies, and (3) alternatives analysis. A fourth strategy not included here is a financial strategy.

Section 1: Setting Sustainability Goals

The first step in sustainability goal-setting is to review and solidify he organization's mission, vision and goals. Management should then conduct an internal analysis to identify priorities and potential opportunities, infrastructure and operations strengths that can enable the utility to achieve that goal. Equally important is a vulnerability assessment. The second step in this section is determination of the sustainability priorities of the community served by the organization. Once these are identified, the third step—coordinating the utility's sustainability activities with those of the community and relevant stakeholders—can result in a synergistic effect that benefits both bodies. The final step is documenting sustainability goals so that they are available to guide following strategy and objective-setting.

The sustainability planning process then proceeds with the organization setting the sustainability goals that emerge from an internal analysis of the barriers to sustainability in the community it serves and the strengths and weaknesses that emerge from an environmental analysis. An example of a goal for a combined water and wastewater system might be: *The utility will reduce the stormwater I&I into the wastewater treatment system that results of discharge of untreated sewage.* I&I—the inflow and infiltration of groundwater and stormwater into wastewater or sanitary sewer systems—can overload the ability of the utility to collect and treat normal sewage inflow, resulting in release of untreated sewage into the environment.

Sustainability goal-setting begins with an internal analysis to identify the priorities and potential opportunities, infrastructure and operations strengths that can enable the utility to achieve that goal. Equally important is a vulnerability assessment. The second step is determination of the sustainability priorities of the community served by the utility. Once these are known, the third step—coordinating the utility's sustainability activities with those of the community and relevant stakeholders—can result in a synergistic effect that benefits both bodies. The fourth step is documenting sustainability goals so that they are available to guide following strategy and objective-setting.

Section 2: Setting Objectives and Strategies

Once a goal is identified, an analysis of the existing and planned activities needed for achieving the goal should be evaluated and a baseline performance level set. Objectives and timetables can then be set for the selected activities to be employed for moving forward from the baseline. For example, a utility might have identified a goal of forging a stable, reliable and knowledgeable long-term management team. The baseline is analysis of the existing operating structure, which in this case might be operating under a contract management system with little say in planning for the future. An objective could be to conduct a search of other regional utilities of the same or similar size and experts at the state professional water management association. Once that data is collected, a second objective would be to select a management structure with a paid permanent general manager with the certifications and the skills necessary for achieving the utility's sustainability goal. Thus, achieving the goal of a more efficient and stronger management system included sustainability considerations into the setting of the objective.

An example for objectives improving the way a utility manages stormwater to lessen the likelihood of flooding from expected stronger storms might be stated this way: "The utility will reduce total I&I inflow to the sanitary system by 30% by 2025." The utility can adopt different strategies for achieving this goal. Inflow is stormwater that enters into sanitary sewer systems from drains, manholes and other access points; infiltration is groundwater that enters sewer systems through cracks and/or leaks in the sewer pipes. Sources of inflow include roof or foundation drains, downspouts, other architectural structure drains including outdoor base-ment stairwells, parking lots, roads and driveways, basement sump pumps, and even urban creeks and streams. Often these sources are improperly or illegally connected to sanitary sewer systems.

Section 3: Alternatives Analysis

Analysis of alternatives to solutions to a strategy for achieving the objective calls for cost–benefit analysis and explicit and consistent strategy selection criteria. An initial action for identifying and measuring the status of the sewer mains could be the installation and monitoring of flowmeters that record limitations to increased flow in sewage lines during storms. Among the alternatives for achiev-ing the objective is the increasingly important strategy of achieving this objective by green infrastructure (Furlong, Phelan and Dodson 2018). Since the 1960s, water and wastewater utilities have been expected to contribute to environmental protection in their communities and, since the 1990s, they have been encouraged to prepare strategic plans for assuring sustainability. Environmental protection options include catch basins, urban green areas and permeable roads and parking lots, and facilities for collecting stormwater that allow it to soak into the ground and recharge an underlying aquifer. Another strategy might be to use a video camera to inspect sewer mains for breaks and for intrusion of root blockages that restrict the higher flow during storms.

Evaluating the cost of a sustainability action for correcting the problem imme-diately or at a later period should include the social and economic costs that could occur from an extreme weather event. The two main sources of funds for operations and infrastructure repair, replacement and expansion are utility rate payments and borrowing. The traditional approach is for repairs and replacement to be paid for by current users through rate revenues; costs for expansion are paid for by loans paid for by new users.

A scorecard approach is often used when analyzing alternative actions. Two alternatives are scored using the same criteria and numeric scale. The alternative with the most favorable score for benefits and for costs is the preferred choice. A transit system operations example of a goal, measurable objectives and strategy for achieving for the objectives and goal is shown in Table 11.1.

As a component in its value management framework, the Ohio Office of Budget and Management (OBM) develops, coordinates and monitors the budgets of state agencies and reviews all state financial transactions. OBM's Office of Value Management provides state agencies with a Value Management Frame-work to use when planning programs and projects. To help agencies improve the likelihood of project success and reduce the risk of project failure, the framework includes a section on conducting an analysis of alternatives. Box 11.2 includes the purpose for the analysis. The Ohio value management framework for an analysis of alternatives includes these major elements.

TABLE 11.1 Transit system goals, objectives, achievement measures, targets and strategies

Goal 1: Improve transit services convenience, reliability and customer service

	Objective	Metric	Target	Strategy
1.1	Improve accessibility to major employment, recreation, educational, healthcare, retail centers and cultural attractions	• Percent coverage of the urbanized area • Amount of transit service route miles within ¼ mile of major health facilities, recreation, education, employment, cultural and social service facilities	• Provide a minimum of 60% transit coverage of the urbanized area • Provide a minimum of healthcare: 50 miles; tourist and special attractions: 100 miles; major employment: 40 miles; retail centers: 90 miles within a ¼ mile	Evaluate achievement of service coverage and route design standards to improve transit access to major destinations in these categories

1.2	Improve transit service reliability	• On-time performance of transit vehicles per mode
		• Percentage of missed pullouts
		• Achievement of mean distance between service failures
			• Metrorail: 95%
			  Metrobus: 78%
			  STS: 80%
			• Agency: 0%
			• Metrorail: 39,000 miles
			  Metrobus: 4000 miles
			  Mover: 6000 miles
				Evaluate achievement of transit reliability target levels

1.3	Match transit service coverage with passenger demand	• No. of average daily boardings
		• Hours of transit service/service population
			• Metrorail: 67,000
			  Metrobus: 241,000
			  Mover: 30,000
			• Minimum of 1.5 hours transit service/service population
				Evaluation of passenger demand measures

Source: MDCTS (2014)

BOX 11.2 THE PURPOSE OF AN ANALYSIS OF ALTERNATIVES

The purpose of an analysis of alternatives (AoA) is to assess the effectiveness, cost, and risks of alternatives that have potential to close or mitigate the capability gaps identified in the business problem and subsequent process analyses. An AoA helps identify more cost-effective alternatives, validate the appropriateness of the selected solution, reduce risks, and improve performance.

The AoA should assess critical technology elements associated with each proposed solution, including technology maturity, integration risk, manufacturing feasibility, technology maturity, and demonstrated needs. It must provide compelling evidence of the capabilities and worth of the alternatives. The results should enable decision-makers to discuss the appropriate cost, schedule, performance, and risk tradeoffs and assess the capabilities and affordability of the alternatives.

Source: Ohio OBM (2018)

Once the data are collected, a second objective would be to select a management structure with a paid permanent general manager with the certifications and the skills necessary for achieving the utility's sustainability goal. Thus, achieving the goal of a more efficient and stronger management system included sustainability considerations into the setting of the objective.

All U.S. government agencies must report on their goal-achievement progress every year. An example of the performance goal summary report issued by the Army Corps of Engineers (USAGE) in 2016 for performance in 2015 is shown in Table 11.3.

1. Identify the technology and legacy systems and modifications capability gaps; determine the existing system baseline before beginning the analysis.
2. State what elements of the agency's mission will be supported.
3. Identify viable alternative or representative system or program solutions.
4. Consider project requirements, including time, cost, security, risk and enterprise compliance.
5. Secure and evaluate data on representative systems deemed viable.
6. Present first-stage findings in a table or spreadsheet format for easy reference and scoring.

Additional analyses that can be included for large-scale projects could include a cost–benefit and return on investment (ROI) solution comparison, weight scale

TABLE 11.2 Example municipal utility sustainability strategies

Goal	Examples of Potential Strategies
Improve compliance	Work with regional laboratories and regulatory agencies to improve state-wide network of testing laboratories
Reduce overall infrastructure costs	Investigate availability of innovative methods for processing and delivering services while repairing and replacing failing infrastructure
Extend projected adequacy of current supplies	Design and implement conservation program and investigate installation of new delivery methods
Reduce extreme storm impacts	Implement green architecture test installations
Enhance community livability	Target critical infrastructure projects needed to support community livability and encourage redevelopment
Reduce long-term operation costs	Where possible, use natural treatment systems such as functioning wetlands
Improve operational resilience	Begin planning for sustainable operations during extreme weather events
Reduce vulnerability of supply	Invest in real-time service quality monitoring, install new delivery methods where appropriate
Ensure a safe, sustainable workforce	Implement safe workplace changes, knowledge retention and new knowledge through regular training
Reduce energy costs	Invest in more energy-efficient equipment

Source: After material in EPA (2008) with local content; McNabb (2019)

TABLE 11.3 Selection of USACE's FY 2015 performance on key sustainability measures

Goal	Description	2015 Target	2015 Performance
1	Reduce Greenhouse Gas (GHG) emissions by 23.1% by FY 2020	−12.6%	−10.3%
2	Sustainable Buildings: Reduce building energy intensity by 30% by end of FY 2015	−30%	−15.1%
3	Achieve 10% renewable energy use	10%	16.6%
4	Water use intensity: Reduce potable water intensity by 26% annually through end of FY2020	−16%	−13.7%
5	Reduce total fleet petroleum consumption by 20%	−20%	20.1%
6	Ensure at least 95% of applicable contract actions demonstrate compliance with sustainability goals	95%	55.6%
7	Ensure at least 50% of non-hazardous solid waste is diverted from the land fill by reduction, reuse, recycling	50%	Not reported
8	Award $12.5 million in energy performance contracts by December 31, 2017	$12.5M	$15.9M
9	At least 95% of monitors, PCs and laptops acquired meet environmentally sustainable electronics criteria	95%	100%

Source: U.S. Army Corps of Engineers (2016)

TABLE 11.4 Example comparison of three alternatives

Decision Criteria	Alternative 1	Alternative 2	Alternative 3
Business process impact	5	5	3
Technical feasibility	5	4	3
Maturity of the solution	5	3	4
Resources required	4	4	4
Impact of constraints	4	4	3
Cost–benefit analysis	5	4	1
Return on investment	5	4	1
Other	5	3	1
Totals	38	31	21

Source: After Ohio OMB (2018) example

of simple scoring data, and an importance or criticalness-weighted analysis of each alternative. An example of the first-level analysis patterned after the Ohio OBM solution comparison format with a five-point rating scale is shown in Table 11.4. The rating scale values are: 1 = very poor; 2 = poor; 3 = fair; 4 = good; and 5 = very good. The alternative with a total score of 38 received the highest score. The following five steps can serve as a guide when implementing the practice of sustainability.

Step 1: Understand the concept and practices of sustainable innovation:

- Sustainability couples environmentalism's protection of natural systems with the notion of business innovation while delivering essential goods and services that serve social goals of human health, equity, and environmental justice.
- Technology and innovation must be a large part of any potential solution to a range of environmental and social issues.
- Sustainable development innovation must incorporate the added constraints of social and environmental pressures as well as consider future generations.

Step 2: Adopt the strategic sustainability planning (SSP) process:

- SSP has been adopted by government agencies to help them plan for meeting such crises as natural disasters and the effects of climate change on agriculture.
- SSP consists of a combination of elements from three planning models, i.e., the combination adopts elements of *strategic planning*, *asset management planning*, and *financial planning*.

Step 3: Prepare for sustainability and planning for sustainable operations:

- Review the organization's mission, the external environment, and the perceived support it has from major stakeholder groups.

- Conduct an internal analysis (e.g., SWOT) and identify and adjust for any disparity between governance goals and persistent attitudes against change.
- Develop a comprehensive asset management plan and a policy and practice of engagement with customers and the community served by the organization.
- Reshape the organizational culture and climate to increase the levels of commitment to the strategy of organizational transformation.

Step 4: Develop and implement a strategic sustainability plan:

- Key components in a sustainability plan:
  - setting sustainability goals;
  - setting objectives and attainment strategies;
  - alternatives analysis (e.g., cost–benefit analysis, explicit and consistent strategy selection criteria, and/or a scorecard approach);
  - financial strategy (i.e., financial resources and strategies sustainable?).
- The organization's tasks, objectives and goals are required to be spelled out in the plan that the strategies for overcoming the increasing severity of obstacles.

Step 5: Build in assessment and review processes for monitoring and modifying strategies in accordance with the changes in the external environment for continuous improvement.

Summary

Public sector organizations are increasingly encouraged to develop a sustainability strategy and plan for implementing the plan. The plan includes three components or tools: a self-assessment, development of a strategy for accomplishing goals and rectifying problems, and an action plan for how to accomplish its strategic sustainability goals. The sustainability concept has two meanings for government administrators. The first is government control of economic development to meet the needs of the current population without compromising the needs of future generations. This results in the three-part inclusion of service to humanity, the economic growth and protection and preservation of the biosphere. A second approach is centered on longevity, seeing sustainability as referring to actions that assure maintenance of a sustainable government and agencies that provide public service, particularly with respect to human health and safety. Thoughtful planning that includes consideration of the future of the natural environment is necessary for meeting the demands of both of these meanings of sustainability.

Strategic sustainability planning (SSP) was adopted by government agencies to help them plan for meeting such crises as natural disasters and the effects of climate change on agriculture. SSP consists of a combination of elements from three planning models: The combination adopts elements of strategic planning, asset management planning, and financial planning.

12

PERFORMANCE MANAGEMENT STRATEGIES

Strategic management concepts as a tool for improving public sector organizations' performance have been tested and documented since at least the 1960s (Ansoff 1965; Andrews 1971; Porter 1991; Ingraham, Joyce and Donahue 2003; McNabb 2009). Public sector performance management as an element in strategic management is now a key component in both the application of strategic management and in the forming of operations strategy (Högland, Caicedo, Mårtensson and Svärdsten 2018; Newcomer and Caudle 2011). The degree that performance measurement influences an organization's success under the environmental conditions under which it must operate is shaped by its capabilities and resources.

Public Sector Performance Management

The beginning of a movement for adopting a means for improving performance in government agencies appeared as early as the 1960s. After several failed attempts at adopting a system for outcome-based improvements, a formal public sector performance improvement program finally took root with passage of the Government Performance and Results Act (GPRA) in 1993. Although not fully implemented until 1996, the GPRA required federal agencies to implement performance management programs that included goal-setting, measuring results in accomplishing those goals, and reporting their progress to both houses of Congress (Wholey 1999). The mechanisms for carrying out those mandates were use of strategic planning and performance measurement systems.

Problems and gaps in the original legislation were resolved with passage of the GPRA Modernization Act (GPRAMA) in 2010 and its full implementation in January 2011. Key changes were requirements to publish their plans and reports in machine-readable formats, and to identify the key external uncontrollable factors that were barriers to achieving their goals and objectives. Also included were adoption of enhanced performance planning, management and reporting activities. Box 12.1 is a short history of the federal adoption difficulties.

The framework for implementing the GPRA is strategic performance management (SPM). Strategic performance management is an organization's system for measuring and reporting how it is accomplishing its objectives and strategies. The International Management Accountants Association describes SPM as a critical

> process for helping a public sector organization to shift its policy goals into reality. SPM enables an organization to achieve an effective "line of sight" from policy formation to front line delivery of services, understanding how and to what extent individual activities throughout that chain contribute to high level goals; and easily identifying those areas that are not contributing, or are contributing poorly so that appropriate action can be taken. SPM is both high level (strategic) and integrated, linking various aspects of the [organization] with management of individuals and teams.
>
> *(Ross 2011, 19)*

BOX 12.1 HISTORY OF THE GOVERNMENT PERFORMANCE AND RESULTS ACT

The Government Performance and Results Act (GPRA) was signed by President Bill Clinton on August 3, 1993. "From the time it was signed, the federal government focused on data collection and preparation for the following fiscal year. The fiscal year for the federal budget always starts October 1 and ends September 30 the following year. Before the GPRA was enacted, there was an attempted law adopted in the 1960s that tried to fulfill the task the GPRA achieved. That earlier attempt was called the Program Planning and Budgeting System."

"Additional similar legislation attempted to introduce performance management. Examples include Zero-Based Budgeting, Total Quality Management, and a few other minor programs. These were some of the many unsuccessful programs that tried to establish Federal Performance Budgeting. Where those earlier bills failed to receive enough legislative approval to be made into law, the GPRA was successfully approved by both Congress and the president. To ensure the GPRA continued to have a lasting impact, president Barack Obama signed the Government Performance and Results Modernization Act of 2010 into law on January 4, 2011. The GPRA requires the GAO to produce an annual report on agency performance. The report is then transmitted to Congress with the President's annual budget request."

Source: GAO (U.S. Government Accountability Office) (no date)

TABLE 12.1 Agency requirements in GPRAMA 2010

N	GPRAMA Requirement	General topic
1	Agency strategic plan	Strategic planning
2	Agency priority goals	Establishing goals
3	Agency performance planning	Performance planning and reporting
4	Agency quarterly reviews	Data-driven performance reviews
5	Transparency of agency performance	Public reporting website
6	Reducing unnecessary plans and reports	Reduced reporting
7	Federal government priority goals	Goals
8	Federal government performance plan	Performance planning and reporting
9	Federal government quarterly review	Data-driven performance reviews
10	Federal government performance website	Public reporting website
11	Leadership at the government level	Leadership roles
12	Agency leadership involvement and accountability	Leadership roles

Source: GAO (n/d)

Table 12.1 lists the components in the federal government's performance planning system.

Key Performance Requirements

The first requirement in the list, developing an agency strategic plan, is the basis for all subsequent strategic management strategies, goals and operational priorities. Requirements 2, 3 and 4 in the list of GPRAMA requirements are the elements that apply to performance management. Agency priority goals, along with regular operational objectives, are the targets against which performance is measured. Agency planning is the first step in a strategic performance management system. Agency quarterly reviews are the framework for periodic performance measurement progress.

Agency Strategic Plan

The Office of Management and Budget (OMB) explanatory document describes the agency strategic plan as a statement that defines the mission of the agency. It names its long-term primary goals and the administrators responsible for guiding progress in accomplishing the goals, the strategies and tactics planned for accomplishing those goals. It includes how the agency proposes to monitor its progress in addressing both the cited priority goals and actions to be taken on other relevant national problems, needs, challenges, and opportunities related to the agency's mission. Administrators are to explain the importance of the goals, enumerate the agency's capabilities and weaknesses, and assess the operating environment

TABLE 12.2 Elements to be included in an agency's performance measurements

Section	Description
1	List measurable strategic (long-term) goals and short-term objectives
2	Description of how the progress on achieving the goals and objectives are to be measured
3	Description of interagency collaboration, if any, to achieve the agency's goals and objectives will be measured
4	Description of how the agency's performance goals and priority goals relate to the general long-term goals and objectives
5	Identification of external environmental factors that could significantly affect performance toward achieving the agency's goals and objectives
6	What program evaluations (metrics) are to be used to establish or review the agency's general (long-term) goals and objectives.

Source: After material in GPRA (2011)

(OMB 2016). The goal of these improvements was better communications to Congress and the Executive Office while fostering improved cooperation with other agencies and reducing duplication. Table 12.2 lists the government strategic management performance requirements included in GPRAMA (GAO n/d).

The strategic plan should include explanations of why the specific goals and strategies were selected and provide evidence supporting the selections. Some programs included in the strategic plan are respected as being to be more reflective of continuations of ongoing basic agency operations, whereas the newer priority goals named in the strategic plan should focus on high-priority goals that have been identified during agency analyses of the operating environment. The plan will therefore provide justification for funding decisions in support of performance goals, priorities, strategic human capital planning, and budget planning.

Agency Priority Goals

Agency priority goals (APGs) are the performance measuring guides that enable agencies to focus on leadership priorities and program outcomes, and then measure results of their programs (performance.gov). APG statements are outcome-oriented, ambitious, and measurable with specific targets set that reflect a near-term result or achievement that agency leadership wants to accomplish within approximately 24 months. In some instances, agencies are also utilizing the APG structure to drive progress and monitor implementation of agency management reforms and priorities, a modification of the traditional APG statement format. The act required the directors of 24 major agencies to identify agency priority goals. The Senate expected the number of goals to be submitted to not exceed 100 and individual agencies to not list more than five, although with the expectation that some larger agencies might need to include more than five. The Department of the Interior, for example, submitted six goals. The Department of Defense and the Treasury Department each listed three priorities; the Department of Agriculture and the Department of Homeland Security each listed only two priority goals.

The chief goals of these improvement programs were the fostering of better communications between Congress and the Executive Office while also improving cooperation between agencies and reducing duplication of efforts. Table 12.3 lists the government strategic management requirements included in GPRAMA (GAO 2010). The three strategic planning projects required by the GPRAMA are an agency strategic plan, specification of agency performance goals, and an agency performance plan for achieving those goals. All three plans must be updated every four years, beginning the first year of every four-year presidential term of office. At least every two years, all agencies are required to consult with majority and minority elements of appropriations and oversight committees of Congress.

Priorities Examples

Agency managers select two or more strategic goals every two years. They then assign teams responsible for achieving the goal. Performance is evaluated quarterly to check progress and identify barriers to progress. They may then make changes to vary or implement new strategies to achieve the desired outcomes. APGs are to be achieved throughout the course of the current fiscal years. Priority goals are to be established by all major federal agencies. In one example, the following four priorities were included in the 2018 fiscal year for the Department of Health and Human Services: (1) human security, (2) reducing opioid morbidity and mortality, (3) combined data analyses, and (4) serious mental illness. The goal statements for each of these four priorities were (Performance.gov 2018):

Human Security: Increase capacity to prevent health threats originating abroad from affecting the United States. By September 30, 2019, HHS will contribute to increasing the surveillance, workforce emergency management, and laboratory capacity of 17 partner countries.

Reducing Opioid Morbidity and Mortality: Reduce opioid-related morbidity and mortality through (1) improved access to prevention, treatment and recovery support services; (2) targeting the availability and distribution of overdose-reversing drugs; (3) strengthening public health data and reporting; (4) supporting cutting-edge research; and (5) advancing the practice of pain management.

Combined Data Analysis: This requires an increase in the combined analysis of disparate datasets to achieve better insights. By September 30, 2019, HHS will develop and implement an enterprise-wide data governance model. Two use cases of interagency data through this process are to be tested.

Serious Mental Illness: Improve treatment for individuals with serious mental illness. By September 30, 2019, HHS wants at least 280 evidence-based coordinated specialty care (CSC) programs providing services to individuals with functional restoration programs (FEP), representing a seven-fold increase in the

TABLE 12.3 Requirements for government agency performance planning

Requirement	Regulation
1	List agency performance goals.
2	Describe how the performance goals contribute to the agency's general (or strategic) goals.
3	Describe how the performance goals contribute to any federal government performance goals.
4	Identify agency priority goals and performance targets.
5	Describe the strategies and resources required to meet the agency performance goals.
6	Specify clearly defined milestones.
7	Identify the organizations, program activities, regulations, policies, and other activities that contribute to each performance goal from internal and external sources.
8	Describe the interagency cooperation for achieving the agency performance goals and the federal government performance goals.
9	Identify goal leaders.
10	Include a balanced set of performance indicators.
11	Provide a basis for comparing results.
12	Describe how the agency will ensure data accuracy and reliability.
13	Describe major management challenges.
14	Identify low-priority programs of the agency.

Source: GPRA (2011)

number of such programs compared with 2014. This target assumes stable funding at the federal and state level and may need to be adjusted if there are major unanticipated changes in either.

Types of Programs

An example of the types of specific programs and objectives associated with each of the goals is the set of specific targets HHS has identified for its reduction in opioid morbidity and mortality priority are:

1. Reduce opioid prescribing by the medical profession as measured by morphine milligram equivalents (MMEs).
2. Decrease by 25% the MME of opioid analgesics dispensed in U.S. outpatient retail pharmacies.
3. Increase by 30% the number of naloxone prescriptions dispensed in U.S. outpatient retail pharmacies. (Naloxone is the medication designed to reverse opioid overdose.)
4. Increase by 25% the number of individual patients receiving prescriptions for buprenorphine in the U.S. (Buprenorphine is a prescription drug used to treat dependence on opioid painkillers such as oxycodone.)

5. Increase by 100% the number of prescriptions for long-acting injectable or implantable buprenorphine from retail, long-term care, and mail-order pharmacies in the U.S.

6. Increase by 25% the number of prescriptions for the extended-released naltrexone from retail, long-term care, and mail-order pharmacies in the U.S.

The OMB guidelines for strategic management activities encourage agency planners to identify priority goals that reflect the agency's highest priorities as determined by the head of the agency. Since agency secretaries change often, the goals should be ambitious but achievable within a two-year period.

Performance Plan Mandates

Strategic Objectives

Agencies must translate the long-term goals in their strategic plans to strategic objectives and then to the policies and actions necessary for accomplishing the targeted goals. Annual performance metrics are to be included in the annual performance plan. Because the strategic plan focuses on long-term objectives, it is important that agencies consider risks and how risks change over time during formulation of the plan.

The positions taken and activities needed to achieve the agency's general (long-term) goals constitute the policies that guide the agency actions. Policy descriptions are the broad government guiding principles that shape the decisions that pertain to the programs and management objectives of the agency. They must be consistent, purposive and action-related to the mission of the agency.

Annual agency performance plans are a mandated activity in federal agency strategic management. Objectives in the annual plan are to be associated with long-term goals spelled out in the strategic plan. Two types of goals are required: mission-focused and mission support goals, each of which covers a different type of problem. Mission-focused collaboration goals identify partners with special knowledge and skills, and with experience in dealing with problems that extend across agency boundaries. Examples include international trade, food safety, sustainable communities, disaster preparedness and intelligence sharing. Mission support goals focus on continuing government efforts for streamlining administrative processes (Fountain 2017).

Rules for preparing all aspects of the plan are monitored by the OMB along with the agency's strategic plan and priority goals. Briefly, the three core elements of the requirement are identifying goals and objectives for the issues and programs for which the agency operates, establishing objectives for programs and policies for objectives and goal-achieving programs, and providing for methods for measuring progress toward accomplishing the short-term objectives.

BOX 12.2 DEFINITION OF PERFORMANCE MEASUREMENT AND ITS PURPOSE

Performance measurement is the process of collecting, analyzing and reporting data regarding the performance of an organization. It is a tool to help local government evaluate the quality and effectiveness of government services. Performance measures include inputs (resources used), outputs (program activities), efficiency measures (ratio of inputs to outputs), and outcomes (the actual results of programs and services). Many performance measurement systems are limited to measuring program inputs and outputs. Ideally, however, performance measurement efforts will also generate information about program results and outcomes.

Source: MRSC (2018)

These elements are contained in the 14 required elements of the annual program performance plan. They include specifying the issues, programs, strategies, activities, goals and objectives, progress measurement metrics, and reporting.

State-level Performance Management

The use of performance measurement and reporting in state and local governments is a result of increased citizen demands for government accountability. This has generated greater interest by local legislators and elected municipality officers to incorporate performance measurement specifications during decision-making on program and resource allocations. Box 12.2 includes a definition of performance measurement and a description of the process prepared for agencies in Washington State.

City-level Performance Measurement

Kirkland, Washington, a city on the shores of lake Washington with a population of nearly 50,000, publishes a performance report, *City Council Goals*, to its citizens each year. The report lists progress on 10 key policy and service priorities for the city government. Council goals are for guiding allocation of budget and capital improvement program resources. The goal plan also describes how work plans and projects are developed to move the community towards the stated long-term goals. The City's ability to make progress toward their achievement is based on the availability of resources at any given time. The allocation of resources reflects the need to balance taxation levels with community service demands and the achievement of stated goals. Similar performance plans and reports are prepared by city, county and special municipal districts throughout the United States.

The 2017 report preamble described the purpose of the report was to:

> articulate key policy and service priorities for Kirkland. Council goals guide the allocation of resources through the budget and capital improvement program to assure that organizational work plans and projects are developed that incrementally move the community towards the stated goals. Council goals are long term in nature. The City's ability to make progress toward their achievement is based on the availability of resources at any given time. Implicit in the allocation of resources is the need to balance levels of taxation and community impacts with service demands and the achievement of goals.
>
> *(City of Kirkland 2018, 5)*

Kirkland's park and recreation unit is an example for which progress on meeting goals to provide and maintain natural areas and recreational facilities and opportunities that enhance the health and wellbeing of the community. Meeting objectives for programs and classes are measured by tracking the percentage of programs and classes that meet minimum numbers to operate. The city uses five measures on park and recreation management; three measures each on the city's level of investment in parks and recreation facilities and on the city's open space plan; and two measures on citizens' ratings of the park and recreation system. More than 87% of recreation classes met the minimum enrollment, which exceeds the city's target, a good indication that the classes offered meet the demands of community members. Community member satisfaction with the parks, recreation and community services, as determined by the Community Survey, provides another measure of how well the park and recreation system meets the community's needs.

Performance Management Systems

Performance management is the process that begins with creating a productive and harmonious work environment in which workers are able to perform to the best of their abilities (Heathfield 2019). A performance management system (PMS) is a continuous process of identifying, measuring and developing performance in organizations. De Rooij, Janowicz-Panjaitan and Mannak (2018) adopted a definition of performance management system developed by Ferreira and Otley (2009, 264):

> [A PMS consists of] the evolving formal and informal mechanisms, processes, systems, and networks used by organizations for conveying the key objectives and goals elicited by management, for assisting the strategic process and ongoing management through analysis, planning,

measurement, control, rewarding, and broadly managing performance, and for supporting and facilitating organizational learning and change.

After an extensive review of the research on performance management systems, De Rooji et al. (2018) reported on a difference between performance management systems and what they termed performance management packages (PMPs). PMSs as elements in a broader organizational management control systems form a system if they are designed independent of a comprehensive management control system. A PMP, on the other hand, consists of the complete set of management control practices in place in an organization.

In practice, a PMS can range anywhere within a structural and focus continuum that ranges from a mechanistic model to an organic model. A mechanistic model relies on formal rules, standard procedures, and routines—all of which are designed to control behavior and rigid system delivery output. This control leads to close monitoring of all activities in an agency's programs and projects. An organic model operates with greater flexibility and responsiveness. Performance measurements ranging across an organization return performance information about an operations team. Rules are basic and procedures are standardized, although they tend to reflect responses to various contingency factors.

Implementing a PMS

Citing a 1996 US GAO release, Newcomer and Caudle (2011) listed these three key steps to follow for adopting a strategy of performance-based management: (1) developing a reasonable level of agreement on missions, goals, and strategies for achieving the goals; (2) deciding how and when to implement performance measurement systems for documenting performance and support decision-making; and (3) plan how to use performance information as a basis for decision-making at various organizational levels. Taking his lead from the GAO guide for implementing a PMS, Wholey (1999, 289) concluded that to implement an effective performance-based management system, managers must achieve a reasonable level of agreement with senior officials and other key stakeholders on agency or program goals and on the resources, activities, and processes required to meet the goals.

The federal government's PMS initiative includes the need to focus on measurable results and a balance scorecard, both of which are important elements in public sector strategic management systems and human resources programs. The recommended balanced scorecard is a strategic management tool that organizations in business and the public sector use to track and manage the organization's goals, its strategies, objectives, performance, target progress measures, and the operational programs and activities for each of these steps.

Three years after the GAO release, David Otley (1999) proposed a five-step or question framework for developing a performance management system. Included were: (1) identify key organizational objectives, methods and process to be used for measuring progress toward achieving the goals; (2) formulate plans, strategies and measurement systems; (3) set performance targets; (4) identify systems for rewards for achieving performance goals; and (5) specify information flows for monitoring performance and supporting learning.

Building on that earlier five-factor framework, 10 years later Aldónio Ferreira joined Otley (2009) to expand the factors list from five to twelve for use when considering whether to develop a performance management system. Abbreviated descriptions of this new framework can also be used as a checklist for use during goal achievement evaluation:

1. Identify the vision and mission of the organization. How are they communicated to managers and staff?
2. Identify the core factors contributing to the organization's success today. What changes are expected in future operations.
3. Identify the organizational structure. How will this structure affect the design and use of the performance measurement system?
4. Identify the strategies and planned operations and how the PMS will be affected by these strategic elements. How are strategies, objectives and goals established?
5. List the key performance measurements needed for determining progress toward achievement of objectives and goals. These are the resources, competencies, activities, and capabilities that management sees as critical for the success of the organization. Their implementation is at the heart of the performance management system.
6. Identify the level of performance at appropriate schedules needed to ensure goals are achieved.
7. Identify how the organization is to evaluate performance of individuals, teams, groups and departments. Are the methods adopted objective, subjective or a combination of the two?
8. Identify and communicate what rewards will be used for performance by managers and staff. Are they to be financial, non-financial or a combination of the two? Alternatively, what punishments are to be used when goals or objectives are not achieved?
9. Identify the means for communicating performance goals and objectives, required changes, and for providing regular feedback.
10. Identify how the performance data is to be used, necessary privacy ensured, and what control mechanisms are in place.
11. Determine when and how the PMS may be altered to reflect changes in the organization, stakeholders, and/or the mission itself. Are these changes implemented reactively or proactively?
12. Finally, how strong and understood are the links between strategies, goals, performance and elements of the performance management system in how they are used?

All in all, performance-based management in a government organization at all levels of operation must begin with agreement on the goals and strategies of the organization; only after this can managers develop performance management systems that prove the information necessary for forming and auditing the effectiveness of its strategies and programs. Performance measurement standards with standardized definitions on goals, objectives, and what constitutes stellar performance must be agreed upon at all levels, departments and units.

Adopting Performance Management

Adopting a performance management system is a fundamental component in the strategic management process. Albeit critical for long-term success, it is often difficult to implement. According to the Chartered Institute of Management Accountants, a variety of characteristics of the public sector often make adopting a performance management system difficult. Some of these items are (Ross 2011, 2):

- Public sector organizations by their nature are not profit motivated. Their mission is to deliver a service or product as efficiently as possible, without any increase in revenue.
- Politics influences what public organizations do, including their governance systems and mandated transformation movements.
- Agencies' complicated delivery chains, networks and multilevel government partners render it difficult for agencies to improve performance by modifying or changing the way programs are managed.
- Difficulties in determining the relationship between the cause of an issue and the results of proposed amelioration actions. Public problems are often the result of a combination of contributing factors. The results of a single solution are therefore difficult to identify and measure.
- The deleterious effects of a decision are often hidden from view for long periods—often decades after their implementation.
- Sections of society often have conflicting attitudes toward a given social trend. Hence, barriers to accountability and transparency arise, making completing a mandated or influential stakeholder group's politically motivated mission difficult to achieve.

Despite these difficulties, performance-based management systems are in use at all levels of government in the United States and many organizations around the globe. Adopters of this approach have adopted many of the management control processes that make PMS work. These include delegating authority, developing incentives and rewards for improved performance, as well as restructuring their organizations to focus on performance, shifting resources and capabilities in support of performance management activities, and partnering with other government agencies and civil society organizations to improve delivery and enhance program value. Following is a list of the possible performance management strategies designed to enhance the effectiveness of public sector performance management (Newcomer and Caudle 2011).

Administrators and managers need to promote stakeholder support and engagement. "Sufficient political capital" from both legislative leaders and external stakeholders is necessary to implement and secure a system of punishments and rewards for performance in government organizations. As they adopt performance management systems, the transition will be easier if the program is commensurate with the existing social and managerial structure—the political, governance and budgetary context in which it will function.

Research has shown that there is no single best performance management system. Each system must be right for the political, legal and human resources systems climate that exists for that organization at the time it is conceived. The organizational structure and support for the performance process calls for strong leadership, excellent communication, and managerial flexibility. Without strong leadership, success will not follow.

Furthermore, in most governments, networking and partnering in design and delivery of services is the way public value is produced. It has become necessary to achieve a "whole-of-government" performance system. Cooperation among different agencies and levels of government, members in strategic alliances, networks and collaborative agreements, and civil society organizations and stakeholder management groups must "buy into" the program, its purpose and promise. Despite the growing need for partnership governance, agencies must still maintain selectivity when selecting, implementing and evaluating performance measurement tools. Successful systems include clear, effective communication, honest and fair application, public participation, strategic plans and performance targets. Achievable performance goals, targets and the strategies and programs needed to achieve them are essential in public sector performance management systems.

Setting performance targets requires understanding what the best practices are in delivering similar public values, then updating them to match an organization's resources and capabilities (Camp 1989). That is, they should not simply be an extension of what has occurred in the past, as described by the following simplification: Continue the past year's programs, adjust for expected changes in the environment by increasing for known activities, add adjustments for inflation and for emergencies and contingencies. Establishing operating targets based on the best possible other agency practices—what is known as benchmarking—is the recommended method for setting performance targets. Benchmarking is "a proactive activity that is the missing ingredient in the kit bag of U.S. [public sector organizations] to correctly establish their goals, objectives, and targets. Its focus in on the search for best practices that will lead to" superior performance and sustainable operations (Camp 1989, xiii).

At the same time, the agency or group for which the PMS will apply must have the capacity and capabilities to accomplish the goals management set forth in its strategic plan. Nothing is more discouraging than goals that look good on paper and satisfy stakeholder interests but are patently too high to achieve. One way to avoid making this painful mistake is to consistently test and publish the appropriateness and quality of the collected performance data.

Finally, performance management is a fruitless activity if, when programmers sit down together to plan the long-term goals, and the strategies and necessary tasks to achieve them, the funds necessary to achieve what will be measured are not available; the whole planning activity is then a waste of time. Moreover, the performance management system should be expected to exist for a long time.

Introducing Strategic Performance Systems

Strategic performance management (SPM) is an organization's system for measuring and reporting how it is accomplishing its objectives and strategies. The following six steps are included to guide readers through the basic application of performance management strategies.

Step 1: Understand the key features of SPM:

- SPM combines strategic planning with performance management by creating an organizational structure based on strategies and functions, aligning resources with the structure, addressing human capital and productivity, and establishing performance measures (Redding and Layland 2015).
- SPM is more about finding ways to leverage system resources to maximize agency goals, i.e., looking to leverage inputs for maximum outcomes, than calling exclusively for cutting spending, increasing efficiency, or finding cheaper ways to do the same things as before.
- SPM provides direction for agency people's work while allowing for innovation and adjustment in due course to produce better results more efficiently.

Step 2: Identify the key performance requirements:

- Develop an agency strategic plan as the basis for all subsequent strategic management strategies, goals and operational priorities.
- Select agency priority goals.
- List the elements to be included in an agency's performance planning and measurements.
- Report progress and review performance periodically.

Step 3: Comply with the mandates for the agency performance plan:

- Annual agency performance plans are a mandated activity in federal strategic management systems.

- Two types of goals are required:
  - Mission-focused collaboration goals identify partners with special knowledge and skills, and with experience in dealing with problems that extend across agency boundaries.
  - Mission-support goals focus continued government efforts for streamlining administrative processes.

Step 4: Select a model for the performance management system (PMS):

- The mechanistic model relies on formal rules, standard procedures, and routines—all of which are designed to control behavior and rigid system delivery output.
- The organic model operates with greater flexibility and responsiveness.

Step 5: Adopt a strategy of performance-based system:

- Develop a reasonable level of agreement on missions, goals, and strategies for achieving the goals.
- Decide how and when to implement PMS for documenting performance and supporting decision-making.
- Plan how to use performance information as a basis for decision-making at various organizational levels.

Step 6: Take action steps to develop and implement a strategic performance management plan:

1. Create vision, mission, and values.
2. Delineate agency's roles and responsibilities.
3. Appraise the situation (e.g., SWOT analysis).
4. Determine strategies (e.g., goal-aligned or emergent).
5. Establish performance measures (e.g., baseline, annual, milestones).
6. Conduct functional analysis (e.g., strategic, unique, overlapping).
7. Conduct structural analysis (e.g., organization, clusters, units).
8. Establish coordinating teams.
9. Assign personnel and funding.
10. Assign milestones for accountability.
11. Manage and review performance.

Summary

Performance management is the process that begins with creating a productive and harmonious work environment in which workers are able to perform to the best of their abilities. A PMS includes formal and informal mechanisms, processes, systems, and networks for assisting the organization and management to carry out analysis, planning, measurement, control, rewarding, and broadly managing performance and supporting organizational learning and change. A PMS can range from a mechanistic model to an organic model. A mechanistic model relies on formal rules, standard procedures, and routines—all of which are designed to control behavior and rigid system delivery output. This control leads to close monitoring of all activities in an agency's programs and projects. An organic model operates with greater flexibility and responsiveness. Rules are basic and procedures are standardized, although tend to reflect responses to various contingency factors.

The performance management system as a means for improving performance in government agencies appeared as early as the 1960s. After several failed attempts to adopt a system for outcome-based improvements, a formal public sector performance improvement program finally took root with passage of the Government Performance and Results Act (GPRA) in 1993. Although not fully implemented until 1996, the GPRA required federal agencies to implement performance management programs that included goal-setting, measuring results in accomplishing those goals, and reporting their progress to both houses of Congress. Performance management became the mechanism for carrying out those mandates through the use of strategic planning and performance measurement systems.

Problems and gaps in the original GPRA legislation were resolved with passage of the GPRA Modernization Act (GPRAMA) in 2010 and its full implementation in January 2011. Key changes were requirements to publish plans and reports in machine-readable formats, and to identify the key external uncontrollable factors that were barriers to achieving their goals and objectives. Also included were adoption of enhanced performance planning, management and reporting activities.

The framework for implementing the GPRA is strategic performance management (SPM). Strategic performance management is an organization's system for measuring and reporting how it is accomplishing its objectives and strategies. It is a process for helping shift policy to specific goals and strategy. SPM is both high level (strategic) and low-level (integrated), linking various aspects of the organization with management of individuals and teams.

Annual agency performance plans are a mandated activity in federal strategic management systems. Objectives in the annual plan are to be associated with long-term goals spelled out in the strategic plan.

Adopting a strategy of performance-based management occurs over three steps: (1) developing a reasonable level of agreement on missions, goals, and strategies for achieving the goals; (2) deciding how and when to implement performance measurement systems for documenting performance and support decision-making; and (3) plan how to use performance information as a basis for decision-making at various organizational levels.

13

STRATEGIES FOR ORGANIZATIONAL TRANSFORMATION

Achieving a strategic transformation involves a process that includes establishing or reviewing the vision and mission of the organization, analyzing internal and external environmental factors, forming both long-term and short-term objectives, and selecting, implementing, and evaluating a strategy to accomplish those objectives. Strategic transformation activities occur over three separate but closely related stages: (1) during environmental analysis and development of a vision and mission for the organization; (2) while identifying and planning the organizational components and processes that enable agency to accomplish its mission; and (3) when crafting, selecting and prioritizing strategies, and implementing performance measurement systems, and controls.

Stage One: Environmental Analysis, Vision, and Mission

The first level of the model includes four fundamental processes. The first two are the preparatory processes of analyzing the internal and external environments. This scanning of events and trends in the environment provides the agency leadership with the background information necessary to construct long-term operational strategies.

Environmental scanning, or SWOT analysis (for strengths and weaknesses, and opportunities and threats), is the strategic management process that managers and administrators go through to identify and analyze the impact of the salient characteristics and trends in their internal and external environments. Strengths and weaknesses refer to internal capabilities, whereas opportunities and threats refer to forces outside of the organization, such as the economy, social and cultural trends, laws and politics, and similar forces beyond the control of agency managers.

This is the most challenging and, in some ways, most important element of strategic management. Anyone can forecast using linear projections of long-term trends; organizations that have the capacity to detect subtle yet important changes, both internal and external, are more likely to make successful strategic choices.

Once carried out only at the beginning of the annual budget cycle, environmental analysis has become an ongoing process in agencies practicing strategic management. The internal environment includes the culture, capabilities, and capacities of the organization that enable it to carry out its core tasks and evolve into the high-performance organizations required in today's fast-changing world. The external environment includes factors beyond the control of the agency, but which serve both as constraints to its operations and opportunities for innovative change. Together, the internal and external environments shape the progress of the agency in the conduct of its mission.

The two activities prior to strategic management are first constructing a long-term vision for the organization and, second, collaboratively forging a statement that describes for all relevant stakeholders the core mission of the organization or firm. Many, even most, public organizations have already completed the hard work of creating a mission and vision; the task for organizations undergoing strategic transformation is to review these statements and aspirations and validate that they are consistent with its changed circumstances.

The mission of the agency is a statement of what it does now, what it does best, and for whom the agency carries out its core activities. The mission statement should clearly establish how the organization's vision will be implemented; the mission-forging process requires collective agreement on the purpose of the agency. It must be a unifying statement, one that helps ensure that everyone in the agency knows where their contribution fits into the larger whole. Because it affects everyone, the mission statement must be a product of collective action. This means an administrative team must agree on the fundamental rationale for the group's existence, often by restating the original reason for which the organization was formed in light of current states of reality. The statement of organizational mission is a key management process; it establishes in everyone's mind the single, core thing that the organization does, and does best. Only under exceptional circumstances do public agencies change their missions.

Organizations engaging in strategic management for transformation engage in a two-phase analysis of their knowledge management practices. The first phase is to ask, "How can improved knowledge management help us respond to our current strategic challenge?" This will require consideration of the ways in which knowledge is collected and used, and what tacit knowledge in the organization or its network may be brought to bear on its strategic problems. The second phase, reflective of double-loop learning, is to ask, "Can improved practices of knowledge management help us prevent similar strategic failures in the future?" Part of the answer may lie in adopting digital government practices that change the interface between the agency and its clients or customers.

The IAD Framework

Institutional analysis and development (IAD) is a framework for analyzing behavior in groups and organizations and how rules, physical and material conditions, and attributes of the community of individuals affect the structure of groups and organizations and the resulting outcomes (Ostrom 2010). This framework has been used to analyze the performance of networks.

The IAD framework has been used to study how people in government organizations collaborate and organize themselves across department, agency, federal–state–local government levels and sector boundaries to manage such programs as sanitation, water resources, prevention of disease, storm damage, farming, and forests and fisheries, which often cross or flow through national boundaries.

Stage Two: Facilitating Components and Processes

The second stage of activities and decisions involves two broad sets of enabling organizational resources and organizational systems. These facilitate the functioning of the agency and provide the resources from which organizational objectives and strategies may be identified, prioritized, and implemented. Organizational resources include the culture of the agency, its distinctive competencies, and the capabilities and knowledge on hand or available to carry out its tasks. Operational systems include the information and communications technology that enhance the efficiency and effectiveness of all agency operations. They are here grouped into three sets of systems: enterprise, delivery and human resources.

Stage Three: Identifying and Selecting Strategies and Controls

The third level of activities and decisions for achieving an organization's transformation begins with using the product of the two earlier levels of analysis to set realistic and attainable agency objectives. It then turns to identifying, selecting, and prioritizing strategies for the agency to follow in order to accomplish those objectives.

The first two levels made it possible for agency leaders to firmly establish what has occurred in the past to establish the agency's "core competencies." During the actions in the third level, the administrative team must now focus on what must be accomplished in the future. In strategic management terms, this requires establishing realistic, attainable long-term objectives for every unit in the agency. The transformation cannot take root if staff members rush from fire to fire instead of working together on a set of activities built on the foundation of a vision of the long-term role of the organization, a clear, concise statement of its mission, and a set of objectives toward which the agency strives to accomplish.

Types of Change

Organizations go through different types of change depending on changes in their internal or external environments. Nadler and Tushman (1995) identified four types of change according to the rate of change (incremental or discontinuous) and scope of the changes (anticipatory or reactive), as illustrated in Figure 13.1. The organization can make the small, incremental adjustments associated with maintaining stability in its operational environment, or it can suffer through the larger, discontinuous changes necessary to adjust to instability or uncertainty in its environment. It can be a planned adaptation to meet an anticipated shift in the external environment, or it can be an unplanned transformation requiring a fundamental re-creation brought on by a threat to the organization's very existence.

Moving from an environment wherein management or staff rebels against or obstructs a change to a new and strategic orientation where the organization thrives on an orientation open to change and where innovation is paramount is not easy to bring about. Making such a move can be difficult, regardless of the motivation, as William Rouse (2005, 1) explained. He pointed out that a "complex nature of factors underlying the need for transformation may come from economic, social, political and/or technological sources." Hence, "the implications of change may be both positive and negative, with the balance between positive and negative depending on perspectives of the particular types of stakeholders impacted by the change."

	Incremental	Discontinuous (Radical)
Anticipatory (Planned)	Tuning	Reorientation
Reactive (Unplanned)	Adaptation	Transformational Re-creation

FIGURE 13.1 Types of organizational change strategies.

Source: After Nadler and Tushman (1995).

The need for a change can be anticipated and planned or it can be forced as in a reaction to unforeseen external political orientation. It can also be incremental or discontinuous change required by a catastrophic external event such as the attack on September 11, 2001, when two hijacked airliners were flown directly into the World Trade Center in New York City, causing the complete collapse of the twin towers, and a third airliner was flown into the Pentagon.

Changes can occur not only from different sources; they can also result in different reactions in the organization. For example, relatively small increments in changes to meet anticipated shifts in the environment or a planned increase in efficiency occur as regular re-tuning of the organization's operational strategies. Little negative reactions from these changes usually result. Unanticipated structural changes, however, may require significant unwelcome internal adaptation, usually occurring as significant adjustments.

When these operational changes become threatening enough, a full-scale reorientation of the organization may be required to assure sustainable delivery of services. This can mean a controversial overhaul of the management team. When the need for such discontinuous change reaches a point where the very existence of the organization is threatened, a complete transformational change for re-creating the organizational system becomes necessary. Often, the need for a complex transformation will need to be implemented in just a matter of months.

A large part of the necessary urgency of implementing a transformational re-creation of the organization occurs because of the traumatic nature of the change. Re-creation includes a change in the organization's existing identity and core values. Often, large portions of the history and goodwill built up over years of successful service will be lost, along with many loyal employees. A "piecemeal approach gets bogged down in politics, individual resistance, and organizational inertia" (Nadler and Tushman 1995, 28).

Changing to Strategic Management

Transformational change to a strategic management structure occurs in response to, or in anticipation of, unplanned, significant changes in an organization's environment, technology or by a major disruption of its organizational structure. These changes often result in a significant revision of an organization's mission and its core strategy. This, in turn, may require modifying the way the organization's members perceive, think and behave at work, as well as its corporate culture to support the new direction and target markets (Cummings and Worley 2014).

Bureaucratic models of public sector strategic management are inadequate as frameworks for planning and implementing the challenging task of organizational transformation. They are no longer comprehensive enough; they omit a knowledge management component and do not explicitly incorporate digital governance. They fail to resolve what Mintzberg (1994) identified as the critical flaw of strategic planning, the assumption that a process of analysis—breaking down reality into its component parts—can accomplish a worthwhile synthesis into adoption of a new strategy.

True transformation of a public agency is a process of change in external form or inner nature, or conversion to a new state. It transcends simple reorganization and, in our view, requires a comprehensive analysis of an organization and its various strategies. This is a relatively rare phenomenon. Audits, evaluations and investigations enable agencies to correct most ongoing difficulties with their programs and systems, while webs of interest groups act as a powerful force for organizational inertia.

In a survey of concepts and processes involved in transformational change in government agencies and private firms, researchers at Scandia National Laboratories found significant commonality between the public sector agencies and private industry in most of the key concepts associated with transformation (Slavin and Woodard 2006, 7). Salient in their findings was the following common premise that underlies transformation in both sectors (emphasis in the original):

> *For organizations facing a significant crisis, successful transformations can be characterized by an effective leader and a supporting coalition.* For the change to occur and succeed, leaders must (1) convince their organization that survival depended on changing the way it performs its core mission; (2) recognize that a new organizational paradigm is needed to bring about the change; and (3) lead the organization down the path to the new paradigm and utilizing metrics to guide the necessary change.

Transforming Work

The innovation strategy adoption process example in Figure 13.2 begins with identification and a prioritization of the problems and challenges that could lead to the need for a radical change. Transformational change processes can occur at four different work activity centers in the organization. The first involves strategies aimed at improving the way work occurs internally. While these business process improvement strategies may improve efficiency, they are least likely to bring about a lasting transformation in the agency or department.

A second body of transformation strategies involves changing the flow of work through an organization. These organization re-engineering strategies are designed to implement dramatic operational changes. Without extensive and lasting changes in the way the organization does its work, these strategies may generate a transformation, but one that is typically far less than the transformation generated by the next group of strategies. A third group of change strategies includes those designed to completely change the work that the organization performs. These organizational culture strategies are designed to transform agencies from traditional, internally focused bureaucratic organizations to client/customer-focused, high-performance, and cost-effective organizations. The fourth

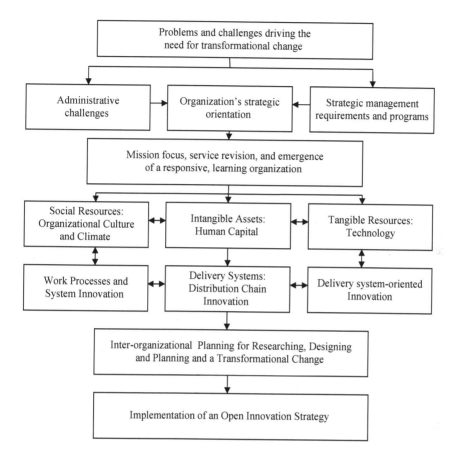

FIGURE 13.2   The processes involved in adopting an innovation strategy.

Source: After concepts in Schot and Kanger (2018).

level of transformation strategies refers to the specific characteristics of the agency's work that are engaged in the transformation process. Five such characteristics were identified: purposes, objectives, function, tasks, and activities.

Public agencies historically have slowly evolved with environmental changes and society's needs and as their own capacities have expanded or declined in response. Such an approach makes intuitive sense in a relatively slowly changing environment, but it does not acknowledge the reality that organizations may have predilections to react in other ways to environmental change. Andrews, Boyne and Walker (2006), for example, suggested that organizations have differing strategic stances that reflect their general approach to staying in alignment with their environment and improving their performance. Their typology suggests that organizations are likely to innovate (prospectors), consolidate (defenders), or wait for instructions (reactors). The "stance" of an agency, they concluded, is a relatively unchanging aspect of organizational culture and behavior.

The challenge for public agencies, however, is that the societal pace of change throughout the world is accelerating, driven by technology, economics and other forces. Data are accumulating that suggest that the increasingly linked nature of the globalized economy increases the risk of sudden systemic crises. In addition, important changes in the environment of public agencies are discontinuous, and as a result require that on occasion public agencies make abrupt changes in their mission, structure and operations. The "punctuated equilibrium" model, featuring periods of stability followed by sudden instability and organizational change, describes this reality better than the placid change of the evolutionary perspective.

Transformation Strategies

Governments have traditionally operated under a relatively inflexible organizational form that resists change. It aims to solve several serious problems, including the need to limit both the influence of special interests and the discretion of public officials, while offering reasonable efficiency. One of the key concepts in transformation research has been identifying and explaining the pillars upon which a transformation strategy is designed. Taking its use from architecture, a pillar is a column, pilaster or pillar that supports a structure. Hence, it is the central, or one of several, core ideas that make up a concept. There can be many pillars supporting the concept. The literature on organizational transformation includes a number of supporting pillars, ranging from three to nine, with four as the most popular number. In a 2014 CIO (Chief Information Officer) newsletter, Charles Araujo identified four pillars of transformation as:

1. Redefining leadership: Transformational change is not a top–down process. It will occur only when every member of [the] entire organization sees themselves as a leader in the process.
2. Bridging organizational silos: Break down negativity and self-interest silos in the organization with transparency and vision.
3. Mastering the customer equation: "The customer equation is a simple formula that says perceived value = business value + customer experience."
4. Catalyzing change: Organization leaders must openly promote their commitment to the proposed change, including a shared vision. Showing doubt and neglecting to educate workers in the changes will result in its failure.

In an article on transformation in organizations' IT operations, *Forbes* magazine contributor Daniel Newman expanded the list of pillars to six, with the notation that all are applicable in all organizations: The six pillars of digital transformation he named were (participant's prior) change experiences, people, change itself,

---

BOX 13.1 BUSINESS MODEL TRANSFORMATION UNDER WAY IN BELGIUM

In 2015, the public employment service agency for the Flemish region of Belgium (VDAB), was in the midst of a transformation designed to change its business model from a new public management model to one of digital era governance (DEG). DEG has three core concepts: bringing issues back into government control, reorganizing government around distinct client groups, and digital storage and Internet communications to transform governance. Beginning in the 1970s, the NPM approach was touted as an answer to what was seen as the gross inefficiency of the traditional bureaucratic operations that characterized the public sector. Governments in much of the world were dealing with financial crises, public discontent with the inflexibility of administrative procedures, and decreasing public trust in government (Pollitt et al. 2007). A model based on private sector management practices was proposed and quickly adopted. Under NPM, governments were expected to become more efficient, more customer oriented, and in sum, provide more value for less money.

However, NPM did not live up to its promised benefits. Administrative complexity increased, agencies became more like closed silos, and service continued to decline. The DEG model was offered as a better solution. The DEG model is said to make possible a transformation to "a more genuinely integrated, agile and holistic government, whose organizational operations are visible in detail both to the personnel operating in the fewer, broader public agencies and to the citizens" (Dunleavy et al. 2006). DEG relies on information technology (IT) to enable the transformation, while also improving the way government interacts with citizens and private sector stakeholders.

Sources: Danneels and Viaene (2015); Pollitt, Van Thiel and Homberg (2007); Dunleavy, Margetts, Bastow and Tinkler (2006)

---

innovation, leadership, and (organizational) culture. Box 13.1 describes an example of an internal transformation.

A Transformation Model

Schalock, Verdugo and Van Loon (2018) developed a model for developing and implementing an organization transformation, in which transformation pillars are combined with transformation strategies, organization capacity and organization outputs and outcomes to form a general model of transformation. Two of the four core components are context-based and two are sustainability related.

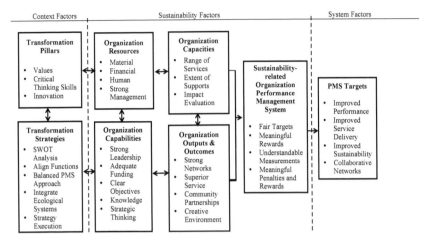

FIGURE 13.3 Organizational transformation model.

Source: After concepts in Schalock, Verdugo and Van Loon (2018).

Context-based Components

Context-based components are "complex, multifaceted, and highly interactive" phenomena that influence adoption of change. They include such factors as social, historical, political, ecological, and cultural forces. The two context-based sections of the context-based component are transformation pillars and transformation strategies. The three transformation pillars included in the Schalock et al. model are (1) the values held by managers and staff, (2) the critical thinking skills of managers and staff, and (3) the level of acceptance to, and development of, innovation in services and processes.

Transformation Pillars

Values include the beliefs, personal assumptions, generalizations and what personnel think of the organization's mission and service recipients. With a clear statement of the mission of the organization, these same values may be the same values included early in the strategic management process. An organization's values are core concepts that guide the way its managers think and act. They are the beliefs and attitudes upon which the organization operates. Its value statements tell people what the organization stands for, why it exists and what its purpose is. An example is the value statement adopted by Steele County, Minnesota: "We are responsible, accountable, respectful, effective, efficient public stewards. We promote honesty, integrity, and openness in all we do. We encourage innovation to meet challenges. We foster an environment of collaboration."

Critical thinking and decision-making are at the heart of transformation. This is because transformation requires making decisions, the results of which can have extensive impact on the organization, its employees and the clients it serves. It is for this purpose that critical thinking is considered a core competency in strategic management. In this application, a competency should be considered the "integration and mobilization of knowledge, abilities and skills, attitudes as well as values which are developed when solving problems" (Bezanilla et al. 2019).

Innovation is the third transformation pillar in the Schalock et al. context-related component. Managers and staff must be open to innovative approaches and methods in how they design strategies for the transformation of an organization. As noted in Figure 13.1, there are two approaches to innovation: incremental (or discontinuous) or radical. Because an incremental change is usually a modification to an earlier approach, it is low risk, usually only mildly innovative, and therefore more popular than a discontinuous change, where a radical approach is more complex and inherently more difficult and with greater risk to the organization's sustainability.

Transformation Strategies

The model lists five context-based transformation strategies that coincide with five critical thinking skills, as shown in Table 13.1.

TABLE 13.1 Critical thinking skills and transformation strategies

Critical Thinking Skill	Examples	Associated Transformation Strategy
Analysis	Examine and evaluate component parts Determine what hinders/facilitates change	Analyze environments
Alignment	Bring processes into logical sequences	Align organization functions
Holism	See transformation as a complete system Incorporate multiple perspectives	Balanced approach to PMS
Systems	Focus on systems that affect human functioning Integrate all systems into thinking	Integrate ecological systems
Synthesis	Integrate information from multiple sources Base strategic execution on communications, multilevel leadership, network partnerships and data engagement	Employ strategic execution

Source: After material in Schalock et al. (2018, 55)

Sustainability Components

Sustainability components are any factors that form the organization's ability to adapt successfully to transformational changes. The two sustainability components are the organization capacity and the organization's outputs and outcomes. Both of these components affect the ability of the organization to deliver its public goods or services and its ability to adopt new or different practices that enhance the value of its outputs and outcomes.

Organizational Capacities

The organization's capacities are the product of the transformation pillars and strategies. Together with the organization's resources, strong capacities make it possible to provide a wide range of services and supports to the individuals and groups it serves. Capacity-building is, therefore, a major focus of transformation. Regular monitoring of the organization's environments and resource base ensure it is able to anticipate changes that require a major transformation of its structure and focus. Analysis and performance feedback ensure the sustainability of its ability to provide the outputs for which it was established and the outcomes reflect the organization's strategic goals.

Figure 13.3 is a conceptual model developed from concepts in Schalock et al. (2018) that lists the components of designing and implementing a performance management system. In the past, many public organizations had the luxury of working in placid environments and making occasional changes to their primary strategies. Conducting a SWOT analysis at the beginning of the process is a step for alleviating these difficulties. Small adaptations to process difficulties unearthed in the analysis can improve performance sufficiently to keep an organization in equilibrium with its environment. They can also satisfy stakeholders that errors are being corrected.

Implementing Strategic Change

In their seven-year study of patterns in strategic change, Dominguez, Galán-González and Barroso (2015) found that changes in an organization's strategic focus are a natural occurring and reoccurring activity, whereas periods of strategic change are relatively rare. Although strategic change is the predominant state of affairs in organizations, the rate of change varies in both intensity and duration.

Strategic changes occur more often as a result of changes in an organization's external environment than as a result of internal changes. The motivation for a strategy change comes from multiple sources, with different levels of influence on the organization. At the federal level, these forces for a change can range from a change of administrations, political changes in either or both Houses of Congress, pressure groups, environmentalists, political parties, lobbyists, or civil society pressures.

Organizational transformation refers to deep, fundamental, often radical changes in an organization's mission, strategy, structures, systems, and culture, rather than incremental change and improvement. Guidance for implementing a transformative change are provided in the following steps:

Step 1: Identify the stages for conducting the strategic transformation process:

- Stage one: Conduct an environmental analysis and develop vision and mission for the organization.
- Stage two: Plan and design the organizational components and processes that enable the agency to accomplish its mission.
- Stage three: Craft, select and prioritize strategies and implement performance measurement and control systems.

Step 2: Select organizational change strategies and processes:

- Choose either one of the four types of change strategies:
  - *Turning*: Initiate incremental changes to meet anticipated environmental shifts, or a planned increase in efficiency occurs as regular re-tuning of the strategies.
  - *Reorientation*: A full-scale organizational change may be required to assure sustainable delivery of (public) services.
  - *Adaptation*: Unanticipated structural changes may require significant unwelcome internal adaptation of the environment.
  - *Recreation*: Transformational change occurs in response to significant changes in an organization's environment, technology or by a major disruption of its organizational structure.
- Transformation change processes can occur in four areas:
  - business process improvement;
  - re-engineering the organizational structure and processes;
  - organizational culture and change strategies;
  - transform organizational characteristics such as purposes, objectives, tasks, and activities.

Step 3: Identify and select the transformation "pillars" to formulate organizational transformation strategies:

- redefining leadership, bridging organizational silos, mastering the customer perceived value, and catalyzing change (Araujo 2014);
- participants' prior change experiences, people, change itself, innovation, leadership, and organizational culture (Newman 2018);
- values (held by managers and staff), the critical thinking skills (of managers and staff), and the level of acceptance to, and development of, innovation in services and processes (Schalock et al. 2018).

Step 4: Implement organizational transformation strategies:

- Apply Schalock et al.'s (2018) *General Model of Organizational Transformation* (Figure 13.3) for developing and implementing organization transformation:
  - context-based components: transformation pillars (i.e., value, critical thinking, and innovation) and transformation strategies (e.g., SWOT, balanced PMS approach, and strategy execution); combined with
  - sustainability components: organizational capacities (e.g., range of services and extent of supports) and organization output and outcomes.
- Alternatively, a *"strategy restoration"* strategy, which is an organization's reinterpretation and re-enactment of discontinued aspects of its historical strategy for present use and for the sake of enhancing future performance, can be implemented for organizational transformation.

Step 5: Continue reviewing and revising the organizational transformation strategies and processes to adapt to the changing environment.

Summary

Designing and carrying out a strategic transformation for adoption of new or revised goals requires a close review of the organization's mission and vision, as well as its internal and external environmental factors. Naturally, the organization's operational leadership must also revise its objectives and select, implement and closely monitor performance toward achievement of those objectives.

Traditionally, managers transforming their organizations follow a pattern of change that leads them from the constraints of a failure-leaning past toward a promised future. Even then, the change will tend to follow an incremental process rather than a dramatic revolutionary 180-degree shift. Incremental change can then be continuous, or it is adaptive, as when an agency suffers a steep reduction in budget allocation. However, a small number of researchers have suggested that some organizations are instead re-evaluating their past strategies and are modifying their historical strategies in what they term "strategy restoration." Strategic restoration is defined as "an organization's reinterpretation and reenactment of discontinued aspects of its historical strategy for present use and for the sake of enhancing future performance" (Miller, Gomes and Lehman 2019, 2).

Three characteristics of the proposed reconsideration of previous strategies are included in the conceptualization: First, strategic restoration is cross-functional, involves multiple members of the organization in pursuit of the organization's goals, and functions at the organization level of strategic design. Restored and revised organization values, beliefs, practices, process and structure may play a role in the transformation.

Second, only discontinued aspects of the organization's own previous strategies are included in the restoration. Nor can the strategies or elements of strategies of other organizations be included in the concept. Third, strategic restoration is not an end in itself, nor is it a strategy in itself. It is not a new strategy; rather, it is undertaken as a contribution to development of a new strategy for enhancing an organization's future operations.

PART IV

Implementing Strategic Management

14

STRATEGIC MANAGEMENT AT WORK

Although the tools associated with strategic management have been available at least since the 1970s or earlier, it was not until the 1990s that its practices and processes became widely used in public agencies. Despite that slow willingness to adopt these practices wholesale, the tools for facilitating strategic transformation are now widely used management practices in public management (Kang 2005). As Ingraham, Joyce and Donahue (2003, 2) note, "effective management is basic to the overall effectiveness of government." Government administrators regularly employ environmental analysis, strategic planning, strategy formulation and implementation, performance measurement, and strategic allocation of resources—admittedly sometimes in piecemeal fashion, but increasingly together in a comprehensive application of the strategic management concept.

Strategic management has been adopted as an integrative approach to managing an organization. It centers on designing enterprise-wide strategies and focusing agency activities toward accomplishment of management-established goals and objectives; it is managing with a purpose. It is particularly important in the public sector in light of the far-reaching shifts taking place in the internal and external environments of government.

Role of Strategy in Strategic Management

To achieve the change needed in many public organizations—to create new ways for coping with altered conditions and for managing resources astutely—organizations must capitalize on the existing, widespread internal commitment of their staff members. Commitment to an organization's mission and structure cannot be expected unless the employees have a belief in, and are ready to accept, the organization's goals and the values held in common. They must become eager to work hard for the organization—behavior that is often expressed in terms of wanting to remain an active member. The good news is that this commitment does exist in varying degrees in most government agencies. Where it has disappeared, bringing it back should be the first goal of the agencies' leaders.

Demand for reform of public management has become a call with which public managers at all levels of government are very familiar. They are besieged with calls by elected officials, candidates for public office, senior executive branch officials, members of public and private organizations lobbying for their interests, and by private citizens who see that changing the way governments operate is the solution to a host of public ills. On one hand, the manager is told that wasting the taxpayers' dollar must stop; on the other hand, the public manager is told to do more with less. A cry heard around the globe is that government must change.

This unwillingness to commit to the organization or a subsequent failure to achieve a transformation initiative was clearly displayed in the inability of the managers of a small unit of the General Services Administration (GSA) to implement a total quality management program. Although they assessed the culture, agency administrators neglected to do the follow-on work necessary to stimulate commitment among the unit's personnel. Senior administrators were not willing to face up to the issues and problems the assessment revealed. As a result, the transformation effort failed before it even began. Similar results were reported in the failure of a local public safety organization to implement commitment measures.

Commitment Antecedents

Balfour and Wechsler (1990, 1996) identified three antecedents to describe their causal model of commitment: (1) identification commitment, where employees describe their agency as valuable and respected by the public, one that makes important public contributions, and is regarded as capable and effective; (2) affiliation commitment, which is perceived by employees when organization members are seen as caring, and who value belonging to a close-knit organization that values the individual and their wellbeing; and (3) *exchange commitment*, which employees accept as more than extrinsic rewards, like money, to mean that public organizations recognize employee contributions, and then show concern by providing support and encouragement for this commitment (Figure 14.1).

Mazouz and Tremblay (2006) examined the role of organizational commitment to strategies for public management and administrative reform by the government of Canada. Successful government reforms depend upon three factors: citizen satisfaction with the outcomes, the flexibility of the new structures, and the commitment of staff to accept the new management methods that include performance measurement, accountability, efficiency and economy (doing more with less), ethics compliance, and evaluation of outputs.

An important finding of their study revealed that the supervisors who created supportive and productive social relationships motivated commitment more than

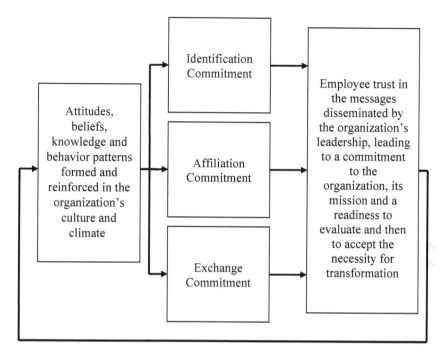

FIGURE 14.1 Antecedents to an organizational commitment to a change initiative.

Source: The authors.

any of the other variables of participation, political penetration, and opportunities for advancement. Whether administrators can bring about this commitment, therefore, depends in large part upon their understanding of what motivates commitment, and whether they can forge a *culture* in their public organization that fosters employee commitment, and rewards this behavior.

To improve their ability to adjust to the changes occurring in their operating environment, administrators at public agencies must find ways to adjust their organizations in ways that will re-establish commitment to public service. Without this commitment, it may not be possible to meet the challenges they face in this new century. The first step in bringing this change about is to reinforce the *service ethos* in the organization. The second is to take cues from the reactions of employees to the revitalized culture to alleviate negative conditions by adjusting the operating climate.

How Cultural Factors Constrain Change Efforts

The forces for change confronting administrators in government organizations are rooted in the distinctly altered economic, administrative and social environments and the organizational cultures that these produce. Among the cultural factors pressing public agency administrators are: (1) an ageing worker population; (2) growth in the numbers of minorities and women entering the public workforce; (3) privatization and outsourcing of once-public services and functions with a loss of a culture of service to society; (4) some perceived decline in government workers' commitment to quality in service and performance; (5) requirements to establish and function by rigid performance standards; (6) restrictions on governments' ability to generate revenue resulting in income demands by workers that cannot be met; and (7) continued erosion in the public's trust in government (Ventriss 2000).

Together, these and other pressures are causing a decline in young workers' commitment to public service, which has resulted in reduced ability to attract and retain skilled employees. Moreover, these changes are diminishing many of the long-term public administration commitments to such service values as equity, stewardship, public spiritedness, and citizenship (Felts and Joss 2000).

Impact on Government Agencies

For public agencies, some of the impacts of these environmental forces have been slashed departmental budgets, competition for shares of the diminishing tax revenues, service delays or breakdowns, scarcity of skilled workers, and heightened demands for environmental accountability. These, in turn, have created the public administrator's dilemma of meeting growing demands for service with fewer resources.

Public agencies that once saw themselves as indispensable and above public reproach have not been protected from these external pressures. The growing gap between rising demand for services and limited resources characterizes many departments at all levels of government, resulting in high turnover and job-related stress. The most severely restricted agencies suffer from a condition called "general service default," where government can no longer deliver the services that enhance or protect the life of their citizens.

How Increasing Diversity Drives Organizational Change

The increasing diversity of the U.S. population is having a large impact on how public agencies hire, motivate, and retain government workers. A more diverse citizenry has meant new client and customer expectations, needs and wants for public agencies. This diversity springs from the shifts occurring in the demographic make-up of society at large. Each group demands their "fair share" of the pool of limited resources; their demands are expressed at the ballot box—without recognition or concern for the costs. An environment of *resource scarcity* with increasing demands for services and the imposition of strict performance measures results in what are called *unfunded mandates*.

The compelling need for organizational transformation has created a simultaneous requirement for shifts in the way human resources policy and strategy is developed and implemented in public organizations. Time has rendered obsolete and ineffective the stable economic and social environments that once fostered tried-and-true ways of doing things (Andrews, Boyne and Walker 2006; Cappelli et al. 1997; Goldsmith 1997).

Need for a New Operating Ethos

Many believe that government organizations are badly in need of a new operating ethos. If not new, then at least a return to the ethos of unselfish commitment to public service that once characterized many in the government workforce. Commitment, however, assumes that those who choose public service have a set of values that prepares them for what is often described as societal disdain for their work and performance.

Pattakos (2004) reminds us that public employees are searching for meaning at work, and while employment security may have been a reason for choosing public service as a career, they truly want to make a genuine difference through their work. It is common for employees to want to add value to their organization and the citizens they serve.

Because of the many changes that have taken place in government over the past decade, the *ethos of service* has lost much of its power to motivate government workers and administrators Some of the more salient changes include privatization, taxing restrictions, mandated reforms such as the Americans with Disabilities legislation and equal opportunity laws, the imposition of user fees, the introduction of total quality initiatives, unique performance measurements, citizen "interference" in government using active involvement in the initiative process, and other actions.

Changing the Management Culture

Three different strategies are possible for changing a management culture in organizations. The commonly heard phrase, "Culture is the way we do things around here," represents one approach in that it refers to reinforcing the good or desired aspects of the existing culture. It occurs internally by appointing trustworthy individuals to promote the existing desired cultural elements.

A second approach occurs when agency managers try to change the values of people in the agency. This is typically a top–down method of instituting a change initiative. This approach fails as often as it succeeds, particularly when the change is mandated from above without first gaining acceptance of the change and commitment to a common goal that includes acceptance of change.

The third process occurs when employees accept that others do things differently "over there." That is, the members of the group come to recognize that other groups function differently—and that the difference is okay. If this idea is accepted, the group is more likely to accept—without changing—the members of the different culture. The third method is followed when public sector managers, like their counterparts in for-profit organizations, practice management by walking around (MBWA), thus communicating the point that they share in the values and actions of the organization.

Once one of these strategies is selected, government managers have greater success in their change process if they bring citizens into the process as co-creators of the service(s) the agency will provide, rather than looking on stakeholders as impediments to their work. Pattakos (2004) illustrated this point by describing the experience of a public manager—who often complained of burnout from dealing everyday with what he called the *mindless bureaucracy*—who has found a way to revitalize his passion for his work. When his frustration resurfaces, he heads to the "front lines," where he works side by side with the employees who provide the agency's service to citizens. By helping citizens find ways to ameliorate community problems, he is able to recharge his commitment to public service. In doing so, he also reinforces this culture element among his staff.

Shifting Administrative Thinking

Critical observers of public administration have often pointed to what they see as the stifling nature of policies and procedures that are perpetuated in the Weberian model of bureaucratic agencies (Thompson 2000). These critics also point to what they term the "mindless repetition" that characterizes many public service occupations—the postal service is often cited as an example.

Unfortunately, it is true that work environments that lack challenge, or are driven by directives from above that never ask for feedback or improvement suggestions, can and do curtail change initiatives. Public managers must be alert, therefore, to any change-inhibitors (policies) that inhibit employees from contributing new ideas for meeting their job responsibilities. They must be alert to reward systems that benefit a few and ignore the many who contribute to the organization's success and structures that promote routine thinking and decision-making.

Public administrators today find themselves forced to refocus their goals, design new strategies and embrace organizational transformation and commitment in order to improve productivity, quality and stakeholder satisfaction. Organizations that have been successful in revitalizing their public service ethos have done so through a process that entails transforming from a bureaucratic to a learning organization culture, together with a renewed shared belief in the future. Public administrators and managers have found that the culture and climate that led to their success in the past renders them ill equipped to launch transformation efforts that are needed today.

Simply acknowledging that a need for transformation exists is, by itself, no guarantee of success. Successful transformation is likely to occur only when key conditions of organizational health are present (Beer, Eisenstat and Spector 1990). Of course, organizational transformation will not eliminate diversity, nor will it automatically result in a coming together of beliefs or values.

Changing the Values of the Government Workforce

In addition to their own distinctive culture, all organizations have their own unique operating *climate*. Climate refers to the valence of values, norms, and attitudes, behaviors and feelings that exist in an organization, and which distinguish it from all other organizations. Climate also refers to the level and form of organizational support, openness, supervisory style, conflict, autonomy and quality of relationships existing in an organization (Lewicki, Bowen and Hall 1988).

Managers in public organizations share a broad common set of values. This ethos holds that public administrators manage for the will of the public, and that government is a public trust to be used for the common good and not for special interests. The shape and strength of these values held in common are a reflection of the degree to which agency members commit to this culture of public service. This ethos of service—the *democratic ethos* of public administration—is based on these key beliefs:

1. Government administrators are servants of the public, not the other way around.
2. Public officials should embody all the public virtues; they are hardworking, honest, wise, sincere, etc.
3. Public administrators are loyal to their superiors and their organization; they subordinate their own interests to those of the group. If they disagree with the mission, they should leave office.
4. Public administrators perform their duties efficiently and economically, with the greater good of the public always in mind.
5. Merit alone should be the basis for appointment to public office, not privilege.
6. Public officials are subject to the law just as are all other citizens.

These and other common values manifest themselves in different ways, depending on the function and mission of each organization and the leadership styles of senior managers. These different manifestations make up what is seen and measured as the *organizational climate* of public agencies.

The attitudes, values and expectations of people in the organization have a direct influence on organizational climate. Many climate problems emerge when staff members perceive that a discrepancy exists between what they believe is the cultural norm of the organization—the attitudes, personal values and expectations—and the way senior managers act.

The term *disequilibrium* can be used to describe this discrepancy in beliefs and norms—what Rouse (2005) referred to as *value deficiencies*. Disequilibrium is exemplified by such symptoms as deteriorating staff morale, supervisors and managers questioning whether the organization can survive under existing strategies, and by increasing demands for autonomy by highly skilled, technical staff members. The operating climate in organizations emerges from an interaction of people functioning in the organization's basic underlying culture. Thus, the active participation of a staff that is committed to the organization's success is a prerequisite for organizational climate to shift from disequilibrium to equilibrium.

Involving the Entire Organization

When administrators fail to involve the entire organization in the process of diagnosing organizations and transformation planning, little long-term gain is achieved. Without a total commitment to change, the transformation attempt may either reinforce disequilibrium in the organization or result only in cosmetic change or short-term gains. A study on changes in the nature of work and work organization sponsored by the National Planning Association contained this caveat:

> [Transformation] actions taken singly, research studies suggest, tend to achieve few enduring gains.... Studies of the introduction of new information technologies, lean production, work force reductions (downsizing) ... for example, reveal that alterations in each of these areas without parallel changes in the culture, compensation, and reporting structure of the (organization) tend to leave the intended effects largely stillborn.
> *(Capelli et al. 1997, 53–4)*

Interaction often obfuscates the deeper, difficult-to-measure, underlying culture. However, climate may serve as a surrogate measure of the organization's culture. An example of the blurred definition of culture and climate may help to underscore the relative importance of both. When moving pictures were first invented, those who began to explore how to turn still pictures into action asked how they could move the still shots quickly enough to give the impression of a life-like moving picture, or how they could move many still pictures rapidly in front of a lens to give the effect of a moving picture.

There in an enduring need to capture still pictures of where the organization is *right now* in terms of the perceptions of organization members regarding an organization's explicit and implicit values, assumptions and practices (Ashkanasy et al. 2000). This also requires keeping track of the changes that take place over time.

Steven Kelman (2005) described the importance of engaging people in the process of implementing changes in the federal government while also suggesting that the conventional idea that people naturally resist change is often oversimplified and misleading. However, he agrees that staff discontent—or disequilibrium—in government organizations is frequently a block to successful organizational change initiatives.

Steps to Follow in the Change Process

Programs to change an organization typically follow a series of clearly defined steps. The elements or pressure points in the organizational culture and climate must be identified and evaluated. Evaluation includes estimating the power of the problem to influence the ability of the agency to perform their mission and accomplish agency goals and objectives. Embarking on the process, base-line measurements of the key disruptive characteristics are taken, using either a diagnostic survey or participant observation process. The complete six-step process is illustrated in Figure 14.2.

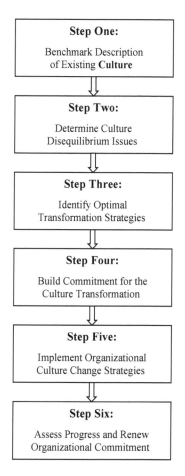

Step One:

Benchmark Description of Existing **Culture**

Step Two:

Determine Culture Disequilibrium Issues

Step Three:

Identify Optimal Transformation Strategies

Step Four:

Build Commitment for the Culture Transformation

Step Five:

Implement Organizational Culture Change Strategies

Step Six:

Assess Progress and Renew Organizational Commitment

FIGURE 14.2 Changing organizational culture for a transformation.

Source: The authors.

Step One: Identify Potential Culture-Based Problem(s)

Step one is the detailed description of an organizational climate in which one or more problems exist or acknowledging a human barrier to needed change. This move may be prompted by disgruntled employees or unhappy citizens, or from higher administrative levels. A typical change driver is when leaders in top government positions decide that they have to finally act on the numerous voter complaints about government incompetence, malfeasance, or money wasting. Harvey and Brown (2001) mentioned some of the normal causes experienced during an organization's lifecycle of this awareness of the need to change, such as rapid organizational growth or precipitous decline in a client population. They also identified problems arising from technology changes or changes in an agency's external environment.

Culture Through the Organization Lifecycle

The idea that every organization has a lifecycle is appropriate here because too many public service agencies are accused of having entered the decline stage. Many government products and services become obsolete, which in turn causes members of organizations to protect resources and avoid confrontation with vocal clients who demand better services. Unfortunately, unlike private sector organizations, where customers can find new and better companies who offer a similar service, there are usually no close substitutes for local, state, or federal services; customers are forced to accept outdated service or methods of delivery.

Before resources are used more effectively, top administrators must feel and be able to react to a real threat. Or, they must experience extreme client or personnel dissatisfaction, or receive notice that a cut in funding will be forthcoming. A transformation process will not be initiated until the severity of the problem attracts the attention of those with power to act.

Threat, or felt need, is only a necessary first step in the process. What is more important is that those in control place the problem in a position of top priority for action to be taken. This must be followed by some means to cause lower-level managers and employees to fully embrace the change as a priority item as well.

Kurt Lewin (1951) described this first part of change as the *unfreezing phase*. This phase requires the introduction of new information, or some new experience that may cause those involved to stop and question their values, or why what they have been doing is now under close scrutiny. Pain need not be the motivator to cause managers to reflect on which values are undermining effectiveness, but something has to signal that a change is needed; without the recognition of disharmony or disequilibrium, no change can begin.

Step Two: Identify Problem Issues

Step two is the first action step in the process: the assessment of issues behind the disequilibrium. This step is where people and their attitudes and behaviors come under scrutiny. It has been stressed that assessment cannot be done successfully without trust in the organization. This step involves three phases that begin with an assessment of organization culture. Estimates have placed the retirement eligibility of senior career government managers at close to 70% by 2010 (Ingraham, Selden and Moynihan 2000), with few individuals seeking public jobs because they have heard too many stories about lazy, dishonest workers on the take, who have few career opportunities.

The ideology of public service, with divergent attitudinal values (Pattakos 2004, 197), makes the changing of values and behavior problematic. The examination must include (1) cultural components, like the rituals (repetitiveness, and the routine nature of most jobs and tasks), (2) the meanings of workplace arrangements and artifacts (the same customer reception area, with sequential numbers creating a long line similar to a bread line during a depression), and (3) the organizational stories that breathe life into the organization. Only then will the manager fully understand what needs to be changed first to start the transformation process.

Another area that must be evaluated is the *external* environment of the agency. This includes the public agencies and private companies that can provide the same or similar services or substitutes for the services government agencies provide. This can become a very complex question, due in part to the partnerships that have been created between public agencies and outside organizations who do some, but not all, of the work.

These difficulties are often experienced in public works departments. For example, private companies who can resurface or repair a road, or install a sewer line, compete for government work—all under the close supervision of public agency personnel.

Step Three: Identify Optimal Change Strategies

Assessment must be done to identify specific public sector performance and needs, for evaluating potential appropriate transformation strategies. Here it involves identifying the barriers to change, building support for a more robust mission statement, identifying the employees in the agency who will not only participate in the needed decisions, and who can solicit and obtain ideas from their colleagues regarding acceptable change strategies. Most stories of public agencies that have taken the transformation journey emphasize the value of proper evaluation in reducing or overcoming resistance to change as a necessary first step.

Research suggests that any potential resistance to change may appear before any official announcement of the changes is forthcoming. Such resistance is often preceded by inaccurate and negative rumors (Smeltzer 1991). Similar to identifying resistance to change, it is also important to try to anticipate which forces in the organization might block the implementation of the transformation program.

Example concepts include: (1) fear of the unknown (not enough information has been provided explaining what will happen, and why); (2) fear of loss of benefits (will I gain something I need, or lose something of equal importance?); (3) fear of a threat to one's security and position power (is there a chance that the power I now have in my current job will diminish, and if so, will I be replaced by someone else?); or (4) fear of being forced to accept new norms, and work with new and different people (will they be people I don't like or who don't like me?).

Harvey and Brown (2001) have created a change model that takes into consideration two variables that occur whenever a change program is considered: the first is the extent of change, and the second is the impact of the change on the culture. Their four-cell matrix displayed in Figure 11.1 illustrates success probabilities and the need for a change manager to consider both variables in terms of their minor and major impact on both variables. For example, if a change is predicted to be major, but the impact on culture is minor, the change manager can expect some employee resistance, with a moderate to high chance of success (Harvey and Brown 2001, 167).

Fortunately, researchers have provided a number of techniques which managers may employ to lessen anticipated resistance to change initiatives. Six methods to reduce resistance, together with notes regarding timing and appropriate use and the advantages and disadvantages for each, are: education and communication, participation and involvement, facilitation and support, negotiation and agreement, manipulation and co-optation, and explicit and implicit coercion.

Harvey and Brown (2001) added five additional methods to the list: creation of a vision, leadership, reward systems, creation of a climate conducive to communications, and power strategies. A list of "grab bag" options for reinvention includes the following:

1.   Empower citizens.
2.   Encourage competitors and government deregulation.
3.   Use mission-driven leaders who follow a more entrepreneurial approach.
4.   Encourage some form of quality initiative.
5.   Decentralize agencies from central administrative decision-making executives.
6.   Suggest privatization as a way to encourage a budgetary and for-profit mentality.
7.   Initiate a top–down reform of the civil service.

Another important consideration for organizations considering a reinvention or transformation program is the target of their efforts—employee empowerment, better control over the budget, reduction in the number of employees, or strategic management initiatives (Durst and Newell 1999).

Step Four: Build Bottom–up Commitment for Change

When administrators talk about building commitment, they generally mean getting employees to buy into the process of a planned change. It has been suggested that if employees were given an active role in structuring the change, they would have a greater commitment to and accountability for the outcomes because they have a practical view of how the organization really works.

Crewson (1997) defined organizational commitment as a combination of three distinct factors: a strong belief and acceptance of the organization's goals and values, eagerness to work hard for the organization, and a desire to remain a member of the organization. Feelings of commitment to organizations are usually due to job experiences or employee perspectives that something important is happening at the workplace, and that they feel respected and capable of doing a challenging job. The process involves encouraging contributions from staff on the question of how to generate a new, better environment in which employees are willing to accept change (Pattakos 2004).

It is necessary to know the causes of resistance before an employee's lack of commitment to the workplace can be changed. Ingraham et al. (2000) summarized the need for a reciprocal relationship that will ensure commitment. If employees are given appropriate rewards, needed incentives, and development opportunities, they will provide the needed skills and expertise, using a solid capacity to reach higher limits of performance. Good leaders should then expect employees to provide high-quality work or services to community customers, base reciprocity on recognition.

Remember that the common definition of employee commitment includes a connection between the relative strength of an employee's identification with the firm and the activity of the organization. This reinforces the concept of the value of employee participation in work-related decisions. Others have supported the view that employee participation in planned organization change helps employees attain higher-order needs and decreases resistance to change. Finally, it may be safe to say that employees—in both public and private sector jobs—will have higher levels of organizational commitment if they also have a high level of intrinsic motivation. This motivation comes from feelings that their jobs are important and that they are recognized for their achievements.

Step Five: Implement Change Strategies

This step requires the organization to first ask employees to help in the change effort, and then to empower them to not only make improvement suggestions, but to be held accountable for the accomplishment of these suggestions, when adopted. This is the *experimentation and search* step. This means that employees are given provisional decision-making authority for some improvement in their department(s), or what is called *trial implementation*. If successful, another department may try an experimental improvement strategy—provided they are given the power to try this in their department before it is tried elsewhere. If step four is done properly, implementation should be relatively easy.

Public managers can ask for employee "ownership" of the needed changes, but employees will not commit to a transformation process until they believe they have the power to change the nature of their jobs and procedures. A major antecedent here is internalization of the desired behaviors and attitudes. This can only happen if public service employees are actively involved in all of the change steps. The experience of the FBI in implementing its transformation initiative after 9/11 is an example of the difficulty government agencies encounter in attempts to transform the way they operate and how they are structured.

The best path in a transformation such as that which the FBI has attempted may be to move slowly, taking incremental steps rather than an immediate upheaval. Administrators must find pockets of support among employees who are eager to try something new. These willing staff members may be new to the organization or may have received the necessary information through the proper channels to eliminate the gossip and stories that precede actual implementation.

It is also wise to try a test case of the chosen transformation initiative, and to remember that even though jobs may be changed in one area and others outsourced, when the employees themselves do the analysis and contribute to the suggested transformation strategy, chances of its success are vastly improved. As employees gain confidence in their own successes, they learn a valuable lesson in self-renewal. When they have seen a change be successful and had a hand in its implementation, they will either use it again or will help others make the change.

This works well until they meet with resistance from their colleagues who were not informed why improvement is needed and question what they will gain if they cooperate. There are many change strategies that can make the improvement process work, but it is up to the top managers to employ competent human resource managers who have the necessary skills to introduce and discuss the needed change strategies, and to allow workers to feel empowered.

Step Six: Assess Progress and Renew Commitment

Regretfully, the assessment step is too often not included in a culture change or renewal program. However, assessing progress is critical if, once the desired change is under way, the culture *refreezing* process is to take hold. An essential part of this step is the use of rewards and other incentives to perpetuate the new system or to revitalize the government agency. To be meaningful, rewards must be tied to the evaluation of the change program. If change is needed, employees must assess adopted solutions and generate new and possibly different strategies to overcome the drawbacks of an adopted solution. If things have changed in the external community/environment or internally due to an influx of new employees with different values and attitudes, there must be a new commitment for a new problem.

Plan, Do, Check, Act

Tying rewards to change commitment is similar to the "plan, do, check, act" process. No process can remain static, but should be constantly re-evaluated so that when needed, new processes to meet new customer requirements are ready. Step six is all about continuously improving the processes that have been improved, because the citizens have changed, or the external community competition has become more influential with customers, or new budgetary restrictions require a belt-tightening to keep the organization afloat.

Harvey and Brown (2001) suggested a somewhat different title for step six, calling it a *continuous improvement process.* This is because they believed that their label clearly stated the objective of the step, which is more than assessment and commitment. It is never being happy with the current situation, but instead being eager to ask if something could be done differently to improve customer service. High-performing agencies recognize that their clients are partners in the improvement process.

This six-step model presents a process to introduce organizational transformation, or reinvention. This process can work and make public service agencies exceptional places to work, providing employees with challenge, ownership of the processes they suggest should be changed, and a desire to remain an active member because they have made a difference in their world, and that of citizens who now have respect for the changed and improved government agency.

Summary

Strategic management has proven itself to be an answer to the need to assess the organizational culture and climate prior to embarking on a strategic planning process. The model illustrates the antecedents of staff commitment to the organization and the change process in organizations. It then introduced a six-step model of the organizational culture change process.

The need for more and more sector inclusive organizational networking has created a requirement for a change in the way public policy and strategy is developed and implemented in public organizations. The once relatively stable economic and social environments that once fostered tried-and-true ways of doing things has been rendered obsolete and ineffective. Government organizations need a new operating paradigm and a revitalized commitment to an ethos of unselfish public service. Commitment, however, assumes that those who choose public service have a set of values that prepares them for what is described as societal disdain for their work and performance. As the study of public organizations mentioned in the chapter illustrate, attaining that commitment and its commensurate readiness to accept change is problematic.

15

STRATEGIC PLANNING REFRESHER

Strategic planning (SP) is the physical demonstration of how to implement strategic goals. It is a required activity in most budget units in the federal, state agency and major municipal departments. SP consists of a combination of elements from three planning models: The combination adopts elements of capital planning, asset management planning, and financial planning. There is no one best way to combine these planning tools, although a traditional set of activities have evolved. This chapter is included as a refresher on the core elements of strategic planning for agency managers by helping provide answers for these fundamental questions:

Who We Are and What is Our Purpose?

Describing an Organization's Mission

In the July–August 1960 edition of the *Harvard Business Review*, marketing professor Theodore C. Levitt suggested that companies often get into trouble because they forget to define the question of what business they are really in when seeking new markets or otherwise adopting a growth or innovation strategy. They base their growth strategies on their own business goals rather than focusing on the needs and wants of customers. Or, they define their operation too narrowly. An example cited by Levitt was the motion picture industry that got into trouble with the advent of home television when the studio leaders defined their business as making movies rather than providing entertainment to their viewers. Myopia was akin to wearing blinders to ensure a limited focus. Accordingly, defining a business or a government service from a myopic perspective results in the company or agency ignoring the many growth or service opportunities and possibilities which might exist. Avoiding mission myopia therefore calls for managers to do the following:

1   Be as client focused as possible when planning.
2   Be always innovative in both services and processes.
3   Regularly monitor the changing needs and wants of clients and stakeholders.
4   Regularly improve core capabilities.
5   Adopt new innovative service delivery strategies depending on client feedback.

Establishing a Vision

Establishing a vision for what you believe an agency or utility will look like at some agreed upon date in the future is perhaps one of the most difficult tasks in the strategic planning process. For a commercial business, that future date could be any time from three to five years in the future. However, water utilities function on a longer time span. Infrastructure projects can take five or more years before they are implemented. Thus, strategic planning for a water utility is often for even longer time periods. A vision must therefore be focused on from 10 to 20 years.

The vision formation step in strategic planning is problematic because no one can predict with total accuracy the impact of all the future forces in the water environment. Too many of both internal and external uncontrollable forces will have an influence on the outcome. A vision is what the organization's administrators and managers want the utility to be in five, ten or twenty years in the future; no one can consistently predict what the future will be. The strategic plan includes the decisions that the leaders will make for that vision to come to pass. The long-term operational decisions for achieving that vision of the future are, in a sense, based on the best guess that the administrators and managers believe will happen, and how the decisions they make now will be affected by what they believe that the future environment will be like. What they can be assured will happen is that changes will occur, and they must be ready to react positively to those changes. Changes will vary in many ways in these and other ways:

*   The regulatory environment changes that utilities will have to do to comply with are influenced by unforeseen political pressures.
*   The utility's service requirements in their community will either be greater as a result of population growth or far less because of outward migration.
*   The population in most of the developed world is ageing; along with this change in demographics are changes in water consumption patterns.
*   Climate change-influenced changes in weather patterns will result in more water for some regions and less for others; for certain, weather extremes will occur more often.
*   The economy will either continue to grow or decline; whichever happens will have different impacts on operational costs and customers' willingness to absorb rate increases.

• Water infrastructure will continue to age, and more will have to be replaced. How much and when it will have to be replaced are hard to predict with any degree of certainty.

Core Values

An agency's core values are what management believes in and how it behaves. They are sometimes referred to as the organization's operating philosophy, its creed, principles or simply values. They can be listed as a few or combination of concepts. They may be simple statements or spelled out in some detail. The values can be constructed from any combination of the concepts described in Table 15.1.

TABLE 15.1 Sample components from which organizational values are drawn

Value Components	Example Value Statements
Key interests or needs to be satisfied or balanced	• Devotion to public interest and/or community • Devotion to volunteer board, donors or key stakeholders • Devotion to employees, suppliers or contractors • Devotion to the support of research in mission-related products and services
Service of good quality or performance excellence	• Commitment to high-quality services or goods • Commitment to maintaining high-quality employees at all levels • Commitment to employing the best technology available and best value for the money
Mission delivery/ operations efficiency	• Dedicated to low-cost, high-productivity delivery • Provides the highest value attainable for budget received • Dedicated to improving and maintaining advanced knowledge base • Dedicated to listening to and reacting to client comments and suggestions
Workplace atmosphere or climate	• Dedicated to providing a good place for people to work • Committed to providing good opportunity for advancement • Providing a management mix that invests in service and process innovation • Maintaining a workplace that encourages teamwork • Dedicated to maintaining leaderships that supports all staff • Dedicated to supporting and investing in developing employee knowledge and skill sets
Observance of codes of conduct	• Belief in honest values and provider integrity • Fairness in all dealings with all we serve

Source: From concepts in Koteen (1997, 129–130)

Mission, Vision and Values Examples

The place to begin planning for sustainable operations is to ensure there is internal organization agreement with, and external stakeholder awareness of, what the organization mission is, what it sees as its future, and what it stands for. The State of California's strategic planning guide for agencies defines an organization's mission as its "reason for existence. [It is] the overarching goal for the agency's existence, usually contained within a formal statement of purpose." It then defines an agency's vision as "a compelling, conceptual, vivid image of the desired future" (CSDF 1998, 13). An agency's core values are also called its principles. Noting that describing an organization's principles often represents a challenge for management, when determined they should reflect the values and philosophy of the director and the executive management team. They should also function as organization-wide values and assumptions:

> [The values/principles] should be compatible and convincing for everyone inside the organization and for customers/clients and stakeholders.... Principles summarize the philosophies or core values that will be utilized in fulfillment of the vision and mission. Thus, principles help form a bridge between where the organization is and where it wants to be.
>
> *(CSDF 1998, 16)*

These are the first three core elements in the strategic plans of large and small public organizations. The following examples were selected at random from published public sector documents.

Federal-level Example

The U.S Air Force Material Command (AFMC 2017) supports the Air Force in its global strategic missions. Its mission is: "Deliver and support agile war-winning capabilities." The mission is further explained as requiring "contributions of all AFMC organizations working together to perform our six Core Mission Areas: Nuclear Systems Management Test and Evaluation Discovery and Development Sustainment and Logistics Lifecycle Management Installation and Mission Support." The Air Force vision statement is "Innovative Airmen, trusted and empowered, creating agile, cost-effective war-winning capabilities for the Nation."

While the plan did not identify a set of individual values, the following explanatory paragraph for its first strategic goal can be said to represent a large element in the Command's values:

> Our people are AFMC's most precious resource; therefore, this goal concisely reflects the commitment to our people. We must strengthen and enhance our total workforce to ensure they have the necessary equipment,

competencies, development, and environment to excel at any mission our nation asks them to accomplish. We remain committed to supporting our Airmen and their families to ensure they can operate effectively while retaining their quality of life and sense of resiliency. AFMC is dedicated to creating an environment where everyone can reach their full potential.

(AFMC 2017, 5)

State Agency Examples

The New Hampshire Department of Information Technology (DoIT) provides information technology (IT) services to state departments and agencies creating statewide efficiencies through the use of information technologies energizing government and business. The department develops the state's IT strategic vision and provides planning and support, enterprise services, technical, operational, infrastructure, and security services, and web and software development services. DoIT's mission and vision statements are:

> Mission: In service to the citizens of New Hampshire, the Department of Information Technology provides comprehensive technical leadership and solutions to agency partners in a secure, transparent and fiscally responsible manner.
> Vision: The NH Department of Information Technology will be recognized as a valued partner to New Hampshire and a major contributor toward innovation and efficiency efforts.

(NH DoIT 2017, 5)

The Arkansas Transportation Department (ARDOT) is the 12th largest state highway system in the United States. ARDOT has more than 3,600 employees and is responsible for more than 16,400 miles of state highways and 7,300 bridges. In its 2017–2022 five-year strategic plan it included the mission, vision and values statements shown in Box 15.1.

BOX 15.1 MISSION, VISION AND VALUES STATEMENTS OF A STATE TRANSPORTATION DEPARTMENT

Mission Statement

Provide safe and efficient transportation solutions to support Arkansas' economy and enhance the quality of life for generations to come.

Vision Statement

Continue to preserve and improve Arkansas' transportation system emphasizing safety, efficiency, quality, trust, and stewardship with a public service focused workforce.

Our Core Values

Safety—Safety first in all we do.
Public Service—Focus on the greater good.
Teamwork—One vision through collaboration and communication.
Quality—Deliver reliable transportation solutions.
Integrity—Commitment to ethics and transparency.
Efficiency—Achieve maximum benefit through fiscal responsibility.

Source: ARDOT (Arkansas Department of Transportation) (2017)

City Strategic Vision and Values

Billings, with a population in 2018 estimated at 109,550, is the largest city in the state of Montana. The city has enjoyed rapid growth as a result of oil production in

---

BOX 15.2 MISSION, VISION AND VALUES OF THE BILLINGS, MONTANA CITY COUNCIL

Vision: The Magic City: A diverse, welcoming community where people prosper and business succeeds.

Values: We, the City Council and staff of the City of Billings, affirm that we perform all of our duties embracing the following values:

Integrity: Through accessibility and transparency, we earn the trust of the community to which we are responsible.

Collaboration: We commit to provide opportunities to achieve common goals through positive communications and interaction with individuals, and with public and private organizations.

Stewardship: We plan and manage resources effectively, responsibly and efficiently.

Service: We deliver services with courtesy and respect while meeting our customers' needs.

Source: Billings, MT (2014, 1)

the eastern section of the state. The 2015–2019 strategic plan of Billings, Montana, skipped the mission statement element in its plan, instead beginning with the city's vision and its values (Box 15.2).

Where Are We Now?

The next step in strategic planning involves carrying out a deeply penetrating analysis—what are called the internal and external environments of the organization. The internal analysis provides information about the ability of the organization to meet the demands of its mission and the principles by which it carries out its actions. Identifying the organization's critical resources and management and personnel capabilities helps bring to light the strengths and the weaknesses and substantial barriers it must overcome to succeed. This analysis process is a systematic analysis of the internal and external factors that shape an organization, the capabilities, customers, competitors, within the organization's current and projected environment and its financial viability.

With agreement on the utility's mission, its vision and core values guiding further planning, it is time to begin a thorough analysis of the current practices and operating environment of the water utility. This step is commonly referred to as an analysis to assure recognition of the utility's strengths, its weaknesses, and the opportunities and threats—or SWOT analysis—that allow or hinder achievement of sustainable operation goals. The analysis must not be unwilling to admit its weaknesses; actions for converting weakness to strengths is what objectives are for. Other ways of conducting the analysis are to focus on understanding the utility's political, economic, social and technological (PEST) environments and their ability to hinder or help achieving the utility's goals and objectives. An abridged example of the key findings of a SWOT analysis for a small water and wastewater district are shown in Table 15.2. Once the SWOT factors are identified, leadership can establish goals that enable it to build on its strengths, overcome the weaknesses, and to use its strengths to take advantage of opportunities while mitigating its threats.

Sources of Situation Analysis Information

Some of the possible sources of information for both the internal and external environment analyses were included in the handbook for Arizona state government departments and agencies.

Sources of internal data listed include agency performance reports, quality assessments, client surveys, program evaluations, and existing agency plans. Some of the sources for information on the external environment are more diverse and difficult to relate to organization operations. However, relevant data can be secured from many federal and state statistical reports, legislation, regulations, executive orders, budgets and policy statements. Nongovernment sources include

TABLE 15.2 Results of a SWOT analysis for a small public utility

Internal Environment

Strengths	*Weaknesses*
Existing staff is dedicated, supportive and committed to cross-training for continuous improvement of their water and wastewater knowledge and skills. Utility has recently installed new $1.3 million water filtration system, added a fourth well and refurbished another well. Customer base is supportive and acceptant of the periodic need for rate increases for infrastructure repair and replacement. Utility has a sound financial status with highly favorable state audits. Utility has reputation for fast, friendly and helpful customer service with water and wastewater issues. Prior leadership and staff have produced good capital improvement plans.	Recent staff turnover has resulted in new leadership and office staff. Organizational structure is lean, resulting in recurring need for part-time workers or outside contract assistance. Utility has never produced a strategic plan. Utility is only beginning its first asset management plan. Maintenance is often more reactive than proactive. Much of the existing infrastructure is at or nearing its expected lifespan. Utility has high debt ratio, precluding low probability of future borrowing. Dependence upon off-site laboratory service delays necessary results and reports.

External Environment

Opportunities	*Threats*
Utility has a growing, financially stable rate base, accustomed to the need for periodic rate increases. Staff has good relationships with all regulatory agencies. Asset management plan and maintenance schedule preparation under way. New leadership and permanent staff with cross-training and dual certification reinforces operational reliability.	Increases in rate of infrastructure failures expected. New regulatory requirements for drinking water. Heavy seasonal water demand periodically approaches authorized water rights. High arsenic levels in some wells. Off-site alternative water supply unavailable.

Source: Authors (2019)

reports by special interest and advocacy groups, professional organizations and associations, court decisions and the media, among many others.

Where Do We Want To Be?

Operational goals are an organization's short-term objectives that contribute to the achievement of its strategic goals. Short-term goals are answers to the question of where it wants to be in the short run and are the focus of performance improvement programs. In 2008, for example, the EPA published a widely used guidebook to help utilities establish their long-term goals and the operational objectives for programs for achieving those goals. Five of the ten EPA-recommended goals with short-term program descriptions are presented below.

The guide recognizes that each utility will have what it believes is its own most important performance targets. The objectives to choose will reflect the utility's own strategic objectives, priorities, and the needs of the community it serves.

1. Product quality: Produces potable water, treated effluent, and process residuals in compliance with regulatory and reliability requirements and consistent with customer, public health, and ecological needs.
2. Customer satisfaction: Provides reliable, responsive, and affordable services in line with explicit, customer-accepted service levels.
3. Stakeholder understanding and support: Encourages understanding and support from regulatory and administrative agencies, community and watershed interests for service levels, rate structures, operating budgets, capital improvement programs, and risk management decisions.
4. Employee and leadership development: Recruit and retain a workforce that is competent, motivated, adaptive, and safe-working, and provides a focus on and emphasizes opportunities for professional and leadership development and strives to create an integrated and well-coordinated senior leadership team.
5. Infrastructure stability: Understands the condition of and costs associated with critical infrastructure assets and maintains and enhances the condition of all assets over the long term at the lowest possible lifecycle cost and acceptable risk consistent with customer, community, and regulator-supported service levels and consistent with anticipated growth and system reliability goals.

Formulate Key Strategic Goals

Strategic goals are what the organization wants to achieve over a longer period, from at least five years, but more often from ten or more years in the future. Table 15.3 is an example of the five-year strategic goals of a collaboration of three federal agencies working together to improve food safety. In 2011, three U.S. federal agencies—the Centers for Disease Control and Prevention (CDC), the U.S. Food and Drug Administration (FDA), and the Food Safety and Inspection Service of the United States Department of Agriculture (USDA-FSIS)—joined together to create the Interagency Food Safety Analytics Collaboration (IFSAC). The purpose was to improve coordination of federal food safety analytic efforts and address cross-cutting priorities for food safety data collection, analysis, and use. IFSAC's focus during its first five years was foodborne illness source attribution: identifying which foods are the most important sources of selected major foodborne illnesses.

Building on first-period accomplishments, the primary focus of the 2017–2021 strategic plan is to continue to improve estimates of foodborne illness source

TABLE 15.3 IFSAC 2017–2021 food safety strategic plan goals and objectives

	Goal	Objectives
1	Improve the use and quality of new and existing data to conduct analyses and develop estimates	1.1: Enhance collection and quality of source data 1.2: Enhance the use of existing foodborne illness surveillance data sources 1.3: Incorporate genomic data and other novel datasources
2	Improve analytic methods and models	2.1: Explore ways to address key gaps in data quality, quantity, methods and models 2.2: Develop new analytic approaches and models to maximize use of already available data 2.3: Expand the availability of technical and scientific expertise through collaboration with internal and external partners
3	Enhance the use of a communication about IFSAC food safety related products	3.1: Enhance relationships and encouragement with both internal and external groups 3.2: Improve the synthesis, interpretation, and dissemination of analytic products for multiple audiences.

Source: After material in CDC.gov (2017)

attribution, and to develop methods to estimate how sources change over time. The three goals that underpin the overarching focus are: improving the use and quality of new and existing data sources; improving analytic methods and models; and enhancing the use of and communication about IFSAC analytic products. The three goals and progress objectives are displayed in Table 15.3.

Agency Priority Goals

Agency priority goals (APGs) are the performance measuring guides that enable agencies to focus on leadership priorities and program outcomes, and then measure results of their programs (performance.gov 2018). APG statements are outcome-oriented, ambitious, and measurable with specific targets that reflect a near-term result or achievement that agency leadership wants to accomplish within approximately 24 months. In some instances, agencies are also utilizing the APG structure to drive progress and monitor implementation of agency management reforms and priorities, a modification of the traditional APG statement format. The act required the directors of 24 major agencies to identify agency priority goals. The Senate expected the number of goals to be submitted to not exceed 100 and individual agencies to not list more than five, with the expectation that some larger agencies might include more than five. The Department of the Interior, for example, submitted six goals. The Department of Defense and the Treasury Department each listed three priorities; the Department of Agriculture and the Department of Homeland Security each listed only two priority goals.

Agency managers select two or more strategic goals every two years. They then assign teams responsible for achieving the goal. Performance is evaluated quarterly to check progress and identify barriers to progress. They may then make changes to vary or implement new strategies to achieve the desired outcomes. APGs are to be achieved throughout the course of the current fiscal years. Priority goals are established by all major federal agencies. In one example, the following four priorities were included in the 2018 fiscal year for the Department of Health and Human Services: (1) human security, (2) reducing opioid morbidity and mortality, (3) combined data analyses, and (4) serious mental illness. The goal statements for each of these four priorities were (Performance.gov 2018):

Human security: Increase capacity to prevent health threats originating abroad from impacting the United States. By September 30, 2019, HHS was to contribute to increasing the surveillance, workforce emergency management, and laboratory capacity of 17 partner countries.

Reducing Opioid Morbidity and Mortality: Reduce opioid-related morbidity and mortality through (1) improved access to prevention, treatment and recovery support services; (2) targeting the availability and distribution of overdose-reversing drugs; (3) strengthening public health data and reporting; (4) supporting cutting-edge research; and (5) advancing the practice of pain management.

Combined Data Analysis: Increase combined analysis of disparate datasets in or to achieve better insights. By September 30, 2019, according to the HHS Action Plan, the enterprise-wide governance model will enable more efficient and effective processes for sharing inter-agency data beyond a data set's primary purpose (US Department of Health and Human Services 2019).

Serious Mental Illness: Improve treatment for individuals with serious mental illness. By September 30, 2019, HHS wants at least 280 evidence-based coordinated specialty care (CSC) programs providing services to individuals with functional restoration programs (FEP), representing a seven-fold increase in the number of such programs compared with 2014. (This target assumes stable funding at the federal and state level and may need to be adjusted if there are major unanticipated changes in either.)

An example of the types of specific programs and objectives associated with each of the goals is the set of specific targets HHS has identified for its reduction in opioid morbidity and mortality priority:

- Reduce opioid prescribing by the medical profession as measured by morphine milligram equivalents (MMEs).
- Decrease by 25% the MME of opioid analgesics dispensed in U.S. outpatient retail pharmacies.

- Increase by 30% the number of naloxone prescriptions dispensed in U.S. outpatient retail pharmacies. (Naloxone is the medication designed to rapidly reverse opioid overdose.)
- Increase by 25% the number of individual patients receiving prescriptions for buprenorphine in the U.S. (Buprenorphine is a prescription drug used to treat dependence on opioid painkillers such as oxycodone.)
- Increase by 100% the number of prescriptions for long-acting injectable or implantable buprenorphine from retail, long-term care, and mail-order pharmacies in the U.S.
- Increase by 25% the number of prescriptions for the extended-released naltrexone from retail, long-term care, and mail-order pharmacies in the U.S.

The OMB (2016) guidelines for strategic management activities encourages agency planners to identify priority goals that reflect the agency's highest priorities as determined by the head of the agency. Since agency secretaries change often, the goals should be ambitious but achievable within a two-year period.

How Will We Monitor Our Progress?

Annual agency performance plans are the third mandated activity in federal agency strategic management. Objectives in the annual plan are to be associated with long-term goals spelled out in the strategic plan. Two types of goals are required: mission-focused and mission support goals, each of which covers a different type of problem. Mission-focused collaboration goals identify partners with special knowledge and skills, and with experience in dealing with problems that extend across agency boundaries. Examples include international trade, food safety, sustainable communities, disaster preparedness and intelligence sharing. Mission support goals focus continued government efforts for streamlining administrative processes.

Rules for preparing all aspects of the plan are monitored by OMB along with the agency's strategic plan and priority goals. Briefly, the three core elements of the requirement are identifying goals and objectives for the issues and programs for which the agency operates, establishing objectives for programs and policies for objectives and goal-achieving programs, and providing for methods for measuring progress toward accomplishing the short-term objectives.

These elements are contained in the 14 required elements of the annual program performance plan. They include specifying the issues, programs, strategies, activities, goals and objectives, progress measurement metrics, and reporting. Table 15.4 lists the plan preparation requirements.

TABLE 15.4 Requirements for government agency performance planning

Requirement	Regulation
1	List agency performance goals.
2	Describe how the performance goals contribute to the agency's general (or strategic) goals.
3	Describe how the performance goals contribute to any federal government performance goals.
4	Identify agency priority goals.
5	Describe the strategies and resources required to meet the agency performance goals.
6	Specify clearly defined milestones.
7	Identify the organizations, program activities, regulations, policies, and other activities that contribute to each performance goal, both from within and external sources.
8	Describe the interagency cooperation for achieving the agency performance goals and the federal government performance goals.
9	Identify goal leaders.
10	Include a balanced set of performance indicators.
11	Provide a basis for comparing results.
12	Describe how the agency will ensure data accuracy and reliability.
13	Describe major management challenges.
14	Identify low-priority programs of the agency.

Source: OMB (2016)

State-level Performance Management

The use of performance measurement and reporting in state and local governments is a result of increased citizen demands for government accountability. This has generated greater interest by local legislators and elected municipality officers to incorporate performance measurement specifications during decision-making on program and resource allocations.

City-level Performance Measurement

Kirkland, Washington, a city on the shores of Lake Washington with a population of nearly 50,000, publishes a performance report, *City Council Goals*, to its citizens each year. The report lists progress on 10 key policy and service priorities for the city government. Council goals are for guiding allocation of budget and capital improvement program resources. The goal plan also describes how work plans and projects are developed to move the community towards the stated long-term goals. The City's ability to make progress toward their achievement is based on the availability of resources at any given time. The allocation of resources reflects the need to balance taxation levels with community service demands and the achievement of stated goals. Similar performance plans and reports are prepared by city, county and special municipal districts throughout the United States.

The 2017 report preamble described the purpose of the report was:

> articulate key policy and service priorities for Kirkland. Council goals guide the allocation of resources through the budget and capital improvement program to assure that organizational work plans and projects are developed that incrementally move the community towards the stated goals. Council goals are long term in nature. The City's ability to make progress toward their achievement is based on the availability of resources at any given time. Implicit in the allocation of resources is the need to balance levels of taxation and community impacts with service demands and the achievement of goals.
>
> *(City of Kirkland 2018, 5)*

Kirkland's park and recreation unit is an example for which progress on meeting goals to provide and maintain natural areas and recreational facilities and opportunities that enhance the health and wellbeing of the community. Meeting objectives for programs and classes are measured by tracking the percentage of programs and classes that meet minimum numbers to operate. The city uses five measures on park and recreation management; three measures each on the city's level of investment in parks and recreation facilities and on the city's open space plan; and two measures on citizens' ratings of the park and recreation system. More than 87% of recreation classes met the minimum enrollment, which exceeds the city's target, a good indication that the classes offered meet the demands of community members. Community member satisfaction with the parks, recreation and community services, as determined by the Community Survey, provides another measure of how well the park and recreation system meets the community's needs.

Preparing the Finance Plan

The last step in the strategic planning process is preparation of a finance plan for ensuring the funds needed to carry out the tasks to achieve the organization's long-term goals. The financial plan is an important element in the strategic planning process because it functions as a roadmap for identifying the agency's financial requirements. By requiring detailed budget reviews, the budget functions as a controlling device. It forces the gathering of financial and operational performance data for all aspects of the operation.

How Will We Transfer the Plan to Operations?

Once the strategic planning process is complete, the organization's managers must design the strategies by which the assets and capabilities of the organization are to be put into operation. The Louisiana state government provides state agencies a detailed guide on operations planning. It describes the process thus:

> An operational plan is an annual work plan. It describes short-term business strategies; it explains how a strategic plan will be put into operation (or what portion of a strategic plan will be addressed) during a given operational period (fiscal year). An operational plan is the basis for and justification of an annual operating budget request.
>
> *(LOPB 2001)*

The operational plan (OP) must be prepared and submitted by each department, agency or budget unit as part of its "total budget request document." The plan is based on agency and program strategic plans, describes agency and program missions and goals, program objectives, and lists program activities and performance measurements.

Steps in the Strategic Planning Process

* Who are we?
* What is the purpose for our organization?
* Where are we now in performing our mission?
* Where do we want to be?
* How will we monitor our progress?
* How will we transform the plan to operations?

Elements of a Strategic Plan

Regardless of how the strategic planning process is applied or the rationales for its implementation, there is general agreement of a set of from five key steps must be followed in every such plan. The strategic planning includes these five steps:

Basic Strategic Planning Process:

Step 1: Identify key stakeholders in the strategic planning process:

* The strategic plan is created with both internal and external stakeholder input.
* The plan is a "living document"—it is used for decision-making and resources allocation.
* The strategic plan is based on the organization's strategy.

Step 2: Develop mission, vision and core values:

* *Mission*: needs to be distinctive, guide decisions, be derived from stakeholders, and be reviewed and revised.

- *Vision*: needs to be inspirational, achievable in the near future, and be easily remembered.
- *Core values*: provide a foundation for vision and mission. Values are an organization's essential and enduring tenets that can be expressed in a set of general principles.

Step 3: Develop specific strategic goals, objectives, and tactics:

- Goals should be SMART: specific, measurable, attainable, realistic, and time-bound.
- Tactics action items are short term (one year is common) and should provide the "how to" details.

Step 4: Identify actions, benchmarks, and resources for each strategic goal.

Step 5: Develop an assessment dashboard or evaluation matrix:

- measures and measurement objectives;
- select and apply the appropriate performance metric;
- identify targets;
- timeline;
- identify the responsible party.

Step 6: Continuous review and revision.

Summary

The strategic plan is a guiding document that defines the mission of the agency, names its long-term primary goals and the administrators responsible for guiding progress in accomplishing the goals, and the strategies and tactics planned for accomplishing those goals. It also describes how the agency proposes to monitor its progress in addressing both the cited priority goals and actions to be taken on other relevant national problems, needs, challenges, and opportunities related to the agency's mission. The strategic plan is expected to explain the importance of the goals, enumerate the agency's capabilities and weaknesses, and assess the operating environment.

Planning for sustainability begins with establishing a framework for decision-making. General utility planning provides this framework. A comprehensive strategic plan can then be used to build on the information gathered in the general planning elements by helping water managers identify what they will do in the future, who will do it and how it will be paid for. Strategic planning is the critical intermediate step in sustainability planning. Sustainability planning then allows the water manager to focus efforts and resources on actions that contribute most to achieving the goal of a sustainable water supply, treatment and delivery system.

The strategic plan includes explanations of why the specific goals and strategies were selected and provides evidence supporting the selections. Some programs included in the strategic plan are respected as being to be more reflective of continuations of ongoing basic agency operations, whereas the newer priority goals named in the strategic plan should focus on high-priority goals that have been identified during agency analyses of the operating environment. The plan will therefore provide justification for funding decisions in support of performance goals, priorities, strategic human capital planning, and budget planning.

BIBLIOGRAPHY

Abell, Derel. 1980. *Defining the Business: The Starting Point of Strategic Planning*. Englewood Cliffs, NJ: Prentice-Hall.

Adams, Pamela, Isabel M. B. Freitas and Roberto Fontana. 2019. Strategic orientation, innovation performance and the moderating influence of marketing management. *Journal of Business Research*, 97(2019): 129–40.

AFMC (U.S. Air Force Material Command). 2017. AFMC 2017 Strategic Plan. Accessed June 27, 2019, at www.afmc.af.mil/Portals/13/documents/AFD-170421-0002.pdf?ver=2017-04-21-143525-987.

Agranoff, Robert. 2006. Inside collaborative networks: Ten lessons for public managers. *Public Administration Review*, 66(S1): 56–65.

Agranoff, Robert and Michael McGuire. 2003. *Collaborative Public Management: New Strategies for Local Governments*. Washington, DC: Georgetown University Press.

Aharoni, Eyal, Lila Rabinovich, Joshua Mallett and Andrew R. Morral. 2014. Insights on program sustainability from the empirical literature. In *An Assessment of Program Sustainability in Three Bureau of Justice Assistance Criminal Justice Domains*. Washington, DC: Rand.

Ajuaj, Allen. 2003. *Innovation Management: Strategies, Implementation, and Profits*. New York: Oxford University Press.

Akan, Obasi, Richard S. Allen, Marilyn M. Helms and Samuel A. Spralls III. 2006. Critical tactics for implementing Porter's generic strategies. *Journal of Business Strategy*, 27(1): 43–53.

Albort-Morant, Gema, Antonio L. Leal-Rodríguez, Vincente Fernández-Rodríguez and Antonio Ariza-Montes. 2018. Assessing the origins, evolution and prospects of the literature on dynamic capabilities: A bibliometric analysis. *European Research*, 24(1): 42–52.

Aldea, Adina, Maria-Eugenia Iacob, Jos van Hillegersberg, Dick Quartel and Henry Franken. 2018. Strategy on a page: An ArchiMate-based tool for visualizing and designing strategy. *Intelligent Systems in Accounting, Finance and Management*, 25(2): 86–102.

Alford, John. 2009. *Engaging Public Sector Clients: From Service-Delivery to Co-Production*. Basingstoke, UK: Palgrave Macmillan.

Alford, John and Carsten Greve. 2017. Strategy in the public and private sectors: Similarities, differences and changes. *Administrative Sciences*, 7(4): 1–17.

Alpkan, Lütfohak and Evrim Gemici. 2016. Disruption and ambidexterity: How innovation strategies evolve? *Procedia—Social and Behavioural Sciences*, 235(2016): 782–7.

Alter, Catherine and Jerald Hage. 1993. *Organizations Working Together*. Newbury Park, CA: Sage.

Amsler, Lisa B. 2016. Collaborative governance: Integrating management, politics and law. *Public Administration Review*, 76(5): 700–11.

Andrews, Kenneth R. 1971. *The Concept of Corporate Strategy*. Homewood, IL: Dow Jones-Irwin.

Andrews, Rhys, Malcom J. Beynon and Aoife M. McDermott. 2016. Organizational capability in the public sector: A configurational approach. *Public Administration Research and Theory*, 26(2): 239–58.

Andrews, Rhys, George S. Boyne and Richard M. Walker. 2006. Strategy content and organizational performance. *Public Administration Review*, 66(1): 52–63.

Andrews, Rhys, George A. Boyne, Jennifer Law and Richard M. Walker. 2012. *Strategy Management and Public Service Performance*. Houndmills, UK: Palgrave Macmillan.

Ansell, Chris and Alison Gash. 2008. Collaborative governance in theory. *Journal of Public Administration Research and Theory*, 18(4): 543–71.

Ansoff, H. Igor. 1957. Strategies for diversification. *Harvard Business Review*, 35(5): 113–24.

Ansoff, H. Igor. 1965. *Corporate Strategy: An Analytic Approach to Business Policy for Growth and Expansion*. New York: McGraw-Hill.

Ansoff, H. Igor. 1980. Strategic issue management. *Strategic Management Journal*, 1(2): 131–48.

Anttiroiko, Ari-Veikko, Stephen J. Bailey and Pekka Valkama. 2013. Outsourcing in Sandy Springs and other US cities: Insights for other countries. *International Public Administration Review*, 11(3/4): 7–24.

AOSPB (Arizona Governor's Office of Strategic Planning and Budgeting). 2011. *Managing for Results Handbook: Strategic Planning Guide for State Agencies*. Accessed May 26, 2019, at www.ospb.state.az.us/documents/pdf/Handbook_ManagingResults_FY2012.pdf.

Araujo, Charles. 2014. The four pillars: Secret to IT transformation, Accessed September 16, 2019, at www.cioinsight.com/it-management/expert-voices/the-four-pillars-the-secret-to-it-transformation.html.

Arbaugh, J. B. and Donald L. Sexton. 1997. Strategic orientation and customer dependency in discontinuously changing environments: A study of the defense industry *Journal of Management Issues*, 9(4): 419–39.

ARDOT (Arkansas Department of Transportation). 2017 Strategic Plan 2017–2022. Accessed September 30, 2019, at www.arkansashighways.com/Trans_Plan_Policy/ARDOT%20Strategic%20Plan-2017-2021%20(2017-08-10).pdf.

Arundel, Anthony and Hugo Hollanders. 2011. A taxonomy of innovation: How do public sector agencies innovate? Results of the 2010 European Innobarometer survey of public agencies. INNO Metrics Thematic Paper. Accessed November 7, 2018, at https://eprints.utas.edu.au/12552/1/A_taxonomy_of_innovation.pdf.

Arundel, Anthony, Garter Bloch and Barry Ferguson. 2019. Advancing innovation in the public sector: Aligning innovation measurement with policy goals. *Research Policy*, 48(3): 789–98.

Ashkanasy, Nneal M., Celeste P. M. Widerom, and Mark F. Peterson. (eds.). 2000. *Handbook of Organization Culture and Climate*. Thousand Oaks, CA: Sage.

Augier, Mie and David J. Teece. 2009. Dynamic capabilities and the role of managers in business strategy and economic performance. *Organization Science*, 20(2): 410–21.

Auka, Daniel O. 2014. Porter's generic competitive strategies and customer satisfaction in commercial banks in Kenya. *Eurasian Business & Marketing Research Journal*, 1(1): 1–31.

Baker, David. 2007. *Strategic Change Management in Public Sector Organization*. Oxford, UK: Chandos.

Balancesmb.com n/d/ What is environmental sustainability? Accessed September 7, 2019, at www.thebalancesmb.com/what-is-sustainability-3157876.

Balfour, Danny L. and B. Wechsler. 1990. Organizational commitment: a reconceptualization and empirical test of public-private differences. *Review of Public Personnel Administration*, 10(3): 23–40.

Balfour, Danny L. and B. Wechsler. 1996. Organizational commitment: Antecedents and outcomes in public organizations. *Public Productivity and Management Review*, 19(3): 256–77.

Balodi, K.C. 2014. Strategic orientation and organizational forms: An integrative framework. *European Business Review*, 26: 188–203.

Barduch, Eugene. 1996. Turf barriers to interagency collaboration. In *The State of Public Management*, Donald F. Kettl and H. Brinton Milward, eds. 169–92. Baltimore: Johns Hopkins University.

Barney, Jay B. 1986. Strategic factor markets: Expectations, luck, and business strategy. *Management Science*, 32(10): 1231–41.

Barney, Jay B. 1989. Asset stock accumulations and sustained competitive advantage: A comment. *Management Science*, 35(12): 1511–13.

Barney, Jay B. 1991. Firm resources and sustained competitive advantage. *Advances in Strategic Management*, 17(1): 3–10.

Barney, Jay B. 1997. *Gaining and Sustaining Competitive Advantage*. Reading, MA: Addison-Wesley.

Barney, Jay B. 2007. Returns to bidding firms in mergers and acquisitions: Reconsidering the relatedness hypothesis. *Strategic Management Journal*, 9(S1): 71–8.

Barrutia, Jose M. and Carmen Echebarria. 2015. Resource-based view of sustainability engagement. *Global Environmental Change*, 34(2015): 70–82.

BC (British Columbia, Canada). n/d. Strategic orientation. Accessed August 2019, at www2. gov.bc.ca/gov/content/careers-myhr/job-seekers/about-competencies/indigenous-relations/strategic-orientation.

Beckhard, Richard, and Reuben Harris. 1987. *Organizational Transitions*, 2nd ed. Boston: Addison-Wesley.

Beer, Russel A., Eisenstat, and Bert Spector, 1990. *The Critical Path to Corporate Renewal*. Cambridge, MA: HBR Press.

Bel, Roland, Vladimir Smirnov and Andrew Wait. 2018. Managing change: Communication, managerial style and change in organizations. *Economic Modeling*, 69(2018): 1–12.

Belbin, R. Meredith. 2012. *Team Roles At Work*, 2nd ed. New York: Routledge.

Benito, Bernardino, Maria-Delores Guyillamón and Ana-Maria Rios. 2018. Public management versus private management in the provision of drinking water: What is cheaper? *Les Localis-Journal of Local Self-Government*, 16(2): 271–92.

Berardo, Ramiro and Mark Lubell, 2016. Understanding what shapes a polycentric governance system. *Public Administration Review*, 76(5): 738–51.

Bernstein, Justin L. 2011. Tender offer taking: Using game theory to ensure that governments efficiently and fairly exercise eminent domain. *Texas Journal on Civil Liberties and Civil Rights*, 17(1): 95–115.

Berry, Francis S. 1994. Innovation in public management: The adoption of strategic planning. *Public Administration Review*, 54(4): 322–30.

Berry, Francis S. and Ralph S. Brower. 2005. Intergovernmental and intersectional management: Weaving networking, contracting out, and management roles into third party government. *Public Performance and Management Review*, 29(1): 7–17.

Bezanilla, María José, Donna Fernández-Nogueira, Manuel Poblete and Hector Galindo-Domínguez. 2019. Methodologies for teaching-learning critical thinking in higher education: The teacher's view. *Thinking Skills and Creativity*, 33(2019): 100588.

Bhuian, Shahid, Bulent Mengue and Simon J. Bell. 2005. Just entrepreneurial enough: The moderating effect of entrepreneurship on the relationship between market orientation and performance. *Journal of Business Research*, 58(1): 9–17.

Billings, MT. 2014. 2015–2019 strategic plan. Accessed June 27, 2019, at https://ci.billings.mt.us/2118/FY2015-2019-Strategic-Plan.

Bloch, Carter and Markus M. Bugge. 2013. Public sector innovation—from theory to measurement. *Structural Change and Economic Dynamics*, 27(2013): 133–45.

Borins, Sandford. 2014. *The Persistence of Innovation in Government*. Washington, DC: IBM Center for the Business of Government.

Bovaid, Tony. 2005. Public governance: Balancing stakeholder power in a network. *International Review of Administration Sciences*, 7(2): 217–28.

Bozeman, Barry. 2007. *Public Values and Public Interests*. Washington, DC: Georgetown University.

Bozeman, Barry and Jeffrey D. Straussman. 1990. *Public Management Strategies: Guidelines for Managerial Effectiveness*. San Francisco: Jossey-Bass.

Bracker, Jeffrey. 1980. The historical development of the strategic management concept. *Academy of Management Review*, 5(2): 219–24.

Brandenburger, Adam M. and Barry J. Nalebuff. 1996. *Co-Opetition: A Revolution Mindset that Combines Competition and Cooperation*. Boston: Harvard Business School.

Bressers, Hans. 2010. *Government and Complexity in Water Management*. Cheltenham, UK: Edward Elgar.

Bridges, Eileen, Anne T. Coughlan and Shlomo Kalish. 1991. New technology adoption in an innovative marketplace: Micro- and macro-level decision models. *International Journal of Forecasting*, 7(3): 257–70.

Brønn, Peggy Simcic and Carl Brønn. 2002. Issues management as basis for strategic orientation. *Journal of Public Affairs*, 2(4): 247–58.

Briggeman, Jason. 2009. Governance as a strategy in state-of-nature games. *Public Choice*, 141(3): 481–91.

Brudney, Jeffrey L. and Robert E. England. 1983. Toward a definition of the coproduction concept. *Public Administration Review*, 43(1): 59–65.

Bryson, John M., Barbara C. Crosby and Melissa M. Stone. 2006. The design and implementation of cross-sector collaborations: Propositions from the literature. *Public Administration Review*, 66, 44–55.

Bryson, John M., Fran Ackerman and Colin Eden. 2007. Putting the resource-based view of strategy and distinctive competencies to work in public organizations. *Public Administration Review*, 67(4): 702–17.

BSI (Balance Scorecard Institute). 2019. Strategic management basics: What is strategic planning? Accessed February 9, 2019, at www.balancedscorecard.org/BSC-Basics/Strategic-Planning-Basics.

Burns, Lawton R., Robert A. DeGraaff, Patricia M. Danzon, John R. Kimberly, William L. Kissick, and Mark V. Pauly. 2002. *The Healthcare Value Chain*. San Francisco. CA: Jossey-Bass.

Burr, Michael, T. 2004. Consolidating Co-ops. *Public Utilities Fortnightly*, 142(June): 71–6.

Buttigieg, Sandra C., Marcus Schuetz and Frank Bezzina. 2016. Value chains of public and private health-care services in a small EU island state: A SWOT analysis. *Frontiers in Public Health*. September 14, 2016. Accessed July 6, 2019, at www.frontiersin.org/articles/10.3389/fpubh.2016.00201/full.

Calabrese, Armando, Roberta Costa, Nathan Levialdi and Tamara Menichini. 2019. Integrating sustainability into strategic decision-making: A fuzzy AHP method for the selection of relevant sustainability issues. *Technological Forecasting & Social Change*, 139(2019): 155–68.

Camarinha-Matos, Luis M. 2009. Collaborative networks contribution to sustainable development. *IFAC Proceedings Volumes*, 42(24): 92–7.

Camp, Robert C. 1989. *Benchmarking*. Milwaukee, WI: ASQC Quality Press.

Capelli, P., L. Bassi, H. Katz, D. Knoke, P. Osterman and M. Usem. 1997. *Change at Work*. New York: Oxford University Press.

Carter, Nicole, Clare R. Sellke and Daniel T. Shedd. 2013. *U.S.-Mexico Water Sharing: Background and Recent Developments*. Washington, DC: U.S. Congressional Research Service.

Carvalho, João M. S., Ricardo V. Costa, Sandra Marnoto, Célio A. A. Sousa and José Carvalho Viera. 2018. Toward a resource-based view of city quality: A new framework. *Growth and Change*, 49(2): 266–85.

CDC.gov. (Centers for Disease Control and Prevention). 2017. IFSAC 2017–2021 Strategic Plan. Accessed June 26, 2019, at www.cdc.gov/foodsafety/pdfs/IFSAC-Strategic-Plan-2017-2021.pdf.

Chandler, Alfred D. 1962. *Strategy and Structure: Chapters in the History of the American Business Enterprise*. Cambridge, MA: MIT Press.

Chaffee, Ellen E. 1985. Three models of strategy. *The Academy of Management Review*, 10(1): 89–98.

Cheng, Colin C.J., Chenlung Yang and Chwen Sheu. 2017. Interplay of strategic orientations, innovativeness, and industrial sectors in enhancing innovation performance. *Journal of Business and Management*, 23(1/2): 25–46.

Chhipi-Shrestha, Gyan, Manuel Rodriquez, and Rehan Sadiq. 2019. Selection of sustainable municipal water reuse application by multi-stakeholders using game theory. *Science of the Total Environment*, 650(Part 2): 2512–26.

Christensen, Tom and Per Lægreid. 2002. A transformative perspective on administration. In Tom Christensen and Per Lægreid, eds. *New Public Management*. Aldershot, UK: Ashgate. 13–39.

City of Kirkland, WA. 2018. *Performance Measures 2017*. Accessed February 2, 2019, at www.kirklandwa.gov/Assets/CMO/CMO+PDFs/2017+Performance+Measures.pdf.

City of Plymouth, MN. 2019. Goals and Objectives. Accessed June 14, 2019, at www.plymouthmn.gov/departments/city-council-/goals-objectives.

Coalition Theory Network – A Portal on Coalition and Network Theory in Social Sciences. [Online]. Available at: www.coalitiontheory.net/research-areas/cooperative-game-theory.

Cockburn, Iain, Rebecca M. Henderson and Scott Stern. 2000. Untangling the origins of competitive advantage. *Strategic Management Journal*, 21(10/11): 1123–45.

Colby, Elbridge A. 2013. Defining strategic stability: Reconciling stability and deterrence. In Elbridge A. Colby and Michael Garson, eds. *Strategic Stability: Contending Interpretations*. Carlisle, PA: U.S. Army War College. Accessed February 28, 2019, at https://ssi.armywarcollege.edu/pdffiles/PUB1144.pdf.

Conboy, Kieron, Patrick Mikalef, Denis Dennehy and John Krogstie. 2019. Using business analytics to enhance dynamic capabilities in operations research: A case analysis and research agenda. *European Journal of Operational Research*, In press. Available at https://doi.org/10.1016/j.ejor.2019.06.051.

Congress.gov. 2018. Government Performance and Results Act of 1993. Accessed May 26, 2018, at www.congress.gov/bill/103rd-congress/senate-bill/20.

Connolly, Jennifer M. 2018. Can managerial turnover be a good thing? The impact of city manager change on local fiscal outcomes. *Public Administration Review*, 78(3): 338–49.

Cooke, Mike. 2012. What makes collaboration initiatives work? Lexington, KY: NASCIO (National Association of state Chief Information Officers). Accessed October 9, 2019, at www.nascio.org/Portals/0/Publications/Documents/NASCIO-What-Makes-Collabo rative-Initiatives-Work.pdf.

Cosens, Barbara (ed.). 2012. *The Columbia River Treaty Revisited: Transboundary River Governance in the Face of Uncertainty*. Corvallis: Oregon State University.

CRA (Canada Revenue Agency). 2016. Strategic orientation. Montreal, Canada: Government of Canada. Accessed August 29, 2019, at www.canada.ca/en/revenue-agency/corporate/careers-cra/information-moved/cra-competencies-standardized-assessment-tools/canada-revenue-agency-competencies-april-2016/strategic-orientation.html.

CRA (Canada Revenue Agency). 2019. About the Canada Revenue Agency. Accessed August 30, 2019, at www.canada.ca/en/revenue-agency/corporate/about-canada-revenue-agency-cra.html.

Crewson, Philip E. 1997. Public service motivation: Building empirical evidence and effect. *Journal of Public Administration Research and Theory*, 7(4): 449–518.

Cristofoli, Daniela, Marco Meneguzzo and Norma Riccuci. 2017. Collaborative administration: The management of successful networks. *Public Management Review*, 19(3): 275–82.

CSDF (California State Department of Finance). 1998. *Strategic Planning Guidelines*. Accessed May 26, 2019, at www.calhr.ca.gov/Documents/wfp-department-of-finance-strategic-plan-guidelines.pdf.

Cummings, Thomas T. and Christopher G. Worley. 2014. *Organization Development and Change*. Mason, OH: South-Western Cengage.

Dahan, Nicolas. 2005. Can there be a resource-based view of politics? *International Studies of Management & Organization*, 35(2): 8–27.

Danneels, Lieselot and Stijn Viaene. 2015. Simple rules strategy to transform government; An action design research approach. *Government Information Quarterly*, 32(4): 516–25.

Day, George. 1990. *Market Driven Strategy*. New York: Free Press.

Day, George and Robin Wensley. 1983. Marketing theory with a strategic orientation. *Journal of Marketing*, 47(4): 79–89.

Deming, W. Edwards. 2018. *Out of the Crisis*, third printing. Cambridge, MA: Massachusetts Institute of Technology.

Demircioglu, Mehmet Akif and David B. Audretsch. 2017. Conditions for innovation in public sector organizations. *Research Policy*, 46(2017): 1681–91.

Denhardt, Janet V. and Robert B. Denhardt. 2002. *The New Public Service: Serving, Not Steering*. Armonk, NY: M.E. Sharpe.

De Rooij, Mariska M.G., Martyna Janowicz-Panjaitan, and Remco S. Mannak. 2018. A configurational explanation for performance management systems design in project-based organizations. *International Journal of Project Management*, 37(5): 616–30.

Deutscher, Franziska, Florian B. Zapkau, Christian Schwens, Matthias Baum and Ruediger Kabst. 2016. Strategic orientation and performance: A configurational perspective. *Journal of Business Research*, 69(2): 849–61.

De Vries, Hanna A., Victor Bekkers and Lars Tummers. 2014. *Innovation in the Public Sector: A Systematic Review and Future Research Agenda*. Speyer: September 9, 2014, EGPA conference.

Domínguez, Eladio, Beatriz Pérez, Angel L. Rubio and María A. Zapata. 2019. A taxonomy for key performance indicators management. *Computer Standards & Interfaces*, 64(May): 24–40.

Dominguez, Marta, Jose Galán-González and Carmen Barroso. 2015. Patterns of strategic change. *Journal of Organizational Change Management*, 28(3): 411–31.

DOE (U.S. Department of Energy). n/d Accessed June 9, 2019, at www.energy.gov/mission.

DPC (Defense Pricing and Contracting). 2015. Defense contracting throughout U.S. history. Washington, DC: Department of Defense. Accessed February 12, 2018, at www.acq.osd.mil/dpap/pacc/cc/history.html.

Drucker, Peter. 1974. *Management: Tasks, Responsibilities, and Practices*. New York: Harper & Row.

Dudley, Emma, Diaan-Yi Lin, Matteo Mancini and Jonathan Ng. 2015. Implementing a citizen-centric approach to delivering government services. Accessed March 29, 2019, at www.mckinsey.com/industries/public-sector/our-insights/implementing-a-citizen-centric-approach-to-delivering-government-services.

Duesing, Robert J. and Margaret A. White. 2013. Building understanding and knowledge: A case study in stakeholder orientation. *Journal of Managerial Issues*, 25(4): 401–15.

Dunleavy, Patrick, Helen Margetts, Simon Bastow and Jane Tinkler. 2006. New public management is dead—Long live digital-era governance. *Journal of Public Administration Research and Theory*, 16(3): 467–93.

Durst, Samantha L., and Chareldean Newell. 1999. Better, faster, stronger: government reinvention in the 1990s. *American Review of Public Administration*, 29(1): 61–76.

Durugbo, Christopher. 2016. Collaborative networks: A systematic review and multilevel framework. *International Journal of Production Research*, 54(12): 3749–76.

Eadie, Douglas C. 1999. Putting a powerful tool to practical use: The application of strategic planning in the public sector. *Public Administration Review*, 33(6): 447–566.

Easterby-Smith, Mark, Marjorie A. Lyles and Margaret A. Peteraf. 2009. Dynamic capabilities: Current debates and future directions. *British Journal of Management*, 21 (2009): S1–S8.

EC (European Community). 2019. Orientations towards the first strategic plan implementing the research and innovation framework programme Horizon Europe. Accessed August 30, 2019, at https://ec.europa.eu/research/pdf/horizon-europe/ec_rtd_orientations-towards-the-strategic-planning.pdf.

Eden, Colin and Fran Ackerman. 2000. Mapping distinctive competencies. *Journal of the Operational Research Society*. 51(1): 12–20.

Eisenhardt, Kathleen M. and Claudia B. Schoonhoven. 1996. Resource-based view of strategic alliance formation: Strategic and social effects in entrepreneurial firms. *Organization Science*, 7(2): 136–50.

Eisenhardt, Kathleen M. and Jeffrey A. Martin. 2000. Dynamic capabilities: What are they? *Strategic Management Journal*, 21(10/11): 11-5-1121.

Eisinger, Peter. 2002. Organizational capacity and organizational effectiveness among street-level food assistance programs. *Nonprofit and Voluntary Sector Quarterly*, 32(1): 115–30.

Ejdys, Joanna. 2015. Innovativeness of residential care services in Poland in the context of strategic orientation. *Procedia: Social and Behavioral Sciences*, 213(2015): 746–52.

EPA. 2008. EPA Sustainability plans. Washington, DC: Environmental Protection Agency. Accessed June 4, 2010, at www.epa.gov/greeningepa/epa-sustainability-plans.

EPA. 2012. Planning for sustainability: A handbook for water and wastewater utilities. Washington, DC: Environmental Protection Agency. Accessed March 14, 2018, at www.epa.gov/sites/production/files/2016-01/documents/planning-for-sustainability-a-handbook-for-water-and-wastewater-utilities.pdf.

EPA Victoria (Environmental Protection Authority Victoria, Canada). 2017. EPA launched new five-year strategy. Accessed September 26, 2019, at www.epa.vic.gov.au/about-us/news-centre/news-and-updates/news/2017/september/07/epa-organizational-strategy.

Essays, UK. 2018. Strategic management and Resource Based View Management essay. Accessed June 1, 2019 at www.ukessays.com/essays/management/strategic-management-and-resource-based-view-management-essay.php?vref=1.

Federal Transit Administration (FTA). 2020. *Transportation Planning: Overview, Office of Planning & Environment,* Washington, DC, United States. [Online] Accessed June 4, 2020 at www.transit.dot.gov/regulations-and-guidance/transportation-planning/transportation-planning.

Felts, Arthur A. and Philip H. Joss. 2000. Time and space: the origins and implications of the new public management. *Administrative Theory & Praxis.* 22(3): 519–33.

Ferlie, Ewan, Lynn Ashburner, Louise Fitzgerald and Andrew Pettigrew. 1996. *The New Public Management in Action.* Oxford, UK: Oxford University Press.

Fernandez, Sergio and Hal G. Rainey. 2006. Managing successful organizational change in the public sector. *Public Administration Review,* 66(2): 168–76.

Ferreira, Aldónio and David Otley. 2009. The design and use of performance management systems: An extended framework for analysis. *Management Accounting* Research, 20(2009): 263–82.

Fiorino, Daniel J. 2010. Sustainability as a conceptual focus for public administration. *Public Administration Review,* 70(S1): S78–S88.

Fitzgerald, Michael, Nina Kruschwitz, Didier Bonnet and Michael Welch. 2014. Embracing digital technology: A new strategic imperative. *MIT Sloan Management Review,* 55(2): 1–12.

Foley, Erik. 2014. *Sustainability Planning Guidebook for Teams.* State College, PA: Sustainability Institute, Penn State University.

Forrer, John J., James E. Kee and Eric Boyer. 2014. *Governing Cross-Sector Collaboration.* San Francisco: Jossey Bass.

Fountain, Jane E. 2016. *Building an Enterprise Government: Creating an ecosystem for cross-agency collaboration in the next administration.* Washington, DC: Partnership for Public Service and IBM Center for Business of Government.

Fountain, Jane E. 2017. Why networked governments are key to better societies. Geneva, Switzerland: World Economic Forum. Accessed February 14, 2019, at www.weforum.org/agenda/2017/02/network-government-society-collaboration.

Fox, Deborah. 1978. An overarching framework for sustainability. *Built Environment,* 35(3): 302–7.

Furlong, Casey, Kath Phelan and Jago Dodson. 2018. The role of water utilities in urban greening: A case study of Melbourne, Australia. *Utilities Policy,* 53: 25–31.

Gagnon, Stéphane. 1999. Resource-based competition and the new operations strategy. *International journal of Operations & Production Management,* 19(2): 125–38.

GAO (Government Accountability Office). n/d. Managing results in government. Accessed January 30, 2019, at www.gao.gov/key_issues/managing_for_results_in_government/issue_summary.

GAO (U.S. Government Accountability Office). n/d. Leading practices in collaboration across governments, civil society [organizations], and the private sector. Accessed March 29, 2019, at www.gao.gov/key_issues/leading_practices_collaboration/issue_summary.

GAO (Government Accountability Office). 2016. *Water Infrastructure.* U.S. Government. Washington, DC: *GAO Reports.*

GAO (U.S. Government Accountability office). 2019. Managing risks and improving VA healthcare. Accessed August 9, 2019, at www.gao.gov/highrisk/managing_risks_improving_va_health_care/why_did_study.

Gatignon, Hubert and J. M. Xuereb, 1997. Strategic orientation of the firm new product performance. *Journal of Marketing Research,* 34(1), 77–90.

Gault, Fred. 2018. Defining and measuring innovation in all sectors of the economy. *Research Policy*, 47(3): 617–22.

Glieske, Hanneke, Arwin van Buuren and Victor Bekkers. 2016. Conceptualizing public innovative capacity: A framework for assessment. *The Innovation Journal: The Public Sector Innovation Journal*, 21(1): 1–25.

Goldsmith, S. 1997. Can business really do business with government? *Harvard Business Review*, 75(3): 110–21.

Goldsmith, Stephen and William D. Eggers. 2004. *Governing by Network: The New Shape of the Public Sector*. Washington, DC: Brookings Institution.

Goodman, Malcom and Sandra Dingli, 2013. *Creative Strategic Innovation and Management*. London: Routledge.

GPRA (Government Performance and Results Act) 1993 and 2010. Public Law 111–352—JAN. 4, 2011: GPRA Modernization Act of 2010. Accessed June 4, 2010, at hwww.congress.gov/111/plaws/publ352/PLAW-111publ352.pdf.

Grant, Robert M. 1996. Toward a knowledge-based theory of the firm. *Strategic Management Journal*, Winter Special Issue: 109–12.

Green, Alison and Jerry Hauser. 2012. *Managing to Change the World: The Civil Society Manager's Guide to Getting Results*. San Francisco: Wiley.

Greer, Bobbi Watt, Jill K. Meher and Michele T. Cole. 2008. Managing civil society organizations: The importance of transformational leadership and commitment to operating standards for civil society accountability. *Public Performance and Management Review*, 32(1): 51–75.

Grizzle, Gloria A. 1999. Measuring state and local government performance: Issues to resolve before implementing a performance measurement system. In *Public Sector Performance*, Richard C. Kearney and Evan M. Berman, eds. Boulder, CO: Westview, 329–40.

Gromark, Johan and Frans Melin. 2013: From market orientation to brand orientation in the public sector. *Journal of Marketing Management*, 29(9–10): 1099–123.

Grotenberg, Sanne and Arwin van Buuren. 2018. Realizing innovative public waterworks: Aligning administrative capacities in collaborative innovation processes. *Journal of Cleaner Production*, 171(2018): S45–S55.

GSA (US General Services Administration). n/d. GSA: Strategically sustainable. Accessed September 7, 2019, at www.gsa.gov/governmentwide-initiatives/sustainabilityprograms/federal-strategic-sourcing-initiative-fssi.

GSA (U.S. General Services Administration). 2018. Federal Strategic Services Initiative (FSSI). Accessed February 15, 2019, at www.gsa.gov/buying-selling/purchasing.

GSA (U.S. General Services Administration). 2019. Strategically sustainable. Accessed February 18, 2019, at www.gsa.gov/governmentwide-initiatives/sustainability.

Gulati, Ranjay, Nitin Nohria and Akbar Zaheer. 2000. Strategic networks. *Strategic Management Journal*, 21(3): 203–15.

Haezendonck, Elvira, Alain Verbeke and Chris Coeck. 2006. Strategic positioning analysis for seaports. *Research in Transportation Economics*, 16(1): 141–69.

Haider, Husnain, Rehan Sadiq and Soloman Tessfamariam. 2015. Multilevel performance management framework for small to medium sized water utilities in Canada. *Canadian Journal of Civil Engineering*, 42(11): 899–900.

Halachmi, Arie. 1996. Strategic Management and Productivity. In *Encyclopedia of Public Administration and Public Policy*, 2nd ed. (Print Version). Accessed October 9, 2019, at www.ebookphp.com/encyclopedia-of-policy-studies-second-edition-public-administration-and-public-policy-epub-pdf/.

Hall, Richard H. 2001. *Organizations: Structures, Processes and Outcomes*. 8th ed. Upper Saddle River, NJ: Palgrave.

Hallin, Carina A., Torben Juul Andersen and Sigbjørn Tveterås. 2017. Harnessing the frontline employee sensing of capabilities for decision support. *Decision Support Systems*, 97(2017): 104–12.

Hambrick, Donald C. 1983. Some tests of the effectiveness and functional attributes of Miles and Snow's strategic types. *Academy of Management Journal*, 26(1): 5–25.

Hansen, Jesper R. and Ewan Ferlie. 2016. Applying strategic management theories in public sector organizations. *Public Management Review*, 18(1): 1–19.

Hansen, Jesper R. and Christian B. Jacobsen. 2016. Changing strategy processes and strategy content in public sector organizations? A longitudinal case study of NPM reforms' influence on strategic management. *British Journal of Management*, 27(2): 373–89.

Hart, Stuart L. 1995. A natural-resource-based view of the firm. *Academy of Management Review*, 20(4): 986–1014.

Hartley, Jean. 2005. Innovation in governance and public services: Past and present. *Public Money and Management*, 25(1): 27–34.

Hartman, Preston, Travis Gliedt, Jeffrey Widener and Rebecca W. Loraamm. 2017. Dynamic capabilities for water system transitions in Oklahoma. *Environmental Innovations and Societal Transitions*, 25(2017): 64–81.

Harvey, Don and Brown, Donald R. 2001. *An Experiential Approach to Organization Change*. 6th ed. Upper Saddle River, NJ: Prentice-Hall.

Hatry, Harry P. 1999. Performance measurement principles and techniques: An overview for local government. In *Public Sector Performance*, Richard C. Kearney and Evan M. Berman, eds. Boulder, CO: Westview, 304–25.

Heathfield, Susan M. 2019. Performance management. Accessed September 8, 2019, at www.thebalancecareers.com/performance-management-1918226.

Heatwole, K.B. 1980. *A Determination of the Association of Competition and Regulation with Hospital Strategic Orientation*. Unpublished PhD dissertation, Virginia Commonwealth University.

Heintzman, Ralph and Brian Marson. 2005. People, service and trust: is there a public sector service value chain? *International Review of Administrative Sciences*, 71(4): 549–75.

Helac, Duygu S. 2015. Multidimensional construct of technology orientation. *Procedia—Social and Behavioral Sciences*, 195(2015): 1057–65.

Helfat, Constance E. and Margaret A. Peteraf. 2003. The dynamic resource-based view: Capability lifecycles. *Strategic Management Journal*, 24(10). 997–1010.

Helfat, Constance E. and Sidney G. Winter. 2011. Untangling dynamic and operational capabilities: Strategy for the (N)ever changing world. *Strategic Management Journal*, 32(11): 1243–50.

Helfat, Constance E. and Jeffrey A. Martin. 2015. Dynamic managerial capabilities: Review and assessment of managerial impact on strategic change. *Journal of Management*, 41(5): 1281–312.

Hempel, Donald J. and Peter J. LaPlaca. 1975. Strategic planning in a period of transition. *Industrial Marketing Management*, 4(6): 305–14.

Herranz, J. Jr. 2006. *Network Management Strategies*. Seattle, WA: Daniel J. Evans School of Public Affairs, University of Washington. Working Paper No. 2006-01: 4–37.

Hill, Alex and Steve Brown. 2007. Strategic profiling: A visual representation of internal strategic fit in service organizations. *International Journal of Operations & Production Management*, 27(12): 1333–61.

Hill, Carolyn J., and Laurence E. Lynn. 2005. Is hierarchical governance in decline? Evidence from empirical research. *Journal of Public Administration Research and Theory*, 15(2): 173–95.

Höglund, Linda, Mikael Holmgren Daicedo, Maria Mårtensson and Fredrik Svärdsten. 2018. Strategic management in the public sector: How tools enable and constrain strategy making. *International Public Management Journal*, 21(5): 822–49. DOI: 10.1080/ 10967494.2018.1427161.

Hough, J. 2011. Supporting strategy from the inside. *The Journal of the Operational Research Society*, 62(5): 923–6.

Hunger, J. David and Thomas L. Wheelen. 1997. *Essentials of Strategic Management*. Boston: Addison-Wesley.

Hunger, J. David and Thomas L. Wheelen. 2015. *Essentials of Strategic Management*, 5th ed. Noida, India: Pearson Education.

Iberra, Hermionia and Mark L. Hunter. 2007. How leaders create and use networks. *Harvard Business Review*, 85(1): 40–7.

IFAD (International Fund for Agricultural Development). 2012. Deepening IFAD's engagement in the private sector. Accessed March 7, 2019, at www.cbd.int/financial/ mainstream/ifad-privatestrategy.pdf.

IGI Global. 2020. Collaborative network. Accessed February 13, 2020, at www.igi-global. com/dictionary/classes-collaborative-networks/4398.

Ingraham, Patricia W., Philip G. Joyce and Amy K. Donahue. 2003. *Government Performance: Why Management Matters*. Baltimore: Johns Hopkins University.

Ingraham, Patricia W., Sally C. Selden and Donald P. Moynihan. 2000. People and performance: Challenges for the future public service: The report from the Wye River Conference. *Public Administration Review*, 60(1): 54–60.

Janesville, WI. 2019. Water utility. Accessed August 30, 2019, at www.ci.janesville.wi.us/ government/departments-divisions/public-works/water-utility.

Janićijević, Nebojša. 2017. Organizational models as configurations of structure, culture, leadership, control, and strategy. *Economic Annals*, LXII(213): 67–91.

Jarillo, J. Carlos. 1988. On strategic networks. *Strategic Management Journal*, 9(1): 31–41.

Johanson, Jan-Erik. 2009. Strategy formulation in public agencies. *Public Administration*, 87(4): 872–91.

Johnson, Åge. 2015. Strategic management thinking and practice in the public sector: A strategic planning for all seasons? *Financial Accountability & Management*, 31(3): 243–65.

Johnson, Jean L., Kelly D. Martin and Amit Saini. 2012. The role of a firm's strategic orientation dimensions in determining market orientation. *Industrial Marketing Management*, 41(4): 715–24.

Johnson, Mary M. Dickens. 2008. Current trends of outsourcing practices in government and business: Causes, case studies and logic. *Journal of Public Procurement*, 8(2): 248–68.

Jones, Candace, William Westerly and Stephen P. Borgatti. 1997. A general theory of network governance: Exchange conditions and social mechanisms. *Academy of Management Review*, 22(4): 911–45.

Jones, Carys, Mark Baker, Jeremy Carter, Stephen Jay, Michael Short and Christopher Wood. 2005. *Strategic Environmental Assessment and Land Use Planning: An International Evaluation*, London: Earthscan.

Joyce, Paul. 2000. *Strategy in the Public Sector A Guide to Effective Change Management*. Chichester, UK: Wiley.

Joyce, Paul. 2012. *Strategic Leadership in the Public Services*. New York: Routledge.

Jucevicus, Ovidijus, 2013. Resource-based view. *Strategic Management Insight* (online). Accessed April 30, 2019, at www.strategicmanagementinsight.com/topics/resource-based-view.html

Kahn, Kenneth B. 2018. Understanding innovation. *Business Horizons*, 61(2018): 453–60.

Kakka, Vishruti, Hitarth Shah, Reema Patel, and Nishant Doshi. 2019. A comparative study of applications of game theory in cyber security and cloud computing. *Procedia Computer Science*, 155: 680–5.

Kamensky, John M. and Thomas J. Burlin. 2004. *Collaboration: Using Networks and Partnerships*. Lanham, MD: Rowman and Littlefield.

Kang, Young Cheoul. 2005. Strategic management in the public sector: Major publications. *Public Performance and Management Review*, 29(1) 85–92.

Katkalo, Valery S., Cristos N. Pitelis and David J. Teece. 2010. Introduction: On the nature and scope of dynamic capabilities. *Industrial and Corporate Change*, 19(4): 1174–86.

Keig, Dawn and Lance E. Brouthers. 2013. Major theories of business strategy. In *Strategic Management in the 21st Century*, Volume 3: Theories of Strategic Management, Timothy J. Wilkinson, ed. Santa Barbara, CA: Praeger, 3–24.

Kelman, steven. 2005. *Unleasing Change: A Study of Renewal in Government*. Washington, DC: Brookings Institution.

Kettl, Donald f. 2005. *The Global Public Management Revolution*. Washington, DC: Bookings Institute.

Kim, Soojin and Sangyub Ryu. 2017. Strategic public management for financial condition: Focus on fund balances of school districts. *The Social Science Journal*, 54(2017): 249–60.

Koch, Per and Johan Hauknes. 2005. Innovation in the public sector. Report No. D20. Accessed November 7, 2018, at aviana.com/step/publin/reports/d20-innovation.pdf.

Koli, Ajay K. and Bernard J. Jaworski. 1990. Market orientation: The construct, research propositions, and management implications. *Journal of Marketing*, 54(4): 1–18.

Koteen, Jack. 1997. *Strategic Management in Public and Nonprofit Organizations: Managing Public Concerns in an Era of Limits*, 2nd ed. Westport, CT: Praeger.

Kraatz, Matthew S. and Edward J. Zajac. 2001. How organizational resources affect strategic change and performance in turbulent environments. *Organizational Science*, 12(5): 632–57.

Král, Pavel and Věra Králová. 2016. Approaches to changing organizational structure: The effect of drivers and communications. *Journal of Business Research*, 69(2016): 5169–74.

Laloux, Frederic and Etienne Appert. 2016. *Reinventing Organizations*. Brussels, Belgium: Nelson Parker.

Larson, Paul D. 2009. Public vs. private sector perspectives on supply chain management. *Journal of Public Procurement*, 9(2): 222–47.

Lau, Chung-Ming, Lynda M. Kilbourne and Richard W. Woodman. 2003. A shared schema approach to understanding organizational culture change. *Research in Organizational Change and Development*, 14(2003): 235–56.

Lee, Chung-Shing and Nicholas S. Vonortas. 2002. Toward an integrated model of strategic formulation for strategic technical alliances. *International Journal of Technology Transfer and Commercialization*, 1(3): 292–312.

Lee, Chung-Shing, Leong Chan, David E. McNabb and Rafaa Khalifa. 2019. Exploring the role of strategic orientation in business innovation. *Journal of Competitiveness Studies*, 27(2): 90–100.

Lehne, Richard. 2005. *Government and Business*, 2nd ed. Washington, DC: CQ Press.

Levitt, Theodore. 1965. Exploit the product lifecycle. *Harvard Business Review*, November 1965. Accessed September 30, 2019, at https://hbr.org/1965/11/exploit-the-product-life-cycle.

Lewicki, R.J., R.D. Bowen, D.T. Hall and F.S. Hall. 1988. *Experience in Management and Organizational Behavior*. 3rd ed. New York: Wiley.

Lewin, K. 1951. *Field Theory in Social Science*. New York: Harper Brothers.

Lieberherr, Eva and Bernard Truffer. 2015. The impact of privatization on sustainability transactions: A comparative analysis of dynamic capabilities in three water utilities. *Environmental Innovation and Societal Transactions*, 15(2015): 101–22.

Liu, Bing and Zhengping Fu. 2011. Relationship between strategic orientation and organizational performance in Born Global: A critical review. *International Journal of Business and Management*, 6(3): 109–15.

Liu, Day-Yang, Shou-Wei Chen and Tzu-Wei Chou. 2011. Resource fit in digital transformation. *Management Decision*, 49(10): 1–10.

Living Economics. n/d. Rivalry and excludability in goods. Accessed March 17, 2019, at http://livingeconomics.org/article.asp?docId=239.

LOPB (Louisiana Office of Planning and Budget). 2001. Operational Plan: Format, guidelines, and instructions. Accessed June 28, 2019, at www.doa.la.gov/opb/faf/OPFormatWord_FY01MWLayout.pdf.

Lynn, Laurence E. Jr. and Carolyn J. Heinrich. 2001. *Improving Governance: A New Logic for Empirical Research*. Washington, DC: Georgetown University.

Madhani, Pankaj M. 2009. Resource based view (RBV) of competitive advantages: Importance, issues and implications. *KHOJ Journal of Indian Management Research and Practices*, 1(2): 2–12.

Mahoney, Joseph T. and J. Rajendran Pandian. 1992. The resource-based view within the conversation of strategic management. *Strategic Management Journal*, 13(5): 363–80.

Mandell, Myrna, Robyn Keast and Dan Chamberlain. 2017. Collaborative networks and the need for a new management language. *Public Management Review*, 19(3): 326–41.

Mann, Pete, Sue Pritchard and Kirstein Rummery. 2004. Supporting international partnerships in the public sector. *Public Management Review*, 6(3): 417–39.

Mazouz, Bachir and Benoit Tremblay. 2006. Toward a postbureaucratic model of governance: How institutional commitment is challenging Quebec's administration. *Public Administration Review*, 66(2): 263–73.

McBain, Luke and Jonathan Smith. 2012. Strategic management in the public sector. *E-Leader International* conference paper. Singapore. Accessed October 30, 2018, at www.g-casa.com/conferences/singapore/papers_in_pdf/mon/McBain.pdf.

McCarty, Nolan and Adam Meirowitz. 2007. *Political Game Theory*. Cambridge, UK: Cambridge University Press.

McGuire, Michael. 2002. Managing networks: Propositions on what managers do and why they do it. *Public Administration Review*, 62(5): 599–609.

McGuire, Michael. 2006. Collaborative public management: Assessing what we know and how we know it. *Public Administration Review*, 66(s1): 33–43.

McGuire, Michael. 2013. Symposium introduction: Challenges of intergovernmental management. *Journal of Health and Human Services Administration*, 36(2): 109–23.

McNabb, David E. 2007. *Knowledge Management in the Public Sector*. Armonk, NY: M. E. Sharpe.

McNabb, David E. 2009. *The New Face of Government: How Public Managers are Forging a New Approach to Governance*. Boca Raton, FL: CRC Press.

McNabb, David E. 2017. *Public Utilities: Meeting 21st Century Management Challenges*, 2nd ed. London: Edward Elgar.

McNabb, David E. 2019. *Global Pathways to Water Sustainability*. Cham, Switzerland: Palgrave Macmillan.

McPhie, Neil. A. G. 2004. *Managing Federal Recruitment*. Washington, DC: U.S. Merit System Protection Board.

MDCTS (Miami Dade County Transit System) 2014. Transit development plan FY 2015–2024: Goals and objectives. Accessed September 23, 2019, at www.miamidade.gov/transit/library/10_year_plan/review/ch-6-mdt-tdp-goals-and-objectives-final-0007.pdf.

Mergel, Ines and Kevin C. Desouza. 2013. Implementing open innovation in the public sector: The case of Challenge.gov. *Public Administration Review*, 73(6): 882–90.

Mettler, Suzanne and Joe Soss. 2004. The consequences of public policy for democratic citizenship: Bridging policy studies and mass politics. *Perspective on Politics*, 2(1): 55–73.

Middle, Gary. 2015. Defining environmental and sustainability planning. Accessed February 15, 2019, at www.garrymiddle.net/defining-environmental-sustainability-planning/.

Mikalef, Patrick, John Krogstie, Ilias O. Pappas and Paul Pavlou. 2019. Exploring the relationship between big data analytics capability and competitive performance: The mediating roles of dynamic and operational capabilities. *Information & Management*, in press. Available at https://doi.org/10.1016/j.im.2019.05.004.

Miles, Raymond E., Charles C. Snow, Alan D. Meyer and Henry J. Coleman Jr. 1978. Organizational strategy, structure, and process. *Academy of Management Review*, 3(3): 546–62.

Miles, Sandra J. and Mark Van Clieaf. 2017. Strategic fit: Key to growing enterprise value through organizational capital. *Business Horizons*, 60(1): 55–65.

Miller, Danny. 1983. The correlates of entrepreneurship in three types of firms. *Managerial Science*, 29(7): 770–91.

Miller, Gerald J. 1989. Unique public sector strategies. *Public Productivity and Management Review*, 13(2): 133–44.

Miller, Kent D., Emanuel Gomes and David W. Lehman. 2019. Strategy restoration. *Long Range Planning*, 52(5): 101855.

Milward, H. Brinton Milward and Keith G. Provan. 1998. Measuring network structures. *Public Administration*, 76(2): 387–407.

Mintzberg, Henry. 1979. *The Structuring of Organizations*. Englewood Cliffs, NJ: Prentice-Hall.

Mintzberg, Henry. 1994. *Rise and Fall of Strategic Planning*. New York: Free Press.

Mišanková, Mária and Katarína Kočišová. 2915. Strategic implementation as part of strategic management. *Contemporary Issues in Business, Management and Education*, 110(2014): 861–70.

Moore, Mark H. 1997. *Creating Public Value: Strategic Management in Government*. Cambridge, MA: Harvard University Press.

Morgan, Robert E. and Carolyn A. Strong. 2003. Business performance and dimensions of strategic orientation. *Journal of Business Research*, 56(3): 163–76.

MPA Collaborative Networks. 2018. Offering local partners an active voice in MPA management. Accessed April 2, 2013, at www.mpacollaborative.org/about/aboutus.

MRSC (Municipal Research and Services Center). 2018. Performance measurement. Accessed September 30, 2019, at http://mrsc.org/getdoc/bafdf54c-b9e3-457d-aa4e-7e8840a77b5c/Performance-Measurement.aspx.

Muggy, Luke and Jessica L. Heier Stamm. 2015. Game theory application in humanitarian operations: A review. *Journal of Humanitarian Logistics and Supply Chain Management*, 4(1): 4–33.

Nabatchi, Tina, Alessandro Sancino and Mariafrancesca Sicilia. 2017. Varieties of participation in public services: The who, when, and what of coproduction. *Public Administration Review*, 77(5): 766–76.

Nadler, David A. and Michael L. Tushman. 1995. Types of organizational change: From incremental improvement to discontinuous transformation. In David A. Nadler, Robert

B. Shaw and A. Elise Walton, eds. *Discontinuous Change*, San Francisco, CA: Jossey-Bass, 15–34.

Nagle, James F. 1999. *A History of Government Contracting*, 2nd ed. Washington, DC: George Washington University.

Nakos, George 2013. The competitive advantage of strategic alliances: Companies profiting from partnerships with competing and noncompeting companies. In *Strategic Management in the 21st Century*, Volume 3: Theories of Strategic Management. Timothy J. Wilkinson, ed. Santa Barbara, CA: Praeger, 197–213.

Nash, John. 1951. Non-cooperative games. *Annals of Mathematics*. 54(2): 286–95.

NCATSC (National Center for Advancing Translational Sciences). 2018. Alliances at NCATSC. Accessed August 26, 2019, at https://ncats.nih.gov/alliances/about.

Newbert, Scott L. 2008. Value, rareness, competitive advantage, and performance: A conceptual-level empirical investigation of the resource-based view of the firm. *Strategic Management Journal*, 29(7): 745–68.

Newcomer, Kathryn and Sharon Caudle. 2011. Public performance management systems: Embedding practices for improved success. *Public Performance & Management Review*, 35(1): 108–32.

Newman, Daniel, 2018. Breaking down the six pillars of digital transformation from the CEO's perspective. *Forbes* (online), May 21, 2018. Accessed September 16, 2019, at www.forbes.com/sites/danielnewman/2019/01/02/breaking-down-the-6-pillars-of-digital-transformation-from-the-ceos-perspective/2/#23fed1cd708e.

Nextgov. 2019. Customer satisfaction drops across federal government. Accessed March 6, 2019, at www.nextgov.com/cio-briefing/2019/01/customer-satisfaction-drops-across-federal-government/154469/.

NH DoIT 2017. (New Hampshire Department of Information Technology). 2017. Information Technology—Strategic Themes, Objectives and Key Initiatives—1–31–2017. Accessed September 30, 2019, at https://www.nh.gov/doit/strategic/documents/strategic-plan-summary-sheet.pdf.

Nichols, Fred. 2019. Three kinds of business strategy. Accessed February 18, 2019, at www.smartdraw.com/strategic-planning/three-kinds-of-business-strategy.htm.

Nidumolu, Ram, C. K. Prahalad and M. R. Rangaswami. 2009. Why sustainability is not the key driver of innovation. *Harvard Business Review*. Accessed February 2, 2020, at https://hbr.org/2009/09/why-sustainability-is-now-the-key-driver-of-innovation.

Noble, Charles H., Rajiv K. Sinha and Ajith Kumar. 2002. Market orientation and alternative strategic orientations: A longitudinal assessment of performance implications. *Journal of Marketing*, 66(4): 25–39.

Norman, Emma S., Alice Cohen and Karen Bakker. 2013. *Canada, the United States, and Shared Waters*. Toronto: University of Toronto Press.

Nutt, Paul C. and Robert W. Backoff. 1995. Strategy for public and third-sector organizations. *Journal of Public Administration Research and Theory*, 5(2): 189–211.

Obeidat, Bader Yousef. 2016 The effect of strategic orientation on organizational performance: The mediating role of innovation. *International Journal of Communications, Network and System Sciences*, 9(2016): 478–505. Available at http://file.scirp.org/pdf/IJCNS_2016111414542384.pdf.

OECD (Organization for Economic Cooperation and Development). 2005. Oslo manual: guidelines for collecting and interpreting innovation data. Accessed October 7, 2019, at https://ec.europa.eu/eurostat/documents/3859598/5889925/OSLO-EN.PDF.

OECD. 2008. Pareto efficiency. *OECD Glossary of Statistical Terms*, 394. Accessed November 22, 2019, at www.oecd-ilibrary.org/docserver/9789264055087-en.pdf?expires=1574 447673&id=id&accname=guest&checksum=376FBBD6DFBEA3165EBD771 D728FEDC4.

O'Flynn, Janine and John Wanna. 2008. *Collaborative Governance*. Canberra, Australia: ANU Press.

Ohio OBM. 2018. Conducting an analysis of alternatives. Accessed September 15, 2019, at https://budget.ohio.gov/doc/VMO/Guidance%20and%20Instructions/3%20Plan/Conducting%20an%20Analysis%20of%20Alternatives.pdf.

OMB (US Office of Management and Budget). 2003. Circular No, A-76 (Revised). Accessed February 12, 2019, at www.whitehouse.gov/sites/whitehouse.gov/files/omb/circulars/A76/a76_incl_tech_correction.pdf.

OMB (US Office of Management and Budget). 2016. Agency Strategic Planning. Section 230 of OMB Circular A-11 2016. Accessed January 31, 2019, at https://obamawhitehouse.archives.gov/sites/default/files/omb/assets/a11_current_year/s230.pdf.

Orley, David. 1999. Performance management: A framework for management control systems research. *Management Accounting* Research, 10(4): 363–82.

Ospina, Sonia M., Rogan Kersh and Jarle Trondal. 2014. Agentification. *Public Administration Review*, 74(4): 545–9.

Ostrom, Elinor. 2010. Institutional analysis and development: Elements of the framework in historical perspective. In Charles Crothers, ed. *Historical Developments and Theoretical Approaches in Sociology*, Vol. II. 261–89. London: Eolss Publishers.

Ostrom, Elinor, Roger B. Parks, George P. Whitaker and Stephen L. Percy. 1978. The public service production process: A framework for analyzing police services. *Policy Studies Journal*, 7(1): 381–9.

Otley, David. 1999. Performance management: A framework for management control systems research. *Management Accounting Research*, 10(4): 363–82.

O'Toole, Laurence J. 1997. Treating networks seriously: Practical and research-based agendas in public administration. *Public Administration Review*, 57(1): 45–52.

O'Toole, Laurence J. and Kenneth J. Meier. 2004. Public management in intergovernmental networks: Matching structural networks and managerial networking. *Journal of Public Administration Research and Theory*, 14(4): 469–94.

Ouenniche, Jamal, Aristotelis Boukouras and Mohammad Rajabi. 2016. An ordinal game theory approach to the analysis and selection of partners in public-private partnership. *Journal of Optimization Theory and Applications*, 169(1): 314–43.

OutsourcingLaw.com. 2019. Definition of government outsourcing. Accessed February 12, 2020, at www.outsourcing-law.com/services-outsourced/customer-care/government/.

Oxford Dictionary of English. 1998. Edited by Judy Pearsall and Patrick Hanks. Oxford: Oxford University Press.

Ozkan-Canbolat, Ela, Aydin Beraha and Abdullah Bas. 2016. Application of evolutionary game theory to strategic innovation. *Procedia: Social and Behavioral Sciences*, 235(2916): 685–93.

Parks, Roger B., Paula C. Baker, Larry Kiser, Ronald Oakerson, Elinor Ostrom, Vincent Ostrom, Stephen L. Percy, Martha B. Vandivort, Gordon P. Whitaker and Rick Wilson. 1981. Consumers as coproducers of public services: Some economic and institutional considerations 1981. *Policy Studies Journal*, 9(7): 1001–11.

Pattakos, Alex N. 2004. The search for meaning in government service. *Public Administration Review*, 64(1): 106–12.

Pavlou, Paul and Omar A. El Sawy. 2011. Understanding the elusive black box of dynamic capabilities. *Decision Sciences*, 42(1): 239–73.

Penn State University (PSU). 2014. *Sustainability Planning Guidebook for Teams.* The sustainability Institute. Accessed February 18, 2019, at sustainability.psu.edu/sites/default/files/SustainabilityGuidebook_final_feb19.pdf.

Penrose, Edith T. 1959. *The Theory of Growth of the Firm*. New York: Wiley.

Performance.gov. 2018. Priority goals: Department of Health and Human Services. Accessed January 31, 2019, at www.performance.gov/health_and_human_services/APG_hhs_2.html.

Perrott, Bruce E. 1996. Managing strategic issues in the public service. *Long Range Planning*, 29(3): 337–45.

Peteraf, Margaret A. and Jay B. Barney. 2003. Unraveling the resource-based tangle. *Managerial and Decision Economics*, 24(4): 309–23.

Peteraf, Margaret A., Giada Di Stefano and Gianmario Verona. 2013. The elephant in the room of dynamic capabilities: Bringing two diverging conversations together. *Strategic Management Journal*, 34(12): 1389–410.

Pine, Jesse M. 2006. The economic role of the emergency department in the healthcare continuum: Applying Michael Porter's five forces model to emergency medicine. *The Journal of Emergency Medicine*, 30(4) 447–53.

PLI (Project Leadership Institute of the U.S. Department of Energy). n/d. Project Leadership Institute. Accessed June 9, 2019, at https://pli-slac.stanford.edu/about/mission-vision.

Poister, Theodore H. and Gregory Streib. 1999. Assessing the validity, legitimacy, and functionality of performance measurement systems in municipal governments. *The American Review of Public Administration*, 29(2): 107–23.

Pollitt, Christopher, Sandra van Thiel and Vincent Homburg. 2007. The new public management in Europe. *Management Online Review*, (October). Accessed September 28, 2019, at www.researchgate.net/publication/228545289_The_new_public_management_in_Europe.

Porter, Michael E. 1979. How competitive forces shape strategy. *Harvard Business Review*, 57(2): 25–40.

Porter, Michael E. 1980. *The Competitive Strategy: Techniques for Analyzing Industries and Competitors*. New York: The Free Press.

Porter, Michael E. 1985. *Competitive Advantage: Creating and Sustaining Superior Advantage*. Glencoe, IL: The Free Press.

Porter, Michael E. 1991. Towards a dynamic theory of strategy. *Strategic Management Journal*, 12(S2): 95–117.

Porter, Michael E. 1996. What is strategy? *Harvard Business Review*, November–December: 61–78.

Porter, Michael E. 2008. The five competitive forces that shape strategy. Special Issue on HBS Centennial. *Harvard Business Review*, 86(1): 78–93.

Potůček, Martin. 2006. Strategic governance in central and eastern Europe: From concepts to reality. Accessed February 9, 2019, at unpan1.un.org/intradoc/groups/public/documents/NISPAcee/UNPAN024312.pdf.

PPS (Partnership for Public Service). 2018. *Time for a Change: How Agencies Are Transforming Business Practices to Meet Customer Needs*. Arlington, VA: Accenture Federal Services.

Prahalad, C. K. and Gary Hamel. 1990. The core competency of the firm. *Harvard Business Review*, 68(3): 79–93.

Priem, Richard L. and John E. Butler. 2001. Is the resource-based "view" a useful perspective for strategic management research? *Academy of Management Review*, 26(1): 22–40.

Provan, Keith G. and Patrick Kenis. 2008. Modes of network governance: Structure, management and effectiveness. *Journal of Public Administration Research and Theory: J-PART*, 18(2): 229–52.

Provan, Keith G., and H. Brinton Milward. 1995. A preliminary theory of network effectiveness: A comparative study of four community mental health systems. *Administrative Science Quarterly* 40(1): 1–33.

Provan, Keith G. and H. Brinton Milward. 2001. Do networks really work? A framework for evaluating public-sector organizational networks. *Public Administration Review* 61(4): 414–23.

Prusty, Santosh K., Pratap K.J. Mohapatra and C.K. Mukherjee. 2017. House of strategy: A model for designing strategies using stakeholders' opinion. *Computers and Industrial Engineering*, 108(2017): 39–56.

Prybil, Lawrence, Paul Jarria and José Montero. 2015. A perspective on public-private collaboration in the health sector. Accessed April 2, 2019, at nam.edu/wp-content/uploads/2015/11/NAM-Public-Private-Collaboration-Perspective.pdf.

PSC (Public Sector Commission). 2018. Public sector governance. Government of Western Australia. Accessed February 9, 2018, at https://publicsector.wa.gov.au/public-administration/public-sector-governance.

PSCSC (Public Service Commission of South Carolina). 2019. 2017–2018 Annual Accountability Report. Accessed June 9, 2019, at https://psc.sc.gov/sites/default/files/Documents/Accountability%20Reports/Public%20Service%20Commission%20 2017-2018%20Accountability%20Report.pdf.

Radin, Beryl. 1996. Managing across boundaries. In *The State of Public Management*, Donald F. Kettl and H. Brinton Milward, eds. Baltimore: Johns Hopkins University, 145–67.

Ram, Padmakumar, Swapna Bhargavi and Gantasala V. Prabhakar. 2011. Work environment, service climate, and customer satisfaction: Examining theoretical and empirical connections. *International journal of Business and Social Science*, 2(20): 121–32.

Ranjan, Ashish. 2019. Modi rewrites history as incumbent BJP registers record 6% rise in vote share. *India Today*, May 24/25, 2019. Accessed August 30, 2019, at www.indiatoday.in/diu/story/election-results-2019-pm-narendra-modi-bjp-vote-share-1534141-2019-05-24.

Rapcevičiene, Daiva. 2014. Modelling a value chain in the public sector. *Social Transformations in Contemporary Society*. ISSN 2345-0126 (online). Accessed February 17, 2019, at http://stics.mruni.eu/wp-content/uploads/2014/08/STICS_2014_2_42-49.pdf.

Redding, Sam and Allison Layland. 2015. *Strategic Performance Management: Organizing People and Their Work in the SEA of the Future*. San Antonio, TX: Building State Capacity and Productivity Center.

Robins, Gerry, Lorraine Bates and Philippa Pattison. 2011. Network governance and environmental management: Conflict and cooperation. *Public Administration*, 89(4). 1293–313.

Rogers, David L. 2016. *The Digital Transformation Playbook: Rethink Your Business for the Digital Age*. New York: Columbia University.

Ross, Don, 2019. Game theory, In *The Stanford Encyclopedia of Philosophy* (Spring 2019 Edition), Edward N. Zalta, ed. Accessed November 20, 2019, at plato.stanford.edu/archives/spr2019/entries/game-theory/.

Ross, Louise. 2011. *Public Sector Performance: A Global Perspective*. London, UK: CIMA (Chartered Institute of Management Accountants). Accessed September 8, 2019, at www.cimaglobal.com/Documents/Thought_leadership_docs/NHS-public-sector/public_sector_report_web_oct_2011.pdf.

Rothaermel, Frank T. 2015. *Strategic Management*, 2nd ed. New York: McGraw-Hill.

Rouse, William B. 2005. A theory of enterprise transformation. *Systems Engineering*, 8(4): 279–95.

Rumelt, Richard P. 1984. Toward a strategic theory of the firm. In R. Lamb, ed. *Competitive Strategic Management*. Englewood Cliffs, NJ: Prentice-Hall, 556–70.

Rumelt, Richard P. 2011. *Good Strategy Bad Strategy: The Difference and Why it Matters*. New York: Crown Business.

Ruokonen, Mika and Sami Saarenketo. 2009. The strategic orientations of rapidly internationalizing software companies. *European Business Review*, 21(1): 17–41.

Sahni, Nikhil, Maxwell Wessel and Clayton M. Christensen. 2013. Unleashing breakthrough innovation in government. *Stanford Social Innovation Review*, 11(3): 27–31.

Samuelson, Paul A. and William D. Nordhaus. 1985. *Economics: An Introductory Analysis*. New York: McGraw-Hill Companies.

Samuelson, Larry. 2016. Game theory in economics and beyond. *The Journal of Economic Perspectives*, 30(4): 107–30.

Santos, Cláudiom, Madalena Araújo and Nuno Carreia. 2015. Towards a classification of technology strategy frameworks. Paper presented at the September 2015 European Conference on Information Systems.

Satell, Greg. 2013. 4 government programs that drive innovation, *Forbes*. Accessed February 24, 2019, at www.forbes.com/sites/gregsatell/2013/07/02/4-government-programs-that-drive-innovation/#71b45b3a3978.

Schalock, Robert L. Miguel A. Verdugo and Jos van Loon. 2018. Understanding organizational transformation in evaluation and program planning. *Evaluation and Program Planning*, 67(C): 53–60.

Schein, Edgar H. 1985. *Organizational Culture and Leadership*. San Francisco, CA: Jossey-Bass.

Schepis, Daniel, Nick Ellis and Sharon Purchase. 2018. Exploring strategies and dynamic capabilities for net formation and management. *Industrial Marketing Management*, 74(2018): 115–25.

Schot, Johan and Laur Kanger. 2018. Deep transitions: Emergence, acceleration, stabilization, and directionality. *Research Policy*. 47(6): 1045–959.

Schotter, Andreas. 2013. Early concepts or strategy. In *Strategic Management in the 21st Century*, Volume 3: Theories of Strategic Management, Timothy J. Wilkinson, ed. Santa Barbara, CA: Praeger, 25–38.

Schwartz, Shalom H. 1992. Universals in the content and structure of values: Theory and empirical tests in 20 countries. In *Advances in Experimental Social Psychology*, Vol. 25, M. Zanna, ed. New York: Academic Press, 1–65.

Schwartz, Shalom H. 2012. An overview of the Schwartz Theory of Basic Values. *Online Readings in Psychology and Culture*, 2(1). https://doi.org/10.9707/2307-0919.1116.

Sen, Barbara. 2014. Multiple strategic orientations: The public library as a societal organization. *Procedia: Social and Behavioral Sciences*, 147(2014): 111–19.

Shapiro, Carl. 1989. The theory of business strategy. *The RAND Journal of Economics*, 20(1): 125–37.

Singh, Anna, Patricia Klarner and Thomas Hess. 2019. How do chief digital officers pursue digital transformation activities? The role of organization design parameters. *Long Range Planning*, in press. Available at https://doi.org/10.1016/j.lrp.2019.07.001.

Skok, James E. 1989. Toward a definition of strategic management for the public sector. *The American Review of Public Administration*, 19(2): 133–47.

Slater, S.F., E.M. Olson and G.T.M. Hult. 2006. The moderating influence of strategic orientation on strategy formation capability-performance relationship. *Strategic Management Journal*, 27 (12): 1221–31.

Slavin A.M. and J.B. Woodard. 2006. *Enterprise Transformation: Lessons Learned, Pathways to Success.* Albuquerque, NM: Sandia National Laboratories Report SAND2006-2228.

Smeltzer, L.R. 1991. An analysis of strategies for announcing organization-wide change. *Group and Organizational Studies*, 16(1): 5–24.

Smith, Kenneth, Walter Ferrier and Herman Ndofor. 2001. Competitive dynamics research: Critique and future directions. In *Handbook of Strategic Management*, Michael Hitt, R. Edward Freeman and Jeffrey Harrison, eds. London: Blackwell, 315–61.

Snidal, Duncan. 1985. The game theory of international politics. *World Politics*, 38(1): 25–57.

Sollosy, Marc D. 2013. The origins of strategy and strategic thought. In *Strategic Management in the 21st Century*, Vol. 1. Timothy J. Wilkinson, ed. Santa Barbara, CA: Praeger, 3–28.

Soltani, Atousa, Rehan Sadiq and Kasun Hewage. 2016. Selecting sustainable waste-to-energy technologies for municipal solid waste treatment: A game theory approach for group decision-making. *Journal of Cleaner Production*, 113(February): 388–99.

Sørensen, Eva and Jacob Torfing. 2005. Network governance and post-liberal democracy. *Administrative Theory and Praxis*, 27(2): 197–237.

Southorn, Graham. 2016. Great expectations: The past, present and future of prediction. *Significance*, 23(2): 15–19.

Stabell, Charles B. and Øystein D. Fjeldstad. 1998. Configuring value for competitive advantage: On chains, shops and networks. *Strategic Management Journal*, 19(5): 413–37.

Stadler, Christian, Constance E. Helfat and Gianmario Verona. 2013. The impact of dynamic capabilities on resource access and development. *Organization Science*, 24(6): 1782–804.

Starling, Grover. 2005. *Managing the Public Sector*, 7th ed. Belmont, CA: Thompson-Wadsworth.

Sterling, Mary Jane. n/d. Important terms in game theory. Accessed February 9, 2010, at www.dummies.com/education/math/important-terms-game-theory/.

Stoker, Gerry. 2006. Public value management: A new narrative for networked governance? *The American Review of Public Administration*, 36(1): 41–57.

Stoyanova, Veselina. 2017. *David Teece's Dynamic Capabilities and Strategic Management.* London: Macat International.

Straffin, Philip. 1993. *Game Theory and Strategy.* Washington, DC: The Mathematical Association of America.

Sunbdo, Jon. 1997. Management of innovation in services. *The Services Industries Journal*, 17(3): 432–55.

Sustainabilitydegrees.com. 2019. What is sustainability? Accessed September 7, 2019, at www.sustainabilitydegrees.com/what-is-sustainability/.

Szymaniec-Mlicka, Karolina. 2014. Resource-based view in strategic management of public organizations: A review of the literature. *Management*, 18(2): 19–30.

Taffinder, Paul. 1998. *Big Change: A Route-Map for Corporate Transformation.* New York: Wiley.

Tang, Pan, Haojia Chen and Shiqi Shao. 2018. Examining the international and interorganizational network of responding to major accidents for improving the emergency management system in China. *Complexity*, 2018(2): 1–16.

Tate, Wendy L. and Lydia Bals. 2018. Achieving shared triple bottom line (TBL) value creation: Toward a social resource-based view (SRBV) of the firm. *Journal of Business Ethics*, 152(3): 803–26.

Teagarden, Mary B. and Andreas Schotter. 2013. Resources and dynamic capabilities: The foundations of competitive advantage. In *Strategic Management in the 21st Century*, Volume 3: Theories of Strategic Management. Timothy J. Wilkinson, ed. Santa Barbara, CA: Praeger, 91–106.

TechTarget. 2018. Strategic management. Accessed June 7, 2019, at https://searchcio. techtarget.com/definition/strategic-management.

Teece, David J. 2000. Strategies for managing knowledge assets: The role of firm structure and industrial context. *Long Range Planning*, 33(1): 35–54.

Teece, David J. 2007. Explicating dynamic capabilities: The nature and microfoundations of (sustainable) enterprise performance. *Strategic Management Journal*, 28(13): 1319–50.

Teece, David J. 2011. *Dynamic Capabilities and Strategic Management*. Oxford, UK: Oxford University Press.

Teece, David J., ed. 2012. *Strategy, Innovation and the Theory of the Firm*. Cheltenham, UK: Edward Elgar.

Teece, David J. 2014. A dynamic capabilities-based entrepreneurial theory of multinational enterprise. *Journal of International Business Studies*, 45(1): 8–37.

Teece, David J. 2018a. Business models and dynamic capabilities. *Long Range Planning*, 51(1): 40–9.

Teece, David J. 2018b. Dynamic capabilities. Accessed August 7, 2019, at www.davidjteece. com/dynamic-capabilities/.

Teece, David J. and Gary P. Pisano. 1994. The dynamic capabilities of firms: An introduction. *Industrial and Corporate Change* 3(3): 537–55.

Teece, David J., Gary P. Pisano and Amy Shuen. 1997. Dynamic capabilities and strategic management. *Strategic Management Journal*, 18(7): 509–33.

Thompson, J.R. 2000. The reinvention laboratories: Strategic change by indirection. *American Review of Public Administration*, 30(1): 46–68.

Torfing, Jacob. 2016. *Collaborative Innovation in the Public Sector*. Washington, DC: Georgetown University.

Tutar, Hasan, Sima Nart and Bursun Bingöl. 2015. The effects of strategic orientations on innovation capabilities and market performance: The case of ASEM. *Procedia – Social and Behavioral Sciences*, 207: 709–19.

UK Forum for the Future. 2006. *Sustainability – A Reporting Framework for the Public Services*. London: Chartered Institute of Public Finance and Accountancy (CIPFA).

UNDP (United Nations Development Program). 2016. Human Development Report Zimbabwe: Governance. Accessed February 9, 2019, at http://hdr.undp.org/sites/ default/files/zhdr2000-governance.pdf.

USACE (U.S. Army Corps of Engineers). 2016. *2016 Strategic Sustainability Performance Plan*. Accessed February 28, 2017, at www.usace.army.mil/Missions/Sustainability/ Strategic-Sustainability-Performance-Plans/.

USAID. 2019. U.S. Government Education Strategy. Accessed September 25, 2019, at www.usaid.gov/education/usg-strategy.

USDA (U.S. Department of Agriculture). 2016. Rural and small systems guidebook to sustainable utility management. Accessed May 10, 2018, at www.rd.usda.gov/files/ RuralandSmallSystemsGuidebook2016.pdf.

US Department of Health and Human Services. 2019. *Top Management and Performance Challenges Facing HHS.* Washington, DC: Office of Inspector General.

Uzochukwu, Kelechi. 2018. Who engages in the co-production of local public services and why? The case of Atlanta, Georgia. *Public Administration Review,* 78(4): 514–26.

Venkatraman, N. and John C. Camillus. 1984. Exploring the concept of "fit" in strategic management. *Academy of Management Review,* 9(3): 513–25.

Venkatraman, V. 1989. Strategic orientation of business enterprises: The construct, dimensionality and measurement. *Management Science,* 35(8): 943–63.

Ventriss, C. 2000. New public management: An examination of its influence on contemporary public affairs and its impacts on shaping the intellectual agenda of the field. *Administrative Theory and Praxis,* 22(3): 500–18.

Vial, Gregory. 2019. Understanding digital transformation activities: A review and research agenda. *Journal of Strategic Information Systems,* 28(2): 118–14.

Vining, Aidan R. 2011. Public agency external analysis using a modified "five forces" framework. *International Public Management Journal,* 14(1): 63–105.

Vinzant Janet C. and Douglas H. Vinzant. 1996. Strategic management and total quality management. *Public Administration Quarterly,* 20(2): 201–19.

Von Neumann, John and Oskar Morgenstern. 1944. *Theory of Games and Economic Behavior.* Princeton, NJ: Princeton University.

Walker, Richard M. 2013. Strategic management and performance in public organizations: Findings from the Miles and Snow framework. *Public Administration Review,* 73(5): 675–85.

Walker, Richard M., George A. Boyne, Gene A, Brewer and Claudia N. Avellaneda. 2011. Market orientation and public service performance: New public management gone mad? *Public Administration Review,* 71(5): 707–17.

Wang, Xiao Hu, Christopher V. Hawkins, Nick Lebredo and Evan M. Berman. 2012. Capacity to sustain sustainability: A study 9 U.S. cities. *Public Administration Review,* 72(6): 841–53.

Warner, Karl S. R. and Maximilian Wäger. 2019. Building dynamic capabilities for digital transformation: An ongoing process of strategic renewal. *Long Range Planning,* 52(3): 326–49.

Watson, Joel. 2008. *Strategy: An Introduction to Game Theory,* 2nd ed. New York: Norton.

Wauters, Benedict. 2017. Strategic management in the public sector. *Report to the European Commission's Public Administration and Governance Network.* Accessed September 27, 2019, at ec.europa.eu/esf/transnationality/sites/esf/files/pag_network_strategy_paper_full.pdf.

Wechsler, Barton and Robert W. Backoff. 1986. Policymaking and administration in state agencies: Strategic management approaches. *Public Administration Review,* 46(4): 331–8.

Wernerfelt, Birger. 1984. A resource-based view of the firm. *Strategic Management Journal,* 5(2): 171–80.

Wheeler, Edward T. 1993. *Government That Works: Innovation in State and Local Government.* Jefferson, NC: McFarland.

Wheelen, Thomas L. and J. David Hunger. 2010. *Strategic Management and Business Policy: Entering 21st Century Global Society.* New York: Prentice-Hall.

Wheelen, Thomas L., J. David Hunger, Alan N. Hoffman and Charles E. Bamford. 2017. *Strategic Management and Business Policy,* 15th ed. Boston: Pearson.

When, Uta and Carlos Montalvo. 2018. Exploring the dynamics of water innovation: Foundations for water innovation studies. *Journal of Cleaner Production,* 171(2018): S1–S19.

White. Michael D., Christopher Fisher, Karyn Hadfield, Jessica Saunders, and Lisa Williams. 2005. Measuring organizational capacity among agencies serving the poor: Implications for achieving organizational effectiveness. *Justice Policy Journal,* 2(2): 1–39.

Wholey, Joseph S. 1999. Performance-based management: Responding to the challenges. *Public Productivity & Management Review*, 22(3): 288–307.

Williams, Wil and Duncan Lewis. 2008. Strategic management tools and public sector management: The challenge of context specificity. *Public Management Review*, 10(5): 653–71.

Winter, Sidney G. 2003. Understanding dynamic capabilities. *Strategic Management Journal*, 24(10): 991–5.

Woiceshyn, Jaana and Loren Falkenberg. 2008. Value creation in knowledge-based firms: Aligning problems and resources. *Academy of Management Perspectives*, 22(2): 85–99.

Wong, Amanda. 2016. The key to keeping up: dynamic capabilities. *California Management Review* blog, August 22, 2016. Berkeley, CA. University of California. Accessed August 11, 2019, at cmr.berkeley.edu/blog/2016/8/dynamic-capabilities/.

Wood, Danielle, Sebastian Pfotenhauer, Wiljeane Glover and Dava Newman. 2013. Disruptive innovation in public service sectors: Ambidexterity and the role of incumbents. Paper presented at the 8th European Conference on Innovation and Entrepreneurship, Brussels, Belgium: ECIE 2013-Volume 1. 669–76. Accessed November 5, 2018, at http://toc.proceedings.com/19354webtoc.pdf.

World Bank. 2012. The World Bank's approach to public sector management 2011–2020: Better results from public sector institutions. Accessed June 10, 2019, at http://siteresources.worldbank.org/PUBLICSECTORANDGOVERNANCE/Resources/285741-1287520109339/PSM-Approach.pdf.

Wu, Shaoyu and Dong Wang. 2017. The influence of local government decision-making competition on enterprise innovation investment under information asymmetry and multiple risk appetite type. *Kybernetes*, 46(5): 802–17.

Xavier, Luciana Yokoyama, Pedro R. Jacobi and Alexander Turra, 2019. Local Agenda 21: Planning for the future, changing today. *Environmental Science and Policy*, 101(11): 7–15.

Yang, Kaifeng. 2016. Creating public value and institutional innovations across boundaries: An integrative process of participation, legitimation, and implementation. *Public Administration Review*, 76(6): 873–85.

Yi, Hongtao. 2017. Network structure and governance performance: What makes a difference? *Public Administration Review*, 78(2): 195–205.

Zhao, Yupan and Bo Fan. 2018. Exploring open government data capacity of government agency: Based on the resource-based theory. *Government Information Quarterly*, 35(2018): 1–12.

INDEX

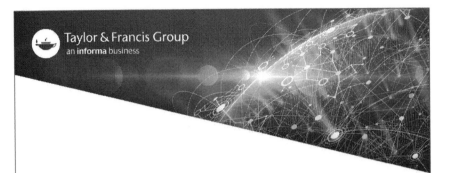

Printed in Great Britain
by Amazon